PUPILLARY DYNAMICS AND BEHAVIOR

PUPILLARY DYNAMICS AND BEHAVIOR

Edited by

Michel Pierre Janisse

Department of Psychology
University of Manitoba
Winnipeg, Manitoba
Canada

PLENUM PRESS • NEW YORK AND LONDON

Library of Congress Cataloging in Publication Data

University of Manitoba Symposium on Pupillometry, Winnipeg, 1973.
  Pupillary dynamics and behavior.

  Includes bibliographies.
  1. Pupillometry—Congresses. 2. Personality tests—Congresses. 3. Mental
illness—Diagnosis—Congresses. I. Janisse, Michel Pierre, ed. II. Title.
QP360.U54   1973   612'.842   74-12062
ISBN 0-306-30812-6

Proceedings of the University of Manitoba Symposium on Pupillometry
held October 17-19, 1973 in Winnipeg, Manitoba

© 1974 Plenum Press, New York
A Division of Plenum Publishing Corporation
227 West 17th Street, New York, N.Y. 10011

United Kingdom edition published by Plenum Press, London
A Division of Plenum Publishing Company, Ltd.
4a Lower John Street, London W1R 3PD, England

Printed in the United States of America

In memory of my father,
OMER E. JANISSE

PREFACE

The University of Manitoba Symposium on Pupillometry was held in Winnipeg, Manitoba, October 17-19, 1973. The seed of the idea was planted in 1967 when Raymond Daly of the University of Windsor first interested me in the utility of the pupil as a dependent measure in psychology. From that time on I have read as much as possible about the pupil and in late 1971 it occurred to me that it might be a good idea to bring together those pupillary investigators whose research had the greatest impression upon me. This book is one of happier consequences of the Symposium.

The guiding principle behind the selection of participants was a blend of three considerations: (1) long standing research or scholarly interest in problems associated with the eye and the pupil; (2) outstanding respect of the participant by his colleagues involved in pupillometric research; and (3) significant contributions to the learned literature.

In due course, nine scientists were contacted and asked to make the trek to Winnipeg. They were encouraged not to report data on one, or few studies, as is typically done at meetings and conventions, but rather to review the findings and theoretical controversies of their specialty area with especial relevance to their own contributions to the field. It was felt that because of the stature of these scholars much more could be gained from their own evaluations of this area and their work, than from the somewhat restricting format of data presentation. They were also encouraged to speculate about what future pupillometric research might have in store for us. With minor variations, this was accomplished and the fruits of their labors are presented in this volume.

Regrettably two of the invited participants, Irene E. Loewenfeld, Ph.D. and Daniel Kahneman, Ph.D. were forced to withdraw at the last minute. Their presence was missed, but their absence was unavoidable. The Symposium participants (with co-authors in parentheses) were: Mathew Alpern, Ph.D. (N. Ohba, Ph.D. and L. Birndorff, Ph.D.), Niles Bernick, Ph.D., Gad Hakerem, Ph.D., Eckhard H. Hess, Ph.D. (Elizabeth Goodwin, Ph.D.), W. Scott Peavler, Ph.D., Leonard Rubin, Ph.D., John Semmlow, Ph.D. (John Hansmann, Ph.D. and Lawrence Stark, M.D.). What follows are the seven papers delivered at the Symposium plus an introductory chapter by the editor.

It is now my most pleasant task to acknowledge all of those wonderful people who contributed so much to making the Symposium a success. Two people stand out above the rest in this regard. My colleague, Frank Shively, helped right from the beginning with planning, organizing and executing several aspects of the Symposium. His ideas and constant positive reinforcement were indispensable. The second person to help so greatly was H. H. Jacobs, Assistant to the Dean of Graduate Studies at the University of Manitoba. His service as a guide through the rough waters of red tape, protocol, university policies and governmental bureaucracy was essential in all aspects of planning. His encouragement and enthusiasm never abated and his knowledge of appropriate funding application procedures was essential. Without his assistance the Symposium would not have been held.

Many other colleagues and students were of help both before and throughout the Symposium. I would like to acknowledge with gratitude the aid of Gary Glavin, Garry A. Hawryluk, John S. McIntyre, Theodore Palys, A. H. Shephard and John H. Whiteley. I would also like to acknowledge the service of Dr. B. A. Gingras of the National Research Council of Canada, for his eloquent address to those in attendance at the Symposium. And thank those officers of the University of Manitoba who participated in various aspects of the Symposium program: Ernest Sirluck, President; Richard A. Lebrun, Associate Dean of Graduate Studies; J. C. Gilson, Vice-President for Research; and John G. Adair, Head, Department of Psychology. Terrence P. Hogan and Richard V. Thysell each chaired a Symposium session, Bernice Lough helped arrange ticket distribution, Ed Labun of the Instructional Media Center at the University of Manitoba provided essential technical assistance, and John F. Neeson of St. Bonaventure University made available a mailing list of American universities.

This manuscript would not have been prepared nor most of the information sent out to those interested in the Symposium had it not been for the excellent stenographic assistance provided by Dorothy McLeod, who was assisted from time to time by Stefanie Madak.

I would like to acknowledge the financial assistance of the Medical Research Council of Canada, the Faculty of Arts and Department of Psychology of the University of Manitoba, Robert Clow of Host Rent-a-Car International, and Harding Bush and George Leonard of the Whittaker Corporation for their assistance with the distribution of the brochures. The aid of the foregoing groups was essential to the success of the Symposium.

And lovingly, I would like to acknowledge the patience of my wife Judy and the children, Jordan and Kier-la, who were almost as enthusiastic about the Symposium as I was.

M.P.J.
Winnipeg, Manitoba
March, 1974

CONTRIBUTORS

M. Alpern, Ph.D.
    Vision Research Laboratory, University of Michigan, Ann Arbor,
    Michigan

Niles Bernick, Ph.D.
    Psychophysiology Laboratory, NIDA Clinical Research Center,
    Lexington, Kentucky

L. Birndorf, Ph.D.
    Department of Ophthalmology, University of Florida,
    Gainesville, Florida

Elizabeth Goodwin, Ph.D.
    Department of Psychology, University of Chicago, Chicago,
    Illinois

Gad Hakerem, Ph.D.
    Department of Psychology, Queen's College of the City Univer-
    sity of New York, Flushing, New York

D. Hansmann, Ph.D.
    Cardiodynamics Laboratory, Beverly Hills, California

Eckhard H. Hess, Ph.D.
    Department of Psychology, University of Chicago, Chicago,
    Illinois

Michel Pierre Janisse, Ph.D.
    Department of Psychology, University of Manitoba, Winnipeg,
    Manitoba

N. Ohba, Ph.D.
    Department of Ophthalmology, University of Tokyo, Tokyo,
    Japan

W. Scott Peavler, Ph.D.
    Human Performance Technology Center, Bell Telephone Labora-
    tories, New Brunswick, New Jersey

Leonard S. Rubin, Ph.D.
   Eastern Pennsylvania Psychiatric Institute, Philadelphia,
   Pennsylvania

J. Semmlow, Ph.D.
   Bioengineering Program, University of Illinois at Chicago
   Circle, Chicago, Illinois

L. Stark, M.D.
   Departments of Physiological Optics and Mechanical Engineering,
   University of California, Berkeley, California

CONTENTS

xiii

CHAPTER I:

PUPILLOMETRY: SOME ADVANCES, PROBLEMS AND SOLUTIONS

Michel Pierre Janisse

Department of Psychology, University of Manitoba

Winnipeg, Manitoba

The study of the pupil has a long history and a rich literature, dating back at least to the ancient Greeks, and scientific
reports of pupillary research go back at least two hundred years.
This introductory chapter will attempt to provide the reader with
an overview of the area by discussing some of its technical,
methodological, and control problems and solutions.

Both technically and empirically research on the pupil has
certainly advanced since the days of the caliper and unaided observation.   There is in this volume, for example, Rubin's evidence
(See, Chapter IV) that pupillary activity may be helpful in understanding psychosis, neuroses and stress in general and Alpern,
Ohba and Birndorf's report (See, Chapter II) that there is more
to the light reflex than meets the iris.   Almost daily new dis-
coveries are being made, old facts validated and updated, and perhaps most important, new scientists are being attracted from
many seemingly disparate disciplines.   Bio-engineering, electronics,
medicine, ophthalmology, optometry, physiology, psychiatry, and
psychology are but a few examples, and it is not by accident that
each of these disciplines is represented in this volume.

A most encouraging advance in pupillometry has been the re-
surgence of interest in the pupil by psychologists in the last
fifteen years.   Much of the impetus for this research has come
from the work of Hess (See, Hess and Goodwin, Chapter VIII).   While
many of his ideas have been controversial (e.g., Loewenfeld, 1966)
others have resulted in productive and fruitful scientific exchange
(e.g., Janisse and Peavler, 1974).   Psychological research on the
pupil (or Pupillometrics, as Hess has called it) has reached the

1

point now that several review articles have appeared (e.g.,
Goldwater, 1972; Hess, 1972; Janisse, 1973). Two of the chapters
in this volume (Bernick, Chapter VII and Peavler, Chapter VI) show
a heavy reliance on Hess' early research.

PROBLEM AREAS

The greatest advances in pupillometry have been in the realm
of methodology, control and technology. Outlined here are six
of the major problem areas in pupillometric research. A consideration of these issues offers solutions to several theoretical controversies and empirical ambiguities which have appeared in the
literature.

Physical Parameter Effects

When studying psychosensory effects upon pupil size, the
most obvious variable to control is brightness. This is a primary
concern, since it has been well established that any change in
luminance causes a change in pupil size. Even so, there are a
number of studies that simply do not consider this powerful
variable, while others try to make use of this brightness effect
to enhance the meaning of their results (e.g., Hess, 1965). For
example, if an experimenter is using slides to present stimuli,
it is quite difficult to equate stimulus and control slides for
luminance; therefore, some researchers make every stimulus slide
brighter than the control slide. The reasoning is that this would
normally make the pupil constrict during the stimulus period,
relative to the control period. However, if the pupil does dilate,
one can be fairly certain that it is because of some quality of
the slide other than luminance (i.e., interest, arousing properties,
etc.). While this method does provide a conservative procedure
when dilation is expected, if constriction occurs, it is difficult
to determine whether it is attributable to luminance or to some
other property of the picture. Also since the various stimulus
slides are not equated for luminance, their effect upon pupil
size will be quite variable and unpredictable in quantitative
terms. Again, the effect of the other, non-luminance, properties
of the stimulus are difficult to judge except in very gross terms.
Finally, the addition of counter-expansion factors to a hypothesized dilation effect, adds further inter- and intra-subject
variation to the already quite variable measurement of pupil size,
since there are already large individual differences in the light
reflex.

A related issue is the problem of relative brightness in
various parts of the stimulus. Woodmansee (1965) has found that
a subject's pupil could constrict 1% to 5% when his gaze shifted

from a relatively dark to a relatively light portion of the test stimulus. To attenuate this effect, he suggests presenting stimuli 'slightly out of focus', thus reducing contrast and the sharp edges of the figure-ground complex. Loewenfeld (1966) speaks to this point, however, and suggests that even this may not be sufficient to reduce significant contrast effects. A related problem lies in the use of color, as opposed to black and white pictures. When pupillary changes occur, it is difficult to specify whether it is because of the content of the picture or the 'emotional impact' of the color itself (c.f., Miller, 1967). The use of non-pictorial visual stimuli considerably reduces or eliminates these difficulties due to luminance, contrast and color. Thus, the most adequate solution to this problem may be to avoid the use of visual stimuli altogether.

If visual stimuli are used, they should be of minimal contrast and be line drawings, words, numbers or other symbols. Above all, the results should be interpreted with caution, for even minimal light reflex effects may contribute variance to the data.

Arousal and Baseline Effects

Another fundamental problem in pupillary research is the subject's level of arousal. This admittedly vague term refers to any of a number of concepts such as drive level, anxiety level, degree of interest and enthusiasm, level of fatigue, etc. All of these factors have an effect upon pupil size that is quite diffi- cult to interpret when one is not specifically studying them. Libby, Lacey and Lacey (1968) pointed to this problem when they asked if a dilation to a slide of presumably negative emotional content was caused by an aversion to the stimulus, or because negative slides are more complex, interesting or attention main- taining. Woodmansee (1966) has pointed out that complexity, interest and attention have all been related to pupillary dilation. He says, "If the general level of autonomic stimulation increases by sensory or emotional stimulation, or by spontaneous thoughts, the pupil widens. Pupil size decreases with decreasing arousal accompanying loss of interest, boredom or falling asleep." (1966, p. 133). While this view might seem simplistic, it is probably fairly accurate and certainly not limited to just pupillary activity among the psychophysiological indices (c.f., Sternbach, 1966). As with any physiological measure, it cannot be assumed that the basal level of pupil size is constant throughout an experimental session.

Baseline variations are always difficult to deal with, but a few methods used to avoid these variations are: to vary the order of stimulus presentation, to avoid lengthy trials and to avoid a large number of trials. Optimal trial length varies a great deal from subject to subject, but after about 100 seconds (Woodmansee, 1966) most subjects begin to lose interest and demonstrate a marked decrease in basal pupil size. This effect, arousal decrement, is probably nothing more than the adaptation phenomenon (Lehr and Bergum, 1966), common to all measures of autonomic activity (c.f., Sternbach, 1966). This same effect occurs over a large number of trials as well as within lengthy trials.

One method of alleviating some of the foregoing problems is to present control slides both before and after each stimulus slide (e.g., Janisse, 1974). Here the unit of measurement is the percentage difference between the pupil size during the stimulus presentation and the average size of the pupil during the presentation of the control slides before and after the stimulus slides. A control presentation typically consists of a plain slide with the numbers one to four printed in each corner and the number five printed in the center, a row of five to ten asterisks printed on a plain background, or a single target (such as a "plus" sign) in the middle of the slide upon which the subject is instructed to focus. One problem with the first type of control slide is that some subjects have been found to add these numbers (Simms, 1967). There is evidence that this type of cognitive work is associated with enhanced pupil size (Daly, 1966), making its use as a control slide questionable. A preferred control slide would be one of the latter two, using asterisks or some other simple symbol. Of course, the luminance of the control and stimulus slides should be equal. When non-visual stimuli are used as test stimuli, some type of control slide should be presented continuously and appropriate measurements taken before and after each presentation. This procedure helps to ensure constant luminance, provide the subject with a fixation point, and obtain an accurate baseline measure.

In addition to the above, statistical methods are available to control for the effects of baseline differences between subjects, especially for the Law of Initial Values (LIV) (c.f., Wilder, 1958). The LIV, "...states that for a standard stimulus there is an inverse correlation between prestimulus values and the magnitude of various organismic responses to that stimulus." (Schmidt, Rose and Bridger, 1974, p. 44). Lacey (1956) has suggested the Autonomic Lability Score, and other authors (e.g., Cronbach and Furby, 1970) have recommended co-variate and multi-variate techniques as means of controlling for the LIV. These suggestions were for use with autonomic indices other than the pupil and unfortunately we are not aware of their application in the pupillometric literature. The time would appear to be propitious for their introduction.

Near Vision Reflex

With constant brightness there is a tendency for the pupil to

constrict when viewing near objects for any length of time. This
effect has to do with convergence of the eyes and accommodation
to near objects. This phenomenon is quite variable among subjects,
and is more pronounced with older subjects, in whom pupil size
compensates for loss of accommodation. The use of college sopho-
mores as subjects may overcome the age factor to some extent.
Also, it is helpful to use an effective viewing distance at which
the subject has little trouble retaining focus for the stimulus
interval. Three or four meters is usually an acceptable distance
(See, Hakerem and Sutton, 1964), but greater distances may be
attained through the use of mirrors (e.g., Sweeney, 1968). As
with the arousal decrement effect, lengthy stimulus presentation
will enhance the near vision reflex.

Iris Color

     Some research into iris color and pupillary activity (e.g.,
Beck, 1967 and Gambill, Ogle, and Kearns, 1967) indicates that
pupils with blue or light irises are generally larger and react
with greater dilation than do pupils with dark irises. Why this
is the case is as yet a mystery. Beck suggests that "....iris
pigmentation is correlated with differences in central sympathetic
reactivity and/or motility of the iris musculature." (p. 2,
1967). In terms of measurement iris color presents an obvious
problem. In many studies only subjects with light irises have
been used, because their pupils are more easily and more accurately
measured. This is done on the assumption that iris color is not
related to pupillary reactivity. It can be seen that if iris
color is related to pupillary activity, generalizations from such
studies is sharply limited. While much research has been done, it
appears that the jury is still out on this issue and it remains
an area of good potential for future research.

High Pupillary Variability

     Loewenfeld (1958) reports that externally effected changes
in pupil size are superimposed on an already varying noise level.
Woodmansee (1966) says that changes in pupil diameter of 1% may
occur from second to second and changes of 10% to 20% may occur
over a period of several seconds. There are no perfect remedies
for this situation, but encouraging reliabilities have been found
using repeated measures designs (Hakerem and Sutton, 1964) and
eight or more trials per subject (Woodmansee, 1966). Another way
of minimizing this effect may be to use Lykken's (1972) Range
Correction, which he suggests is useful for heart rate and electro-
dermal response measures. Issues related to variability are discussed in more detail by Hansmann, Semmlow and Stark in this
volume (See, Chapter III).

Measurement

An infrequently mentioned problem in pupillometry is the
question of what measure of pupillary activity is most appropriate
to use. A widely used index to date has been the average size of
the pupil for the duration of the stimulus presentation. With
photographic methods, this involves about two pictures per second
during both the stimulus and the control periods. The average
pupil size for the stimulus period is then related to the pupil
size during the pre- or post-control periods, or to the pupil
size during both periods, to form an index of pupillary activity.
This relation between the stimulus and control sizes may be in
terms of the absolute difference, a percentage, a ratio, etc.
The use of size alone as a measure of pupillary activity is not
surprising. It is simple, direct and suggests a one-to-one relationship between pupil size and the activity of interest. But,
this is wishful thinking. That size itself may be somewhat mis-
leading is evident from the fact, mentioned earlier, that pupillary
activity is affected by the same types of confounding variables
as are other physiological indices.

It remains to be determined which is the "best" measure of
pupillary activity: average size (diameter or area), peak size,
latency to peak size, minimum size, or variance. Although only
five measures have been mentioned here, it is likely that ingenious
researchers will come up with others before long. The solution
to this question of the sensitivity (and even of the appropriate-
ness) of different indices of pupillary activity may be found in
specificity rather than generality. That is, it is likely that
no one index is adequate nor appropriate for all types of experimental situations, but rather specific measures are more suited to
individual tasks than are others. For example, variance (c.f.,
Daly, 1966) may be the best measure of concentration, latency,
(c.f., Simpson, Molloy, Hale, and Climan, 1968) the best measure
of task difficulty and size (c.f., Hess, 1972) the best measure
of arousal. Again, this is an empirical question and best answered
by further research.

A major methodological problem is that of actually monitoring
the pupil. Several methods have been developed (e.g., photographic
and electronic), but most, as yet, have not been both economical
and convenient. For a more detailed exposition of these problems
the reader is referred to Hakerem (1967 and in the present volume,
Chapter V) for excellent reviews of the technical problems in
this area.

IN CONCLUSION

We have outlined a number of difficulties that need to be

considered by any scientist interested in research on the pupil. That these issues are important is evident from the controversies surrounding several of them. These controversies, however, have for the most part, led to productive exchanges between investigators seeking to ask the right questions in the correct way. Like all good research, pupillometry has a tradition of generating more questions than answers. With the current burgeoning interest in the pupil this tradition should continue.

We trust that the following pages will provide the reader with many more questions about the function of the pupil.

ACKNOWLEDGEMENTS

For their helpful comments on this chapter and other portions of this volume I would like to acknowledge: John G. Adair, Averil E. Karlsruher, David G. Martin, John S. McIntyre, W. Scott Peavler, Daniel Perlman, and John H. Whiteley. A grant from the University of Manitoba Research Board (431-1665-05) aided in the completion of the manuscript.

REFERENCES

Beck, B. B. The effect of the rate and intensity of auditory click stimulation on pupil size. Washington, D. C.: APA September, 1967.

Cronbach, L. J., and Furby, L. How should we measure "change" - or should we? *Psychological Bulletin*, 1970, *74(1)*, 68-80.

Daly, R. M. Pupillary size and its relationship to the problem solving process. Unpublished doctoral dissertation. Loyola University, Chicago, 1966.

Gambill, H. P., Ogle, K. N., and Kearns, T. D. Mydriatic effect of four drugs determined with pupillograph. *Archives of Opthalmology*, 1967, *77*, 740-746.

Goldwater, B. C. Psychological significance of pupillary movements. *Psychological Bulletin*, 1972, *77*, 340-355.

Hakerem, G. Pupillography. In, P. H. Venables and Irene Martin (Eds.), *Manual of Psycho-physical Methods*. Amsterdam: North Holland, 1967.

Hakerem, G., and Sutton, S. Pupillary reactions during observations of near light threshold stimuli. Los Angeles: APA, September, 1964.

Hess, E. H. Attitude and pupil size. *Scientific American*, 1965, *212*, 46-54.

Hess, E. H. Pupillometrics: a method of studying mental, emotional and sensory processes. In N. S. Greenfield, and R. A. Sternbach (Eds.), *Handbook of Psychophysiology*, New York: Holt, Rinehart and Winston, 1972, 491-531.

Hess, E. H., Seltzer, A., and Shlien, J. M. Pupil responses of heterosexual and homosexual males to pictures of men and women: a pilot study. *Journal of Abnormal Psychology*, 1965, *70*, 165-168.

Janisse, M. P. Pupil size and affect: a critical review of the literature since 1960. *Canadian Psychologist*, 1973, *14(4)*, 311-329.

Janisse, M. P. Pupil size, affect and exposure frequency. *Journal of Social Behavior and Personality*, 1974. (In press).

Janisse, M. P., and Peavler, W. S. Pupillary research today: emotion in the eye. *Psychology Today*, 1974, *7(9)*, 60-63.

Lacey, J. I. The evaluation of autonomic responses: toward a general solution. *Annals of the New York Academy of Sciences*, 1956, *67*, 123-164.

Lykken, D. T. Range correction applied to heart rate and to GSR data. *Psychophysiology*, 1972, *9(3)*, 373-379.

Lehr, D. J., and Bergum, B. A. Note on pupillary adaptation. *Perceptual and Motor Skills*, 1966, *23*, 917-918.

Libby, W. I., Jr., Lacey, Beatrice, and Lacey, J. I. Pupillary and cardiac activity during visual stimulation. Paper presented at 8th Annual Meeting of the Society for Psychophysical Research, Washington, 1968.

Loewenfeld, Irene E. Mechanisms of reflex dilation of the pupil historical and experimental analysis. *Documental Ophthalmologica*, 1958, *12*, 185-448.

Loewenfeld, Irene E. Comment on Hess' findings. *Survey of Ophthalmology*, 1966, *11*, 291-294.

Miller, R. L. The clinical validation of the pupillary response: Effect of chromatic and achromatic stimuli upon pupillary responsivity. *Dissertation Abstracts*, 1967, *27(7-B)*, 2515.

Schmidt, K., Rose, S. A., and Bridger, W. The law of initial value and neonatal sleep states. *Psychophysiology*, 1974, *11(1)*, 44-52.

Simms, T. M. Pupillary response of male and female subjects to pupillary difference in male and female picture stimuli. *Perception and Psychophysics*, 1967, *2*, 553-555.

Simpson, H. M., Molloy, F. M., Hale, S. M., and Climan, M. H. Latency and magnitude of the pupillary response during an imagery task. *Psychonomic Science*, 1968, *13*, 293-294.

Sternbach, R. A. *Principles of Psychophysiology*. New York: Academic Press, 1966.

Sweeney, J. Unpublished masters thesis, University of Windsor, Windsor, Canada, 1968.

Wilder, J. Modern Psychotherapy and the law of initial values. *American Journal of Psychotherapy*, 1958, *12*, 199-221.

Woodmansee, J. J. An evaluation of the pupil response as a measure of attitude toward Negroes. Unpublished doctoral dissertation, University of Colorado, 1965.

Woodmansee, J. J. Methodological problems in pupillographic experiments. Proceedings of the 74th Annual Convention of the American Psychological Association, Washington, D. C., APA, 1966, 133-134.

CHAPTER II:

CAN THE RESPONSE OF THE IRIS TO LIGHT BE USED TO BREAK THE CODE

OF THE SECOND CRANIAL NERVE IN MAN?

M. Alpern, N. Ohba* and L. Birndorf**

Vision Research Laboratory

University of Michigan, Ann Arbor Michigan

The sphincture muscle of the vertebrate iris develops tension causing the aperture stop of the eye to become small in the light, and loses tension making it expand in the dark. In this way, the light available to the sensory retina can alternatively be diminished when the world is too bright and increased when it is too dim. This elegant servomechanism is a textbook example, so we are told, of a homeostatic mechanism maintaining the exquisite sensitivity of the vertebrate retina constant while environmental light fluctuates. Nonsense! The maintenance of good retinal sensitivity over a range of 10,000,000,000,000 fold from the one extreme near the theoretical limit of detection to the other extreme at which the light becomes so intense that the retina starts to burn, is no doubt a prize achievement of Mother Nature as a bioengineer, but the photopupillary response has precious little to do with it. The small fluctuations of pupil area available (about 1.2 $\log_{10}$ units, for example, for the human eye) is trivial in this context.

For Denton (1956) the light reflex is important in adjusting the aperture of the eye in such a way that it is always optimum for the highest acuity possible at a given light level. If this is so, it is a curious development for the eyes of all vertebrates (whether nocturnal or diurnal) behave similarly though for some teleosts, reptiles and amphibia -- indeed for some mammals as well (Bito, 1973) -- the retina is by no means a necessary feature of

---

*Now at Department of Ophthalmology, University of Tokyo
**Now at Department of Ophthalmology, University of Florida

the phenomenon.

SENSITIVITY OF THE IRIS SPHINCTURE TO LIGHT

In such animals, the common laboratory frog *Rana Pipiens* for
example, the iris may be dissected free of the eye, suspended in a
bath and attached to a tension transducer so that muscle tension
may be recorded isometrically (Barr & Alpern, 1963).

Figure 1 shows the tension built up by such a preparation when
light shines upon it. The action spectrum of this response measured by the number of photons required to produce a fixed tension
is reasonably similar to the absorption spectrum of the frog pink
rod visual pigment, rhodopsin (Figure 2). Moreover none of the
pharmacological agents, such as atropine, which influence the
nerve-muscle junction of the iris spincture have any effect on the
tension the muscle generates when the iris absorbs light. Evidently
somewhere in the iris--Barr & Alpern's evidence suggests very close
to the contractile apparatus--absorbed quanta cause the muscle to
build up active tension. This preparation may well represent a
model of photoreceptor processes in vertebrate rods and cones.
For example, Barr & Alpern (1963) found that calcium ions play an
important role in this response. In Figure 3, the results of one
of their experiments emphasizing this point is illustrated. The
normal increase in tension evoked by a 10 sec. flash of white
light $(4.12(10)^4$ lumens m^{-2}) decreases systematically when the
calcium in the bath is washed away, or if (as in Figure 3) the
solution bathing the iris is not only calcium free, but contains
2.67 mm Na citrate, a substance which kelates any calcium bound to
the external membrane. This decline in tension in calcium free
solution is too slow to be due simply to sweeping calcium from the
extracellular space. Rather it is as though there is a store of
internally bound calcium. When the cell rhodopsin absorbs photons
some of this bound calcium is released and this causes the tension
generated by the contractile apparatus of the muscle to increase.
In Figure 3, this interpretation is supported by the fact that the
rate of decline of photon evoked tension in Na citrate solutions
depends upon the rate of stimulus presentation. The faster the
store is depleted by successive flashes, the faster the decline in
tension evoked. The release of bound calcium by quantum absorption
in the iris is exactly analogous to the process proposed by Hagins
(1972) for photon excitation in vertebrate rods.

In the frog, at least, absorption of quanta by the rhodopsin
in the iris is not the only way to cause the sphincture muscle to
generate tension in response to light. If light is directed into
the eye of an alert unanesthetized frog in such a way that it goes
through the pupil without touching the iris, after a latent period

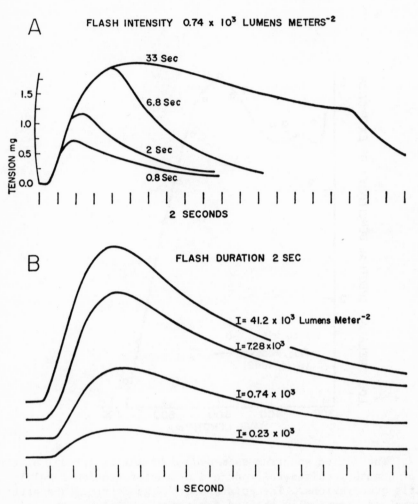

Figure 1. (A) Isometric contractions of the frog iris resulting from flashes of white light of the same intensity, but of different durations. The number on each curve represents flash duration. The separation of the marks on the time scale is 2 sec. (B) Isometric contractions resulting from flashes of white light of the same duration, but of different intensities. Same tension scale, but different time scale. Note that the response to a 2 sec. 0.74×10^3 lumen m^{-2} flash appears in both (A) and (B). From Barr & Alpern, *Journal of General Physiology*, 1963, *46*, p. 1252.

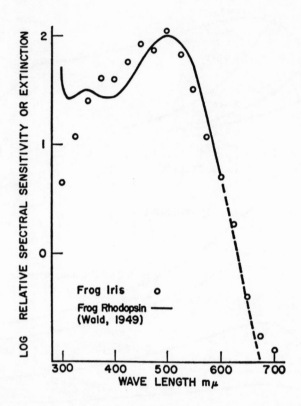

Figure 2. The action spectrum as measured by the reciprocal of the number of quanta required to produce a criterion tension level in three iris preparations. The points are the geometric means after the curves were vertically shifted for superimposition with minimum scatter. The smooth curve is the extinction of frog rhodopsin *in vitro* (Wald, 1949). The sensitivity measurements at 675 nm and 700 nm are probably erroneously high because of monochromator stray light. From Barr & Alpern, *Journal of General Physiology*, 1963, *46*, p. 1258.

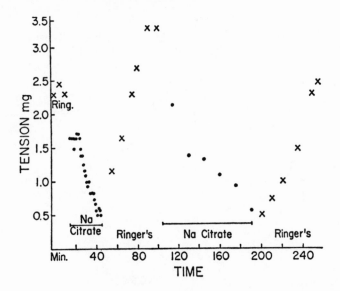

Figure 3. The maximum tension of twitches elicited by 10 sec. flashes of white light $(41.2(10)^3$ lumen m^{-2}) plotted against time when the incubating solution is either normal Ringer's or calcium-free, citrated Ringer's. The twitch amplitude decreases when calcium is washed out. Moreover, the decrease is much faster if the frequency of stimulation is greater. From Barr & Alpern, *Journal of General Physiology*, 1963, *46*, p. 1259.

the pupil becomes smaller as long as the light is on and then (again following a latent period) becomes wider again when the light is turned off. The open circles in Figure 4 illustrate typical results of such an experiment.

But, how do we know that light quanta producing the response in Figure 4 are absorbed by visual pigment in the retina and not in the iris? True enough microscopic examination of the incident stimulus light pencil showed that the focused light beam entered the eye in the very center of the dilated pupil and did not even approximate the iris edge of the pupil, but can we be sure that the physiologically important light was not scattered (either in the apparatus, the eye, or perhaps both) to be caught by the iris rhodopsin? The filled circles in Figure 4 exclude this possibility. They illustrate the results of repeating the experiment producing the unfilled circles following a very strong dose of atropine. Atropine prevents the activation of the sphincture muscle by its motor nerve, but it does not obviate the contraction of the iris evoked by quanta absorbed in the muscle. The triangles show that

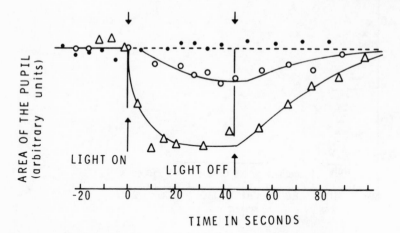

Figure 4. A pupil light reflex evoked by retinal excitation in the frog. The open circles show the change in pupil area evoked by a small pencil of light focused on the center of the pupil (in Maxwellian view). The filled dots show a repetition of the experiment about one hour later after the frog had been dark adapted and exposed to 26 drops of 1% atropine sulfate (2 drops every 5 minutes). The triangles were obtained immediately after the dots by opening the aperture stop so that the stimulus light fell on iris as well as on the pupil. The response evoked by retinal stimulation has been blocked by atropine, but the response evoked by direct iris stimulation remains.

the iris is still responsive to light absorbed by its own rhodopsin; they depict a good contraction (under the influence of atropine) once the aperture stop of the stimulating beam was opened so that the light fell upon iris as well as pupil.

The results in Figure 4 demonstrate, for the frog at least, that the pupil widens or narrows as environmental light wanes and waxes by light absorption in a visual pigment (or pigments) located in two different places (*i*) retinal photoreceptors and (*ii*) iris. To what extent this is true for the other vertebrates (some of them very nocturnal animals with poor acuity) whose iris muscles also contract when they have been isolated in a muscle bath, remains to be shown. If the results in Figure 4 are quite general for such animals, one wonders how it happens according to Denton's view of the light reflex, that such lowly creatures need two independent

regulators of their aperture stops to light, while *Homo sapiens*
must settle for one.

THE HUMAN PUPIL LIGHT REFLEX IN STEADY STATE VIEWING

In man there is probably no rhodopsin in the iris; certainly
there is no direct response of the atropinized sphincture muscle to
light. The human photopupil response depends alone upon nerve
signals leaving the eye over the very limited number of optic nerve
fibers which also must convey a host of visual messages to the
thalamus coding information about the forms, the positions, the
brightnesses and the colors of retinal images. It is not yet known
whether the pupil and visual fibers stem from one and the same set
of ganglion cells, but with only one or two million ganglion cells
and 126 million photoreceptors, mere economy of precious optic nerve
space would argue that perhaps they do. If so, then the nerve fibers for the light reflex might only be small branches of the axone
terminals of the "visual" fibers and therefore contain the same
coded messages about the retinal image which are so crucial for
human vision. Is it the outside chance that this may be the case
which excites the curiosity of many of us to probe the mysteries
of the human light reflex?

So the light reflex survives (in man utilizing valuable nerve
pathways to that end) despite the lack of any convincing survival
value in it as an adaptation mechanism. This may be for Denton's
acuity optimization as Campbell & Gregory (1960) argue, but a
colleague, Professor Stephen Easter, has suggested another possibility: the protection of visual pigments from bleaching. Figure
5 shows how good it is at this. There are two curves in the figure;
each indicating the amount of human rhodopsin present as a function
of environmental luminance. The left hand curve illustrates how
much rhodopsin would be present if the pupil were fixed at its
dark value; the other shows the way in which a healthy normal
binocular light reflex preserves rhodopsin at higher light levels.
Since all of rod vision occurs at relatively trivial bleaching
levels, this hypothesis is viable for rhodopsin only if significant
rhodopsin bleaching in the absence of rod vision is somehow dele-
terious. There is evidence (Noell & Albrecht, 1971; Kuwabara &
Gorn, 1968) that this may be the case for the albino rat, at least,
but whether or not it is also true for man has yet to be shown.
But cone pigments are an entirely different matter. The light
intensity needed in the steady state to bleach half of erythrolabe
(or chlorolabe)--the red and green cone pigments--is within the
precision of the measurement, the same as that shown in Figure 5
for human rhodopsin. Thus the relation shown applies both to cones
and rods. Viewed in this light, Figure 5 emphasizes an important
role of the pupil light reflex in preserving significant cone
pigment for useful vision at high light levels.

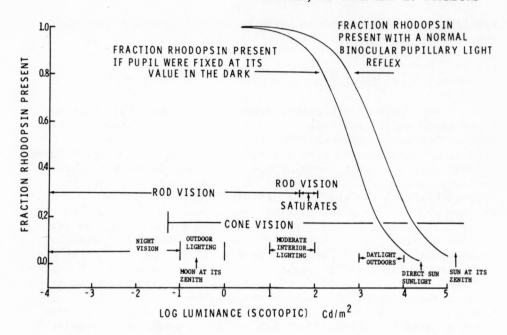

Figure 5. The fraction of human rhodopsin bleached by environmental light of different luminances. The left hand curve shows
the result if the pupil had its size in full dark adaptation; the
right hand curve shows the result if the pupil size in steady state
viewing follows the pattern ten Doesschate & Alpern (1967) determined for subject R. W. using a 12° field in binocular vision. The
curves are essentially unchanged when the calculation is done for
chlorolabe or erythrolabe, the respective human green and red cone
pigments.

A. *The photoreceptor of the steady state light reflex*. The
calculations producing the results in Figure 5 were based upon
measurements of the pupil size of a subject (ten Doesschate &
Alpern, 1967) exposed to a steady level of illumination. Under
such circumstances, the action spectrum is dominated by rods
(Wagman & Gullberg, 1942; Alpern & Campbell, 1962a; Bouma, 1965).
Bouma, in fact, argues from this that in the steady state, rods
alone activate the light reflex, a position that has the difficulty of explaining how in Figure 5 the rhodopsin protection
function of the light reflex continues above levels where rod
vision saturates. Bouma's way around this difficulty is to suppose
that signals "...for the steady state pupil bypass the scotopic
bottleneck which implies that at least some of the rods do not
saturate at 3.0 log scot td..." At first thought this seems to be
a relatively wild hypothesis. For one can easily demonstrate the

more probable alternative under steady state viewing by measuring
the directional sensitivity of the pupillomotor photoreceptors for
a small foveal fixed test. Figure 6 depicts Alpern & Benson's
(1953) measurements of the log of the intensity of a light through
the center of the pupil necessary to produce the same pupil
response as a fixed intensity light through various other points of
pupil entry. The curve falls off with point of pupil entry in the
expected way if the stimulus excited cones alone and not at all in
the way predicted if it excited rods alone. Thus for steady state
viewing (under these conditions) the directional sensitivity of the

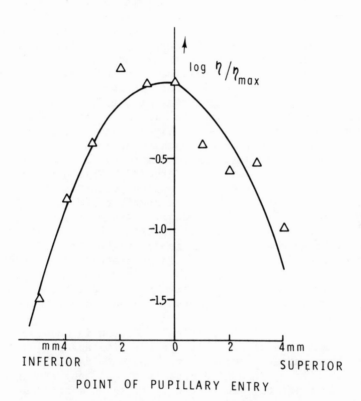

Figure 6. The log of the intensity of light (η) through the center
of the human pupil needed to produce the same steady state pupil
size as that obtained by putting a less than 1° spot of light of
constant luminance (1.5×10^5/ft-L) through various pupil entry
points vertically traversing the horizontal pupil diameter. The
equation of the curve log $\eta/\eta_{max} = p(r - r_m)^2$ was used by Stiles
(1939) to describe the directional sensitivity of foveal cones
measured psychophysically. In the figure, $p = -0.075$, $r_m = 0.5$ mm
inferior. Points calculated from Figure 5 of Alpern & Benson,
American Journal of Optometry, 1953, *30*, p. 577.

photoreceptors which make the pupil small is that of cones, not
rods. Spring & Stiles (1948) showed that this was not the case if
the stimulus field was large rather than small. Under their conditions, the response evoked by rods was so large that it swamped
the signals elicited by cones and almost no directional sensitivity
was observed.

Hence for steady state viewing exciting either rods or cones
can make the pupil small. But how is it that its action spectrum
is that of rods? The answer is instructive for those who will use
the pupil light reflex to decode optic nerve messages. Unlike the
visual central nervous system, the midbrain nuclei which drive the
light reflex cannot discriminate between signals evoked by excitation of the retinal photoreceptors in the focal image of the test
light and those excited by entoptic or exoptic scatter. Usually
this stray light is very weak, but since the absorption of a single
quantum (scattered or focused) suffices for rod excitation and
since the retina contains $120(10)^6$ rods and only $6(10)^6$ cones it is
small wonder that the action spectrum for steady state viewing is
almost always dominated by rods. To circumvent this difficulty one
might put the small steady stimulus light in the center of a large
rod saturating background; if the background does not itself
saturate the muscle, the action spectrum to evoke some criterion
response with the small spot can be studied. This experiment has
yet to be done. Alternatively, the entire retina may be uniformly
flooded with monochromatic light in a ganzfeld and the action
spectrum of the steady state photopupil response measured in this
way. For small responses this will certainly be that of rods; but
will it still be so when the field is so bright that (if all rods
are alike) every rod in the retina has saturated? Bouma (1965)
found that it was and Adrian (1971) that it was not. The C.I.E.
scotopic spectral sensitivity function is a good fit to Bouma's
results and the C.I.E. photopic curve fits Adrian's results.

Thus, even the simplest empirical question is unanswered.
Both answers cannot be right. Without reaching any prejudged
decision on this matter, however, it is easy to demonstrate that
the dilemma that Bouma struggled with is a real one. It is one
purpose of this paper to show that this is so; a second is to
suggest a fresh way of dealing with it.

B. *The size of the pupil in the dark*. Alpern & Campbell
(1962b) showed that in the dark after a full rhodopsin bleach, the
pupil recovered its size only very slowly, as though the unregen-
erated rhodopsin provided a bleaching signal B which served to keep
the pupil small. This interpretation was confirmed when Alpern &
Ohba (1972) measured the regeneration of rhodopsin and the recovery
of pupil size in the same eye (in the dark) after a full rhodopsin
bleach. Figure 7 shows typical experimental results. Pupil size

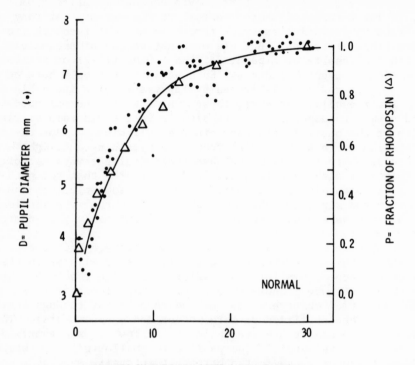

Figure 7. Correlation of the recovery of pupil size (dots ordinate scale to the left) and rhodopsin regeneration (triangles--ordinate scale to the right) in the dark following full rhodopsin bleach. The smooth curve is a simple exponential with a time constant of 400 seconds.

recovery (dots, ordinate scale to the left) and rhodopsin regeneration (triangles, ordinate scale to the right) go together hand in hand. That the pupil size is sensitive to, and recovers together with, the fading of the rod after image of a full bleach, is perhaps not surprising. But the observation is of interest because according to dark adaptation theory, it is precisely this bleaching signal which is responsible for rod threshold elevation (Barlow, 1964; Rushton, 1965b). It does this, according to Barlow, by providing a source of increased intrinsic noisy background against which the test becomes more difficult to detect and, according to Rushton, by attenuating the output signal of an automatic gain control (though not attenuated by it).

Barlow's view has support from evidence accumulating from intracellular records of photoreceptors to the extent that they show bleaching elevating receptor threshold without feedback from the more proximal retina. But his explanation cannot adequately deal with the results of Alpern, Holland & Ohba (1972) on patients with stationary night blindness. Such patients not only have no rod vision, but rod signals evoked by light are quite incapable of driving their pupils. However, these subjects have normal rhodopsin and normal rhodopsin bleaching signals to the midbrain driving the size of the pupil in the dark after a full bleach. Any theory of adaptation (such as Barlow's) requiring bleaching and light signals everywhere to follow the same anatomical pathways cannot adequately deal with this result. It demonstrates that the pathways for rod bleaching signals are separate at some place in the retina from rod signals evoked by light. In Rushton's terminology, these patients have a disease of the retinal automatic gain control.

C. *The size of the pupil in the steady state*. With the entire retina fully and evenly illuminated, the pupil size in the steady state becomes smaller and smaller as the light gets brighter and brighter. Figure 8 shows results of an experiment of this kind on two normal observers and one rod monochromat (though these results have been confirmed on three other rod monochromats). The response is recorded in one eye while its fellow views a ganzfeld with a fully dilated pupil. The pupil gets smaller with increased light even (or nearly) up to the brightest intensity available (100,000 scotopic trolands). This is 20 or 30 times brighter than the rod saturation level of Aguilar & Stiles (1954). For the normal, we might suppose Bouma's scotopic action spectra for such high intensity responses, wrong (and Adrian's photopic curve, right). But that explanation does not help very much when we try to understand the results obtained with rod monochromats. The few rhodopsin filled cones Falls, Wolter & Alpern (1965) found in a retina of this kind are quite inadequate to account for the remarkable similarity of the monochromat's behavior to that of the normal under these testing circumstances. Are we left then, both for normals and rod monochromats, only with Bouma's *ad hoc* reconciling hypothesis that the rod signals for steady state narrowing of the pupil "by-pass the saturation bottleneck"? How else can we account for the fact (as Figure 8 shows) that the monochromat's pupil continues to become smaller in the steady state under levels of retina illuminance at least one order of magnitude greater than Aguilar & Stiles' results suggest that every rod in this retina is saturated?

Bouma's idea is unappealing because with it we resurrect the idea of separate rod receptors for the steady state photopupillary response and have no way of explaining the directional sensitivity results in Figure 6. Moreover, it says nothing about the way

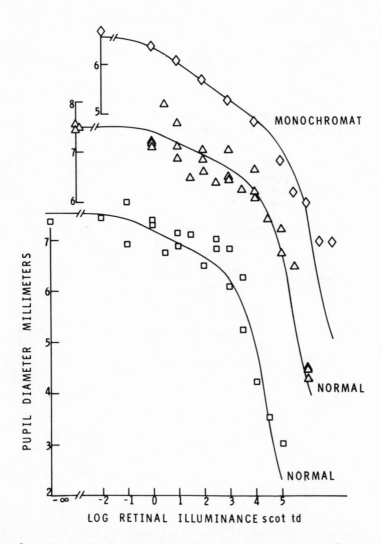

Figure 8. Size of the pupil in the steady state to full ganzfeld illumination for two normal subjects (squares and triangles) and one rod monochromat K (diamonds). Note that the pupil continues to get smaller after every rod in the retina has saturated even in a retina which has virtually no other receptors.

bleaching signals influence pupil size. But if bleaching can make
the pupil smaller in the dark, why can it not also do so in the
light? If it does, this provides a much more satisfying explanation for the rod monochromat's results in Figure 8 than Bouma's
ad hoc hypothesis.

Figure 9 illustrates these ideas more specifically. Bleaching

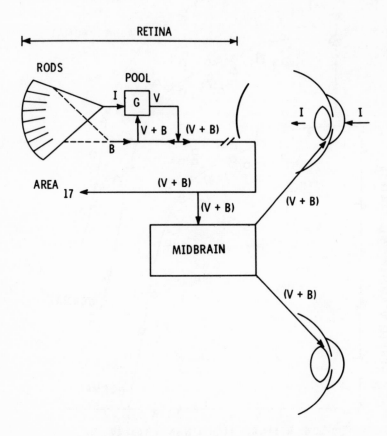

Figure 9. Schematic drawing of the model used to explain the effect
of bleaching and backgrounds on pupil size. Rods feed signals to
the pool proportional to the background intensity I. The output
V is passed to the optic nerve and is fed back to regulate sensitivity. Bleaching signals (B) proportional to the unbleached
rhodopsin enter the gain control from the feedback, but also pass
to the brain via the optic nerve. The change in pupil diameter is
proportional to the sum $(V + B)$. Reprinted with permission from
Alpern & Ohba, *Vision Research*, 1972, *12*, p. 946.

signals B are viewed as regulating retinal sensitivity by adjusting the feedback of an automatic gain control. Signals from real light are attenuated by the automatic gain control (Rushton, 1965b). The input to the gain control device is proportional to the quanta caught from the steady stimulus light (I), but the output (V) is nearly proportional to the logarithm of I. The output signal not only goes to the brain to signal the brightness of the light (and to the midbrain to drive the pupil), but also is fed back into the gain control to adjust the attenuation of retina sensitivity. Bleaching signals (added to the output signals) pass to the brain to signal brightness (as the visibility of rod after images attest) and to the midbrain to make the pupil small (as the results in Figure 7 prove).

The physiology of rod saturation has been analyzed by Alpern, Rushton & Torii (1970). They showed that it was a necessary consequence of the fact that rod signals (N) evoked by flashes cannot increase indefinitely with the light intensity, but only over a range of intensities. The actual equation describing the relation of the two is,

$$N = \phi/\phi + \sigma .$$ (1)

Where ϕ is the intensity of a light flash and σ is a constant. Upon passing through the retinal automatic gain control, these signals are attenuated (but not by their own feedback) and emerge as the output V.

$$V = \frac{\phi}{\phi + \sigma} \cdot \frac{I_D}{I + I_D} .$$ (2)

In equation (2), I_D is a constant, the intensity of the *eigengrau* or receptor noise and I is the intensity of the background. Equation (2) describes how the gain control scales down the output voltage of a flash which gets through before it is attenuated by its own feedback. Once the background becomes so bright (i.e., of the order 3,000 to 5,000 scotopic tds) the V signal evoked by a test flash which emerges from the gain control is too weak to be detected. No amount of increase of the test intensity ϕ will increase V to a detectable level; the rod system is saturated. For normal people, cone vision functions at these levels and rod saturation goes unnoticed; but rod monochromats have virtually no cones and high contrast vision disappears for them at these background brightnesses. As a result, they avoid bright lights (photophobia) not because such lights are painful, but because the monochromat's visual field washes out under these circumstances.

It is this process which Bouma would have us believe is
"bypassed" by rod signals driving the steady state pupil size.
But this *ad hoc* reconciling hypothesis is unnecessary. The
bleaching signals B, as well as the output signals V, drive the
pupil and it is the former which continue to make the rod monochromat's pupil smaller when the light increases to levels where
the latter have saturated.

A quantitative analysis of this process has been developed by
Alpern & Ohba (1972). They derived an equation for the size of
the pupil (D) in steady state viewing of a ganzfeld illuminated
uniformily by a light of intensity I.

$$D = D' - \Delta D_0 \left\{ \frac{I}{I + I_0} + \frac{1}{a} \log (I + I_D) + k \right\} . \qquad (3)$$

In this equation ΔD_0 is the maximum difference in pupil
diameter from full bleaching to its size (D') in full dark adaptation, a is the magnitude of rod log threshold elevation produced
by full bleaching and k is a constant. The smooth curves drawn
through the results in Figure 8 all have this equation and provide
a satisfactory description both of the normal's and the rod
monochromat's results.

This is a more satisfying way of explaining the continued
decrease of diameter of the rod monochromat's pupil in the steady
state above levels where every retinal rod is saturated (Figure 8).
But it does rely on Rushton's (1965b) concepts of adaptation pools,
feedback and gain control, ideas which are now temporarily out of
fashion as a consequence of recent studies of the effects of
bleaching on receptor sensitivity *in vitro*.

PHOTOPUPIL RESPONSE TO TRANSIENT STIMULATION

Turn now to the response of the pupil to flashes of light.
When it comes to transient stimulation, the problem of scattered
light is no less trivial than is the case for the steady state.
However, here the answer is less confused. Alpern & Campbell
(1962a) showed that both rods and cones make a contribution. They
found either with a small foveal field or a 20° centrally fixed
test that rod and cone signals pooled their respective sensitivities logarithmically with each having about equal weight. Only
by adapting the eye to a large (at least 15°) rod saturating
background did a small fovea test evoke a response which had the
action spectrum of cones and cones alone.

To study responses to flashes it is sometimes instructive
once more to obviate scattered light by using uniform stimulation

of the entire retina. We do this by focusing a test flash
uniformly on a homogeneous 'ganzfeld' in the form of a semi ping-
pong ball placed against the open eye with its pupil widely
dilated (with a suitable mydriatic). The pupil movements of its
fellow are studied with an infra-red pupillometer (Green &
Maaseidvaag, 1967).

A. *Normal Subjects*. Responses of the pupil of the normal
eye to light flashes of different intensities are presented in
Figure 10 for a particularly sensitive subject (L. B.). The flash
is a one msec. pulse which occurs at the very beginning of the
trace. The numbers identifying each response is the density of
the neutral filter used to attenuate the stimulus flash. As the
stimulus intensity increases the response amplitude increases and
the latency decreases. Figure 11A shows the relation between
maximum change in pupil size (in millimeters) and flash intensity.
For this subject, under these testing conditions, there was an
exact correspondence between the consensual photopupil response
threshold and the visual threshold. Visible flashes always made
the pupil of the other eye smaller; invisible flashes never did.

Thus, it is not surprising that at low intensities the
response is due to rods and rods alone. To substantiate this, the
experiment was repeated with red and blue test flashes. If the
intensities of the red, white and blue flashes are equated for
rods (Figure 11C), not cones (Figure 11B), the three amplitude
intensity curves superimpose.

At higher flash intensities, cones come into play. To
determine precisely where and how, we have resorted to the following ruse: Figure 12 shows an ordinary dark adaptation curve
measured on this same subject with a 10^{0} test flash 20^{0} in the
peripheral retina after 95% of the visual pigment in every retinal
rod and cone had been bleached. The curve has the familiar two
branches reflecting the recovery first of cones, then rods. The
rod curve, as Rushton (1965a) showed, follows an exponential
recovery even for time intervals in the dark shorter than those
usually studied (because of the normally superior cone sensitivity at these intervals). Therefore, we can follow the cone
contribution to the pupil response unhampered by the rod
contributions by beginning our measurements at 4 minutes--and
terminating them at 10 minutes--in the dark after every retinal
rod and cone has been fully bleached. In this 6 minute interval,
we record responses to light flashes whose intensity range between
the cone threshold and the upper limits provided by the extra-
polation of the rod exponential threshold recovery curve. The
amplitude intensity relation obtained under these conditions is
shown by the right hand curve in Figure 13A. This curve now has a
photopic (Figure 13B0, not a scotopic (Figure 13B), action spectrum.

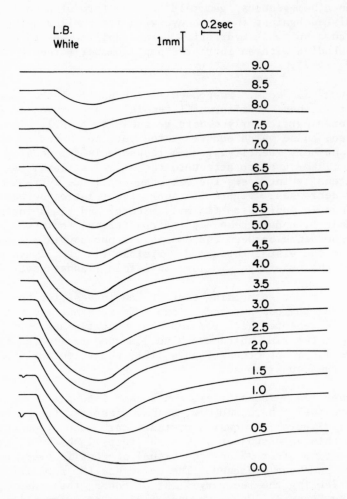

Figure 10. Pupillographic traces of responses to brief (about
1.0 msec.) Xenon flashes of different intensities exposed in a
ganzfeld to the fully dark adapted eye viewing with a widely
dilated pupil (produced by 2 drops 1% Mydriacil, 30 minutes prior
to the beginning of the experiment). The numbers on each trace
represent the density of the neutral filter used to attenuate
the light flash. The flash triggered the start of the trace.
Each curve has been arbitrarily displaced downward, but the dark
value for each was approximately the same (between 8 and 9
millimeters). Data were always obtained in sequence, brighter
flashes always following dimmer ones.

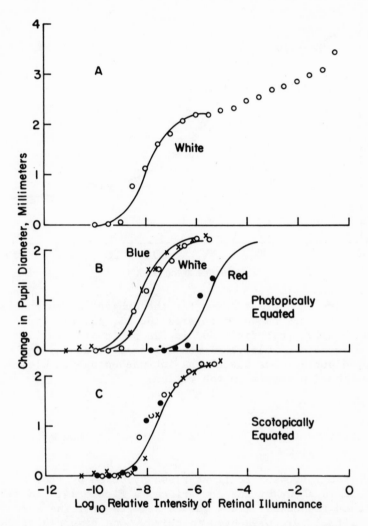

Figure 11. A. Maximum change in pupil diameter plotted as a function of logarithm of retinal illuminance produced by the flash. Each point is the mean of nine repetitions of experiments like those producing the traces in Figure 10. (B) and (C) similar plots of the lower part of the curve when the experiments were repeated with a red (Wratten #92) or a blue (Wratten #47) filter in the test beam. In (C) the flash intensities have been equated for scotopic, in (B) for photopic, vision.

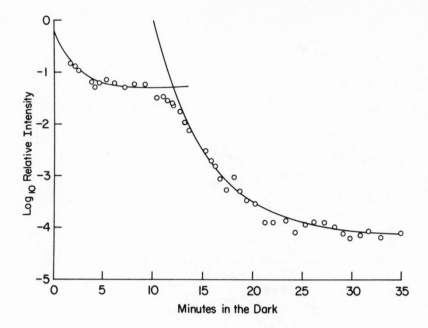

Figure 12. Dark adaptation curve for the subject whose pupillographic records are shown in Figures 10, 11, 13, 14 and 17
measured with a 10° test field 20° in the peripheral retina
following a 'ganzfeld' bleach viewed for 45 seconds through a
fully dilated pupil. The bleach was intense enough to bleach 95%
of all the visual pigments in the retina.

Responses obtained in this way result from excitation of cones
alone.

    How do the responses to light flashes evoked by rods and cones
differ? This is shown by the comparison in Figure 14. In this
figure matched responses, i.e., curves selected for the same
maximum amplitude, are presented in pairs. One response of each
pair was taken in the dark (preceded by a number representing the
log test flash filter density and the letter B). The other was
obtained 4--10 minutes after a full bleach (filter density followed
by the letter A). In the latter case the response is due to cones
and cones alone. In Figure 13A it is seen that flashes obtained
by filter densities equal to or greater than 6B excite rods and
rods alone. The comparison of the matched amplitudes of all
responses to flashes equal to or less than this intensity show
that rods alone give slower responses which have a longer latency
and peak later than equal size responses evoked by cones alone.
For flashes of intensity greater than 6.0B, the B response must be

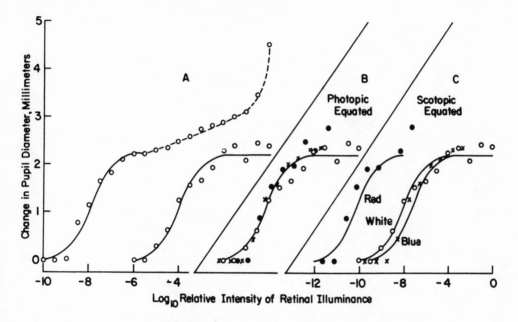

Figure 13.   A. Amplitude of the pupil response as a function of
intensity for a white test target.   The left hand set of data is
replotted from Figure 11A, the right hand set are results obtained
following a repetition of that experiment between 4--10 minutes in
the dark after a full bleach confining the flash intensities to
levels below the extrapolated rod threshold (measured in terms of
the number of log units above the cone photopupillary threshold).
(B) and (C) show results obtained by repeating the same experiment
between 4--10 minutes in the dark after full bleach with a colored
test flashes in (B) equated for the photopic, in (C) for the
scotopic, density of the red (Wratten #92) and blue (Wratten #47)
filters.

evoked by a signal pooled from both rods and cones.   Perhaps
these signals are mixed in the way Alpern & Campbell (1962a) found,
but it is by no means easy to convince oneself of this.   The higher
amplitude responses in Figure 14, for example, show only very
slight differences between those due to cones alone and those due
to a mixture of rods and cones.   What happens to the rod contributions?   Do they disappear?   Clearly it would be useful to study
the contributions that rods alone make to the response at these
higher light levels.   There is no way to do this in the normal eye,
but we can get some idea, by studying the photopupil response in
rod monochromats (who have normal retinal rods, but precious few
cones, Falls, Wolter & Alpern, 1965; Alpern, Falls & Lee, 1960).

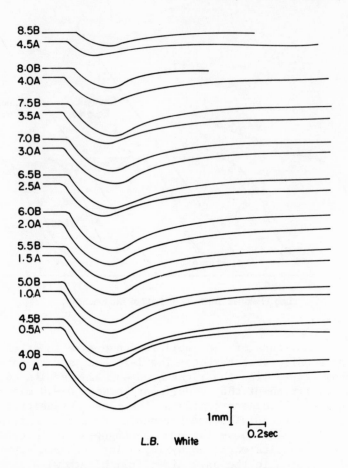

Figure 14. Pupillographic responses to a white test flash. The responses have been grouped in pairs, each number of the pair having about the same maximum change in pupil diameter. One member of the pair (labelled B) has been obtained as in Figure 10 after full dark adaptation, the other (labelled A) between 4--10 minutes in the dark after a full bleach. The number beside each curve represents the density of the neutral (Wratten #96) filters used to attenuate the stimulus flash which initiated the trace.

B. *Rod Monochromatic Subjects*. The size of the pupil of rod monochromatic subjects to steady backgrounds of different intensities has already been described. For the responses to light flashes Geldard (1933) described "...only a very minute and immeasurable twitch..." In his more recent monograph he states that "...pupil reactions are sluggish and greatly diminished in extent..." (Geldard, 1973) although the only intervening study on

this subject to come to our attention (Alexandridis & Dodt, 1967)
provides no justification for either view. None of these authors
document their findings with pupillographic records, so we have
repeated and extended earlier (unpublished) measurements on four
such observers. All of these responded in a similar way. The
traces reproduced here are from the two who were studied most
extensively in the dark.

Figure 15 shows the vigorous pupil response of one dark

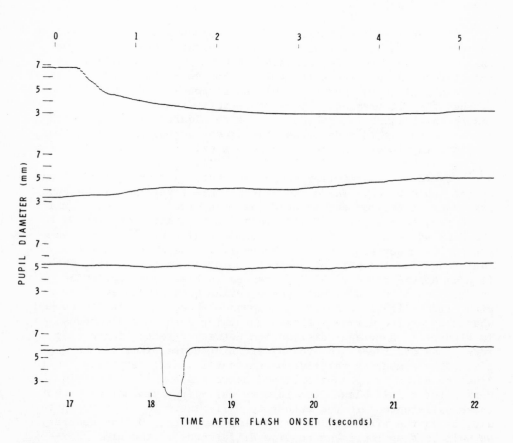

Figure 15. Record of the pupillographic response of a rod monochromat to a single maximum intensity flash. The record begins at
the top left and is continuous to the bottom right. Note that
the pupil size has not returned to its full dark value even after
22 seconds. Subject K.

adapted rod monochromat (K) evoked by an intense flash of light
(compare this to the normal response to 0 intensity flash in
Figure 10). Far from disappearing at these high intensities, this
response of a rod monochromat's pupil to the flash is clear. The
latency of this response (265 msec.) is a good 85 msec. longer than
that of the normal; the response reaches a peak diameter 3.5
seconds after the flash onset (instead of 1.4 seconds in the normal)
and only very slowly does the rod monochromat's pupil recover its
initial size in the dark. (For the example shown, the experiment
terminated after one half minute because the subject could no
longer hold her eye steady in the pupillometer field of view. The
normal pupil also recovers very slowly after these bright flashes,
but it typically reaches the size shown at the end of the trace in
Figure 15 in about 15 seconds.)

In Figure 16 a comparison of the responses of a second set of
subjects to flashes of a variety of different intensities shows
these same features. For flashes below the normal (solid line)
cone threshold the traces for (M) the rod monochromat (dotted line)
are identical to the normal's (0) rod responses. For brighter
flashes the differences in time characteristics of the pupil
responses of these two subjects is quite clear. In keeping with
normal responses to rods alone, the latent period is longer, the
response is slower, the peak reached later.

Figure 17 is a similar comparison between monochromat (K) and
normal subject (B). The solid line in this figure shows the pupil
responses of the monochromat and the open circles matched normal
responses, to a variety of different flash intensities exposed to
the dark adapted eye. These two subjects also had about the same
rod pupillomotor sensitivity, though it is somewhat higher than
that found for the pair of subjects compared in Figure 16. Both
figures document the clear differences in time characteristics of
the responses evoked by exciting a retina with virtually no cones
with bright lights compared to responses those same flashes evoked
when they excite normal retinas containing both rods and cones.
In Figure 17, a crisper distinction between effects of exciting
rods alone and those achieved by exciting cones alone can be
gleaned by comparing the rod monochromat's (dark) responses (solid
line) to normal responses obtained between 4 and 10 minutes in the
dark after a full bleach (solid circles). It seems unlikely that
these differences are due either to differences in the nerve pathways or in the iris muscles in the two subjects. On the contrary
we believe they represent genuine differences in the time characteristics of the relevant photoreceptor discharges themselves.
This view is substantiated to some extent by intracellular records
from vertebrate rods and cones (Fain & Dowling, 1973; Norman &
Werblin, 1973). Figure 18 shows, for example, the quick recovery
of cones and the slow recovery of rods to 180 msec. pulses of light

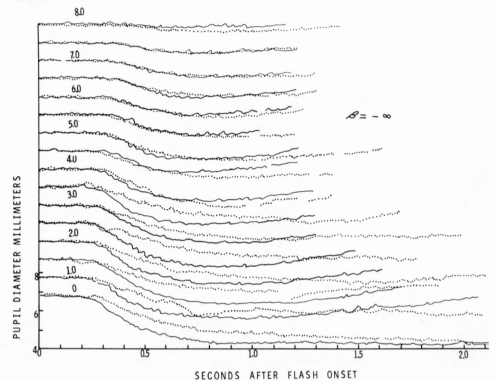

Figure 16. Tracing of the records of the pupillographic responses of a second rod monochromat (M) and a separate normal (O) to light flashes of different intensities presented to the fully dark adapted eye. The rod sensitivities of these two subjects were identical as were the responses to flashes below the normal cone threshold. At higher intensities the monochromat's responses (dotted line) have a longer latency and slower early velocity than the normal (solid line) though the maximum change in size is about the same. The numbers represent the density of the filter used to altenuate the flash intensity. Successive flashes have been vertically displaced; the base line for the two subjects were more or less the same, but in the figure they have been arbitrarily shifted to make them coincide.

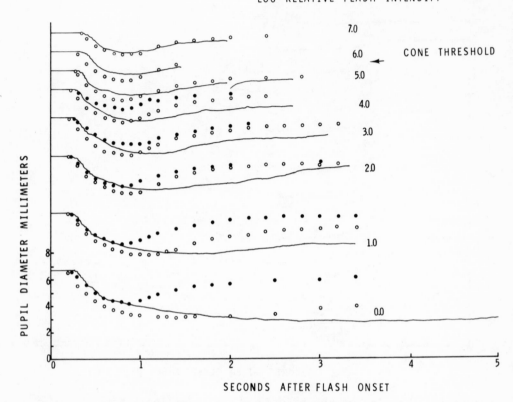

Figure 17. Comparison of the pupillographic records of the responses of normal B (open circles) and rod monochromat K (solid line) to flashes of different intensities presented to the dark adapted eye. The normal is the same subject whose responses are shown in Figure 10. The monochromat is the subject whose response is shown in Figure 15. The filled circles are the normal responses between 4--10 minutes after a full bleach under conditions which insure that cones alone were under test. The base lines have been arbitrarily shifted for coincidence, the lower most curve for the monochromat is correctly placed, all of the other curves have been shifted vertically.

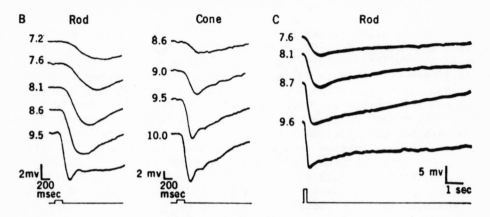

Figure 18. Intracellular recordings of responses of mudpuppy rods
and cones to 180 msec. flashes of light of different intensities.
Note the differences in recovery rate of cones and rods. Compare
these features to the cone and rod responses in Figure 17. Records
from Fain, G. L. & Dowling, J. E., *Science*, 1973, *180(4091)*,
pp. 1178-1180. Copyright 1973 by the American Association for the
Advancement of Science.

obtained in this way by Fain & Dowling (from the retina of the
mudpuppy *Necturus Maculosus*). Of course, iris contractions
involve nerve conduction, synaptic and muscle delays unknown to the
photoreceptor records. No doubt such delays account for the long
latent period of the photopupil response. However, after allowance
is made for these differences, the records in Figure 17 and Figure
18 are remarkably alike. This similarity between results from two
quite different kinds of experiments on different vertebrate
species is too striking to be fortuitous, but the difficulties in
the way of making the unequivocal case that both sets of results
have one and the same physiology are nonetheless formidable.

Perhaps even more difficult is to work out (assuming the
responses of different sense cells are alone responsible for the
differences in the responses in Figure 17 to the same test flash)
the laws of how the nervous system pools the information from
cones and rods, to bring about the results shown by the open
circles. Whatever the outcome of such an analysis, mere inspection
of the figure suffices to exclude as a class all hypotheses which
predict a convex combination of rod and cone inputs (such as, for
example, the weighted geometrical mean of the rod and contributions
which Alpern & Campbell (1962a) used to describe the spectral
sensitivity of the light reflex).

SUMMARY

The pupil light reflex is what engineers call a very "noisy"
system, because the tension of iris muscles can be influenced by a
host of non-retinal factors. Moreover, however clever the visual
central nervous system is in discriminating signals generated by
scattered light from those evoked by a focused retinal image, the
pupil control centers are quite incapable of making this distinction. This makes the task of using the pupil to decode optic
nerve messages both tedious and difficult. So far, very little
understanding has emerged from this approach. However, the ability
in this way to *(i)* exclude hypotheses as to how bleaching influences sensitivity in dark adaptation *(ii)* specify the nature of the
defect in stationary night blindness *(iii)* detect differences in the
time characteristics of human rod and cone receptor discharge
patterns and *(iv)* exclude several likely models as to how these
patterns are pooled, offers some hope that pursuit of this
objective is not without promise.

ACKNOWLEDGEMENTS

Assisted by a grant EY-00197-15 from the National Institutes
of Health. We are indebted to Professor Stephen Easter of the
Department of Zoology, University of Michigan for suggestions
regarding the plotting of Figure 15.

REFERENCES

Adrian, W. K. Proceedings of ARVO, 1971.
Aguilar, M. and Stiles, W. A. Saturation of the rod mechanism of
    the retina at high levels of stimulation. *Optica Acta*, 1954, *1*,
    59-65.
Alexandridis, E. and Dodt, E. Pupillenlichtreflexe und pupillen-
    weite einer stabchenmonochromatin. *Albrecht Von Graefis Archiv
    Fuer Klinische Und Experimentelle Ophthalmologie*, 1967, *173*,
    153-161.
Alpern, M. and Benson, D. J. Directional sensitivity of the
    pupillomotor photoreceptors. *American Journal of Optometry*,
    1953, *30*, 569-580.
Alpern, M. and Campbell, F. W. The spectral sensitivity of the
    consensual light reflex. *Journal of Physiology*, 1962, *164*,
    478-507(a).
Alpern, M. and Campbell, F. W. The behavior of the pupil during
    dark-adaptation. *Journal of Physiology*, 1962, *165*, 5-7P(b).
Alpern, M., Falls, H. F. and Lee, G. B. The enigma of typical total
    monochromacy. *American Journal of Ophthalmology*, 1960, *50*, 996-
    1011.

Alpern, M., Holland, M. G. and Ohba, N. Rhodopsin bleaching signals
   in essential night blindness. *Journal of Physiology*, 1972, *225*,
   457-476.
Alpern, M. and Ohba, N. The effect of bleaching and background on
   pupil size. *Vision Research*, 1972, *12*, 943-951.
Alpern, M., Rushton, W. A. H. and Torii, S. The attenuation of
   rod signals by backgrounds. *Journal of Physiology*, 1970, *206*,
   209-228.
Barlow, H. B. Dark adaptation: A new hypothesis. *Vision Research*,
   1964, *4*, 47-58.
Barr, L. and Alpern, M. Photosensitivity of the frog iris.
   Journal of General Physiology, 1963, *46*, 1249-1265.
Bito, L. Personal communication to M. Alpern, 1973.
Bouma, H. "Receptive systems mediating certain light reactions of
   the pupil of the human eye." Thesis, 1965, Eindhoven, The
   Netherlands.
Campbell, F. W. and Gregory, A. H. Effect of size of pupil on
   visual acuity. *Nature*, 1960, *187*, 1121-1123.
Denton, E. J. The responses of the pupil of gekko gekko to ex-
   ternal light stimulus. *Journal of General Physiology*, 1956, *40*,
   201-216.
Fain, G. L. and Dowling, J. E. Intracellular recordings from
   single rods and cones in the mudpuppy retina. *Science*, 1973,
   180, 1178-1181.
Falls, H. F., Wolter, J. R. and Alpern, M. Typical total mono-
   chromacy. *Archives of Ophthalmology*, 1965, *74*, 610-616.
Geldard, F. A. The description of a case of total color blindness.
   Journal of the Optical Society of America, 1933, *23*, 256-260.
Geldard, F. A. *The Human Senses* (2nd ed.) New York: John Wiley
   and Sons, 1973, p. 110.
Green, D. G. and Maaseidvaag, F. Closed-circuit television
   pupillometer. *Journal of the Optical Society of America*, 1967,
   57, 830-833.
Hagins, W. A. The visual process: Excitatory mechanisms in the
   primary receptor cells. *Annual Review of Biophysics and Bio-
   engineering*, 1972, *1*, 131-158.
Kuwabara, T. and Gorn, R. A. Retinal damage by visible light.
   Archives of Ophthalmology, 1968, *79*, 69-78.
Noell, W. K. and Albrecht, R. Irreversible effects of visible
   light on the retina: Role of vitamin A. *Science*, 1971, *172*,
   76-80.
Norman, R. A. and Werblin, F. S. Proceedings of ARVO, 1973, p. 98.
Rushton, W. A. H. The rod dark adaptation curve measured above
   cone threshold. *Journal of Physiology*, 1965, *181*, 641-644(a).
Rushton, W. A. H. The ferrier lecture: Visual adaptation.
   *Proceeding, Royal Society, Series B: Biological Sciences,
   London,* 1965, *162*, 20-46(b).

Spring, K. H. and Stiles, W. S. Variation of pupil size with
  change in the angles at which the light stimulus strikes the
  retina. *British Journal of Ophthalmology*, 1948, *32*, 340.
ten Doesschate, J. and Alpern, M. Effects of photoexcitation of
  the two retinas on pupil size. *Journal of Neurophysiology*,
  1967, *30*, 564.
Wagman, I. H. and Gullberg, J. E. The relationship between monochromatic light and pupil diameter: The low intensity visibility
  curve as measured by pupillary measurements. *American Journal
  of Physiology*, 1942, *137*, 769-778.
Wald, G. The photochemistry of vision. *Documenta Ophthalmologica*,
  1949, *3*, 94.

CHAPTER III:

A PHYSIOLOGICAL BASIS OF PUPILLARY DYNAMICS

D. Hansmann*, J. Semmlow**, and L. Stark***

*Cardiodynamics Laboratory, Beverly Hills, **Bioengin-
eering Program, University of Illinois at Chicago Circle
***Departments of Physiological Optics and Mechanical
Engineering, University of California at Berkeley

Motor activity of the human iris provides an increasingly
useful data source to a growing number of research and clinical
fields. In addition to studies concerning physiology of the
pupillomotor system itself, pupillary activity has become an important tool in sensory physiology (Cartevette and Cole, 1962;
Eijkmann and Vendrile, 1963), neurological diagnosis and research
(Stanten and Stark, 1960; Stark and Cornsweet, 1958), pharmacology
(Carlson, 1957; Loewenfeld, 1963) and psychology (Hess, 1965).
The usefulness of this motor output system is a result of the
variety of brain stem mechanisms which contribute to its innervation and the complexity of the pupillomotor neuromuscular apparatus.
With the advent of instrumentation to provide continuous monitoring
of pupillomotor output, quantitative studies, both static and dynamic, were possible and a great deal of behavioral information has
been gathered. The ability to quantitatively control certain inputs encourages servoanalytic approaches adding to the richness of
material on this organ (Stark, 1968). However, this fecundity also
presents special problems; the wealth of published data often
appears confusing and contradictory, and has occasionally led to
heated controversy.

In an effort to simplify, we confine our study to motor
processes, here to include muscular mechanisms and final common
pathway. Our first objective is to isolate from the complexity
of pupil behavior, such as found in the light reflex, those characteristics attributable to motor processes. A definition of the
major features of the motor system is, in its own right, a valuable
contribution, since such characteristics may play an important role
in all studies using pupillomotor output as a data source. We then

determine from experiments on isolated smooth muscle the likely
behavioral characteristics of iris muscular components, while an
analysis of the mechanical apparatus provides a structure for
these components. Finally, to link together mechanical and muscular characteristics with gross motor behavior, we will use an
analog type model which can be 'experimented on' using digital
computer simulation. The model will also provide a convenient
framework for organizing isolated data regarding the motor system
or its components.

In addition to organizing and defining motor characteristics,
we expect a quantitative model with its forced consistency to
expose incompatible concepts and, in some cases, to rationalize
seemingly contradictory data. Comparing model simulation results
with experimental data provides a test for possible motor mechanisms and may also suggest new experimental designs. Finally, a
quantitative description of motor characteristics would aid in
separation of pupillomotor responses from behavior attributable to
nonmotor processes, and thus, may provide a valuable tool to the
several disciplines which use pupillomotor activity as a data
source.

MOTOR BEHAVIORAL CHARACTERISTICS

Response Asymmetry

To isolate motor characteristics from those of sensory or
other origin, our approach is to compare and contrast pupil responses from more than one sensory input. In general, those
characteristics unique to a particular input modality are probably
of sensory origin while those common to several inputs are likely
due to motor processes. Three motor reflexes have sensory inputs
which can be quantitatively controlled in the laboratory environment; the light reflex, near response and fusional vergence pupil
response. While the light reflex has been one of the most analyzed
of pupillomotor responses, we present it here with particular regard to characteristics which may be of motor origin. Figure 1
shows average response of the pupil to an increasing and decreasing step of light intensity presented, along with velocity, as a
time function, and as a phase plane trajectory (Semmlow and Stark,
1973). The phase plane display, a concept borrowed from a general
method of nonlinear analysis plots first derivative against output
and produces a succinct presentation of response characteristics
emphasizing transient behavior (Semmlow and Stark, 1971). The light
reflex on-step response shows a rapid constriction attaining a relatively high peak velocity immediately followed by a redilation
movement (sometimes referred to as pupillary escape). The off-
light response is considerably slower resulting in a marked
asymmetry in the phase trajectory and shows none of the overshoot

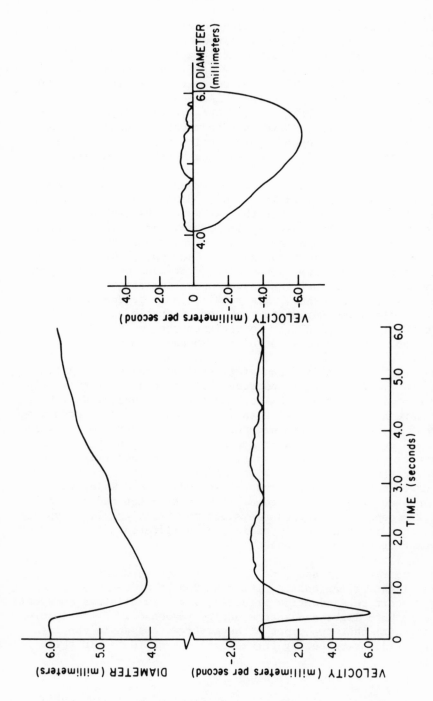

Figure 1. Averaged pupil light reflex movements to a 2-sec on, 4-sec off step change in light intensity from 3.5 to 4.5 log td. presented as time plots (left) and phase plane trajectory (right). Note the marked overshoot in the on response and the slower dilation movements. Semmlow and Stark, 1973)

dynamics seen in the on-step response. In contrast, the response
of the pupillomotor system to a similar stimulus pattern presented
through accommodative sensory pathways shows quite different dynamical features, Figure 2. The on-step response* is slower, even
though the overall response is somewhat larger than the light response, with little overshoot while the off-step response is
slightly faster than its light reflex counterpart leading to a more
symmetrical phase trajectory. While this response is less complex
than the light reflex, lacking significant overshoot characteristics, it still demonstrates different dynamical features for constrictive and dilatative movements indicating the presence of a
nonlinear, direction dependent process somewhere in this system.

In the response of Figure 2 the net excursion of each movement
is equivalent (the entire dilation is not shown), only the velocities
and hence, the times required for the two movements, are unequal.
Thus the nonlinear process responsible for this behavioral feature
acts only on the dynamic aspects of the movement and has been shown
to be independent of static motor levels (Semmlow, 1970). That is,
the effect of this mechanism is not altered by mean pupil size, its
action remains the same over the entire operating range of the
pupillomotor system, and thus, this behavior must be due to elements
which have little or no influence from, or on static behavior. This
observation will be particularly appreciated when we discuss possible
mechanisms for direction-dependence or response asymmetry.

Since the "asymmetrical" behavior involves only the transient
portion of the movement it is described by parameters relating only
to system dynamics. Further, as both constrictive and dilative
movements have been shown in servoanalytic studies to be overdamped,
second order systems, only two parameters are necessary to uniquely
describe each movement, the major and minor time constants. These
time constants may be determined directly from the phase plane and
the values obtained from four subjects showed a minor time constant
for both movements between .08 and .15 seconds, and a major time
constant between .25 and .45 seconds for constriction and between
.75 and 1.2 seconds in dilation (Semmlow and Stark, 1973). Response
asymmetry, then is quantatively defined as a difference in the major
time constant of the two responses.

Comparing Figures 1 and 2 we note that the overshoot is seen
only in the light reflex and is likely a product of sensory elements
(possibly a short term adaptive process), yet slow dilation movements
are common to both light and accommodative responses. It is important to note here that two types of asymmetry are seen in the light
reflex: a rapid, overshooting on-response not reflected in the off-

---

*Due to increasing dioptric stimulation (Semmlow and Stark, 1973).

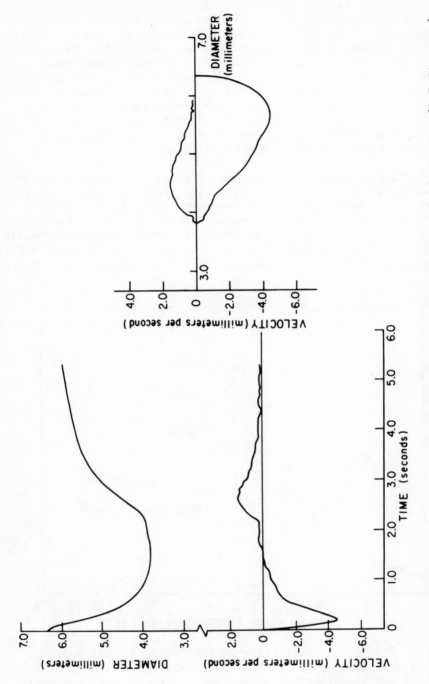

Figure 2. Averaged response of the pupil to a 2-sec on, 4-sec off, 6-diopter (1-7 diopters) step change in accommodative stimulation. Note the marked direction-dependent behavior. (Semmlow and Stark, 1973)

response to light, and slower movement during dilation than found
in constriction, whether produced by redilation after constriction
overshoot or the off-response. The former is stimulus dependent
and almost certainly due to retinal elements so we term it retinal
asymmetry, while the latter appears to be movement or output dependent and falls into the category of a response asymmetry.
Whether the response asymmetry of the light reflex is due to the
same processes which produce asymmetry in the near response (or,
alternatively, a deep sensory process) cannot be determined without a complete systems model integrating both sensory processes
with pupillomotor system; however, we will comment later on
this behavior with regard to our motor model.

     Possibly relevant to the asymmetry of gross responses are the
findings reported by Terdiman, Smith, and Stark (1971) working with
an isolated, though intact motor system in the cat. Stimulating
either sympathetic or parasympathetic final common pathways (the
motor nerves were sectioned just distal to their respective ganglia
forming an isolated system) produced a steady change in pupil size,
(Figure 3) demonstrating the ability of both innervational compon-

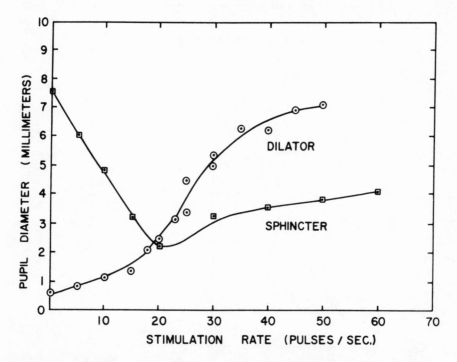

Figure 3. Static characteristics of the isolated pupil motor
system in cat produced by electrical stimulation of sympathetic
(dilation) and parasympathetic (sphincter) final common pathways.
(Terdiman, Smith and Stark, 1969)

ents to effect pupillomotor control over the entire behavioral
range of the pupil. Though the two components, the sympathetic
presumably acting through dilator muscle, and parasympathetic
acting through sphincter muscle, are not identical in response to
electrical stimulation they are certainly capable of functioning
as agonist-antagonist competitors. Again, this data will be discussed with regard to a motor system model.

Range Nonlinearity

Though response asymmetry is independent of static pupil size,
not all pupillomotor features are unaltered by changes in mean
pupil size. Thus if the mean or average pupil size is reduced by
a steady accommodative effort, Stark (1964) showed the motor response to a constant pulse of retinal light decreased presumably
as a result of the change in average pupil size (Figure 4). This
result suggests a decreasing motor system responsiveness, or gain
at the smaller pupil sizes, though well above the normal limits of
pupillary constriction. This variation in responsiveness will
affect static characteristics and is likely responsible for the
familiar "S" shaped curve reported in the literature. To investigate and quantify this "range behavior", so-called because its
activity is a function of, or related to the current operational
range of the pupil, we again make use of the multiple input features of the pupillomotor system; that is three independent stimulus
inputs evoke pupil movement and can be quantitatively controlled
in the laboratory environment. We use one stimulus modality to
create a controlled, repeatable signal to the motor system while
another input is used to vary the mean, or baseline level of motor
output (Semmlow, Hansmann and Stark, submitted).

Essentially, one input is used to "set" the baseline level
while the other "reads out", that is, provides a test of motor responsiveness. In other words, we ask the question: "If mean (or
initial) pupil diameter is varied, but the type and extent of the
stimulus is kept the same, does pupil response change, and if so,
can we establish a quantitative description of that change?" Any
such change would be related to the operating range of the pupillomotor system and thus, we call it 'range nonlinearity'.

Though any of the three quantitatively controllable stimuli
may, in theory, be used to set the level or test responsiveness
certain practical considerations regarding stimulus generation and
the stability of a particular sensory pathway make some combinations unfeasible. We chose retinal light to set the baseline level
which leaves us free to use either accommodative or fusional vergence stimulation to test motor responsiveness.

Another important condition regarding the stimuli is that they
be truly independent, and although fusional vergence stimulation

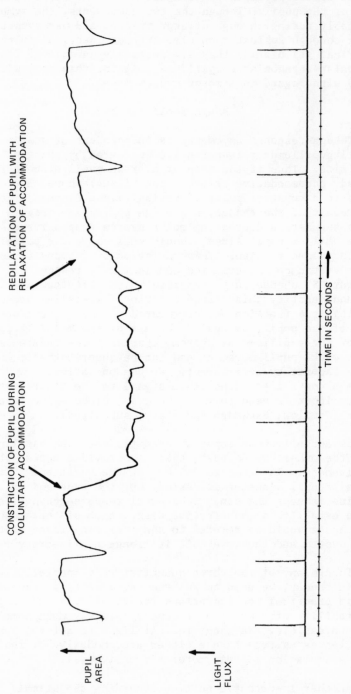

Figure 4. Light reflex movements in response to a constant amplitude pulse showing a reduction in amplitude as mean pupil size is reduced by a steady accommodative effect. (Stark, 1964).

has no known interactions with the other pupil inputs and hence,
satisfies the above criterion, there is a possibility that light
stimulation may affect accommodative input due to an increased
depth of field at smaller pupil sizes. However, experiments on
the accommodative convergence eye movement showed no change in
response over the value of light levels and pupil sizes encountered
indicating independence of the accommodative input from light stimuli in this experiment (Semmlow, Hansmann and Stark, submitted).

Pupil responses to a 5 diopter step change in accommodative
stimulation at various mean pupil diameters are presented as time
plots in Figure 5. Responsiveness of the pupillomotor system is
clearly dependent on operating range, the responses between 4 and
6 mm being more extensive than those at either 3 or 7 mm pupil
size. A quantitative description of this change in iris motor
responsiveness, or gain, can be constructed by plotting response
amplitude against mean pupil size for the entire experimental set

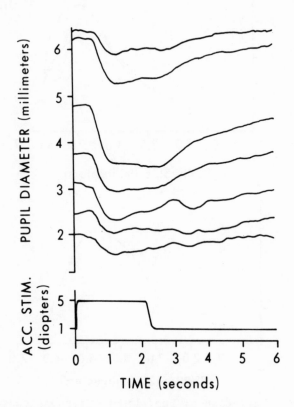

Figure 5. Averaged pupil responses to a 5-diopter accommodative
stimulus for several values of mean pupil size. The dependence of
responsiveness on pupil size is clearly demonstrated. (Semmlow,
Hansmann and Stark, submitted)

as in Figure 6A. The results for two subjects show the response
peaks between 4-5.5 mm pupil diameter, falling off smoothly on
either side.

We can repeat the series of experiments described above using
the third, independent pupillomotor stimulus, fusional vergence.
Again, mean pupil size is set by light input, but the dynamic
accommodation stimulus is replaced by a 3 meter-angle step change,
from 1 to 4 meter angles, in fusional vergence. The resultant
pupillary movement is associated with the change in eye position
necessary to bring to fusion two similar objects and though there
is considerable evidence demonstrating the independence of fusional and accommodative systems they normally interact in binocular
vision. The results of this set of experiments displayed as in
Figure 6A below are seen in Figure 6B.

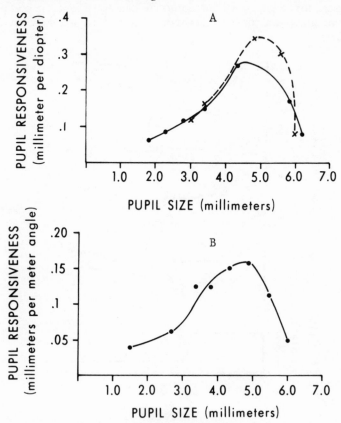

Figure 6A and 6B. Variation of pupillomotor responsiveness, or
gain, as a function of mean pupil size. A) Upper: Range behavior
averaged for two subjects as determined by using accommodative
stimulation. B) Lower: Similar behavior produced by dynamic
fusional stimulation for a single subject.

A qualitative agreement with responses produced by accommodative
stimulation provides additional support to the argument that the
range behavior is of motor origin.

A general description of pupillomotor range behavior is
important both in terms of future experimentation involving pupillography, and clinical diagnostic applications, since it is a motor
process and the changes in responsiveness it describes would affect
all pupillomotor data. Though a precise quantization of responsiveness variation is subject to experimental errors, our results
indicate an "expansive range nonlinearity" producing substantially
reduced gain (by a factor of 2 or more) in movements away from
mid-pupil sizes. The generality of this nonlinear process may be
best demonstrated by its ability to explain a number of indepen-
dently observed pupillomotor phenomena. Thus, Stark's "A multiplier"
(Stark, 1964) appears to be a direct manifestation of the "expansive range nonlinearity" on the light reflex when viewed over a
limited range of pupil size. Similarly, when Stanten and Stark
(1960) studied pupil noise they found interesting variations in
the noise characteristics with changes in mean pupil size. Usui
and Stark (in preparation) plotting random pupil movements as a
function of instantaneous pupil size found a variation in activity
which paralleled the "expansive range nonlinearity" (Figure 7).
The influence of this nonlinearity on the incoming noise signal
clearly demonstrates the action of this mechanism on all signals
processed through the pupillomotor system. Additionally, a single
mechanism, the "expansive range nonlinearity" can now be used to
explain the complex noise multiplicative behavior first described
by Stanten and Stark (1960). Doubtless, other observations unknown to these authors, may be directly or indirectly related to
the range behavior described here.

We have represented pupil range dependent behavior by a function which varies continuously as the mean value of pupil size
varies (Figure 6A and 6B). There is no indication from our experimental results of a linear range separated from a nonlinear range
by a distinct "breakpoint" as suggested by Loewenfeld and Newsome
(1971). Their technique which utilized strong light stimulation
and drug induced ansicoria involved some assumptions concerning
the motor input derived from light stimulation (as well as the
primary muscular action of various pharmacologic agents). Rather,
our data demonstrate the existence of a nonlinear process which is
active throughout the entire pupillomotor range, though it is certainly most noticeable toward the extremes of pupil size. However,
our data and that of others have points which are too widespread
to exclude the possibility of abrupt changes in the action of this
process as a result of slight changes in size. A more detailed
use of the described technique involving more subjects and more data
points (particularly in the critical regions around 4 and 6 mm)

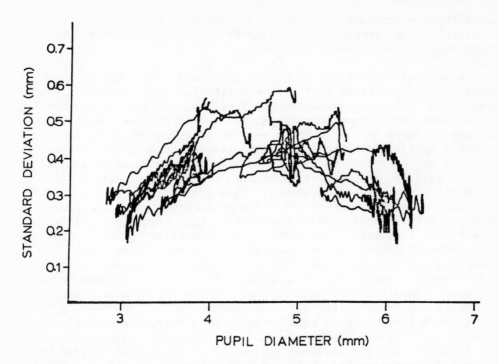

Figure 7. Random movements of the pupil displayed against instantaneous pupil size shows variation in activity produced by the
"expansive range nonlinearity." (Usui and Stark, in preparation)

would be required to settle this matter. In the study mentioned
above Loewenfeld and Newsome (1971) concluded that the pupillomotor
system was effectively linear within a range of 3.5-6.0 mm outside
of which responsiveness decreased. Though at no point within its
normal range of operation can this system be considered truly
linear, in the range of 3.5 to 6.0 millimeters variations in responsiveness are limited to about ±10%. Thus, if in a particular
measurement situation an accuracy of ±10% is acceptable, and if
pupil size is maintained between 3.5 and 6.0 millimeters, the
assumption of approximate linearity is justified.

With regard to specific mechanisms, though our accommodative
convergence eye movement control data eliminates the possibility
that sensory processes of either retinal or accommodative origin
are responsible for pupil range behavior, we have not (nor can we

based on these experiments) ruled out the possibility that the range characteristics are a manifestation of nonlinear interaction between signals summing at the motor nucleus. However, the nonlinearity's strong dependence on output level and the alterations produced by drugs found by many, implies it is associated with a mechanical process. In another study of iris structure, Newsome and Loewenfeld (1971) suggest a decrease in the compressibility of the iris stroma occurring at both large and small pupil sizes may be responsible. Again, we will examine alternative mechanisms for this behavior in light of the model to be presented in the next section.

Summary of Behavior

An analytic presentation of pupil responses to light and accommodative stimulation has demonstrated several behavioral features of interest to all who work with pupillomotor activity. Response asymmetry, characterized by variation in movement dynamics dependent on response direction, is found in both the light reflex and near response and may be a result, at least in part, of motor processes. Additionally, the complex light reflex also exhibits retinal asymmetry wherein behavior is dependent on stimulus direction. Quantitative isolation of the two asymmetries in the light reflex awaits the development and simulation of a comprehensive light reflex -- near response system model.

Variation in pupillomotor responsiveness with mean pupil size was isolated through the use of multiple stimulus inputs, one to vary mean size while the other measured responsiveness. The expansive range nonlinearity so defined is a motor process which influences all pupillomotor activity. This basic behavioral characteristic must be incorporated into the methodology of any experiment involving a range of pupil sizes. Thus, while a given light flash input may produce, say, a 1 millimeter maximum response in a 5 millimeter pupil the same input would be expected to produce only a .7 millimeter response in a 4 millimeter pupil. Therefore, variation in pupillomotor response to a dynamic input, such as the flash so often used in clinical situations, may be more of a test of mean pupil size than of a change in actual pupillomotor responsiveness. This does not negate the value of such data, but suggests that the information lies not in response amplitude, but in the related parameter, mean pupil size. Indeed, since absolute measurements are usually more difficult than relative ones, particularly in the clinical environment the use of response amplitude as an approximate measure of mean pupil size is a sound and expeditious procedure.

THE MATHEMATICAL MODEL

The several experiments described above demonstrated that the pupil range nonlinearity is a real phenomenon which is observed

using different physiological inputs (e.g., vergence, accommodation).
The obvious question was whether this behavior could be attributed
to (1) mechanical iris sphincter/dilator characteristics and known
smooth muscle properties; or (2) whether the non-linearity was due
to neurological preprocessing. To suggest an answer a homeomorphic
model was constructed based on the following assumptions:

1. The iris can be modeled by a rectilinear push-pull system
   representing sphincter and dilator muscle components with
   identical properties.

2. Iris sphincter and dilator characteristics are similar to those
   of other multi-unit, smooth contractile tissue.

3. Multi-unit muscle can be modeled by the Carlson (1959) equation
   for force-velocity relationships (variable spring-constant).

4. Iris innervation can be characterized by a single parameter,
   E, related to pulses per second. Further, sphincter and dilator muscles are reciprocally innervated.

These assumptions were developed and defended in the following
manner:

   Kinematics. It is appropriate to begin this discussion with
a few comments on nomenclature. The terms: tension, force, and
stress are often used interchangeably in the muscle physiology
literature*.

   Discrete-Element Model. If we consider the sphincter and
dilator muscles to be composed of a finite number of elemental
fibers then the iris can be visualized as the network in Figure 8.
The model is drawn with an equal number of sphincter and dilator
fibers but this is not essential to the argument. The only assumption is that T_s be the total tension in the sphincter muscle, and

---

*Some literature references confuse force with stress, N, which is
force per unit area. Stress has a definite physical significance
in muscle mechanics, but is often difficult to work with because
of the large cross-sectional area changes associated with muscle
contractions and relaxations. For a single muscle the number of
contractile elements remains constant despite large area changes.
Hence, total force provides a more convenient measure of the mechanical state of the muscle than does stress. In this study, we
define tension, P, as the scalar component of the force vector, P.
Tension will be the predominant measure of the mechanical state of
a muscle. This is reasonable since directionality, if required, is
determined by the axis of the component muscle fibrils.

that $n.T_d$ can be defined as the total tension, $T_D(n)$, in the dilator muscle, where n is the number of elemental dilator fibers. For steady state conditions, the sum of the forces must equal zero. Considering a particular junction point,

$$T_d = 2T_s \sin(\alpha) \qquad\qquad 1$$

or
$$T_D(n) = 2nT_s \sin(\alpha) \qquad\qquad 2$$

but
$$\alpha = \theta/2 = \pi/n$$

and
$$\underset{n \to \infty}{\text{Lim}} \; n\sin(\pi/n) = \pi$$

Hence

$$T_D = \underset{n \to \infty}{\text{Lim}} \; 2T_s n\sin(\pi/n)$$

$$T_D = 2\pi T_s \qquad\qquad 3$$

Equation 3 gives us the rather surprising result that, for equilibrium, the ratio of total sphincter tension to total dilator tension is a constant, and is not affected by the changing geometry at various pupil diameters. On the other hand, the characteristic sphincter and dilator muscle lengths ℓ_s and ℓ_d are related to pupil diameter, x, by the expressions:

$$\ell_s = \pi x \qquad\qquad 4$$

$$\ell_d = \frac{L-x}{2} \qquad\qquad 5$$

where L = iris root diameter

The sphincter muscle, of course, is not a single idealized muscle fiber as assumed in the derivation of equation 3, but is a matrix of fibers having a finite width, w, and thickness, h, as illustrated in Figure 9. Using the methods of continuum mechanics the equation of motion in polar coordinates for the axisymmetric, plan strain case is

$$N_{r,r} + \frac{N_r - N_\theta}{r} = 0 \qquad\qquad 6$$

where N_r and N_θ are the radial and tangential components of stress as shown in Figure 9 and the "," implies partial differentiation.

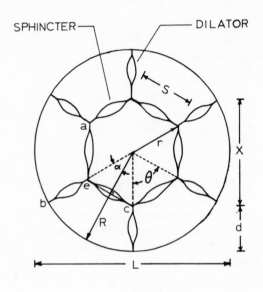

SPHINCTER   DILATOR

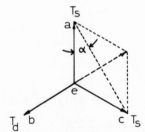

$$T_d = 2 T_s \sin(\alpha) \quad \text{for equil.}$$

Figure 8. Finite-element model of sphincter-dilator muscle system.
Upper: Outside circle represents iris root attachment (limbus).
Spindle shapes represent individual muscle fibers (radial = dilator; circumferential = sphincter), although assuming them to be
fractions or multiples of actual fibers does not effect the argument.

    S = distance between dilator attachment points
    d = length of dilator muscle
    L = diameter of iris (= 2R)
    x = diameter of pupil (= 2r)
    $\Theta = 2\pi/n = 2\alpha$
    n = number segments in model (= number of dilator fibers)

Actual iris structure is approximated by allowing n to approach
a very large number.

Lower: Free-body force diagram at a particular sphincter-dilator
junction for conditions of static equilibrium. T_s is the tension
in the sphincter muscle. T_d is the tension in a single dilator
fiber.

Assuming isotropy and the boundary conditions:

$$N_r \ (r = a) = 0 \tag{7a}$$

$$N_r \ (r = b) = P \tag{7b}$$

it can be shown than

$$N_\theta = \frac{Pb^2}{(b^2 - a^2)} \left(1 + \frac{a^2}{r^2}\right) \tag{8}$$

where P can be interpreted as the "pressure" (force per unit area-
h.b.dθ) exerted on the sphincter by the dilator muscle, and N_θ is
the tangential, or hoop stress within the sphincter muscle, at
radius, r. Choosing nominal values for a and b in equation 8 (a =
5 mm, b = 6 mm), we have

$$N_\theta \ (5) = 6.55P \tag{9a}$$

$$N_\theta \ (6) = 5.55P \tag{9b}$$

or $$N_\theta \ (a = 5, \ b = 6) \cong 6P \tag{10}$$

In comparing equations 3 and 10 we see that, although "total"
dilator tension is 2π times greater than sphincter tension (at equilibrium), sphincter "stress" (force per unit area) is 6 times greater

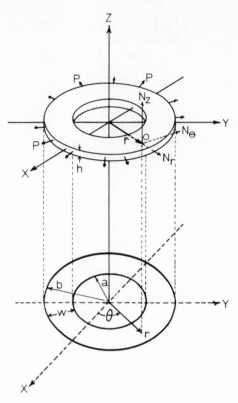

Figure 9. Continuum model of iris sphincter muscle. Position vector, $\bar{r}$, of an arbitrary point, 0, within the muscle is expressed in cylindrical coordinates (r, θ, z); h = thickness; w = width; N_r, N_θ, N_z are the components of stress (force/area) at the point, 0; and P is the rth-component of stress at the sphincter boundary (r=b) provided by the dilator muscle. Stress at the inside boundary (r=a) is zero.

than dilator stress (pressure). This implies that the concentration of muscle fibers must be greater in the sphincter than in the dilator. This is supported histologically and may explain the experimental results of Apter (1960) who had difficulty in observing dilator muscle activity. Relative thickness of the two muscles must be taken into consideration to be able to make realistic calculations.

As the width of the sphincter decreases the sphincter stress, N_θ, increases and, in the limit as a → b, it becomes unbounded. However, if we observe that

$$P = \frac{T_D}{2\pi bh} \qquad\qquad 11$$

and

$$N_\theta \cong \frac{T_s}{(b - a)n} \qquad\qquad 12$$

and substitute 11 and 12 into 8, we have

$$T_D = \frac{(b + a)\pi T_s}{b}$$

and in the limit as $a \to b$

$$T_D = 2\pi T_s \qquad\qquad 13$$

which is the same result we obtained in equation 3.

   The Push-Pull Model. On the basis of equations 3 and 13, then,
the sphincter/dilator system can be thought of as a push-pull system where one muscle has a mechanical advantage. An appropriate
analogy might be a lever arm as imagined in Figure 10. If we now
make the arbitrary definitions that

$$\ell_{s'} = \ell_s / \pi$$

$$\ell_{d'} = 2\ell_d$$

$$P_s = 2\pi T_s \qquad\qquad 14$$

and $\qquad P_d = T_D$

then equation 3 and 4 can be written

as $\qquad\qquad P_s = P_d \qquad\qquad\qquad 15$

and $\qquad\qquad \ell_{s'} = x \qquad\qquad\qquad 16a$

$$\ell_{d'} = L - x \qquad\qquad 16b$$

Mechanically this is equivalent to two muscles hooked together in
a rectilinear push-pull manner which was the basic Semmlow model
assumption (Semmlow and Stark, 1971). The prime super scripts in equation 16 will be dropped in the future with the understanding that the
definitions in 14 still hold. Here x can be thought of as a charac-

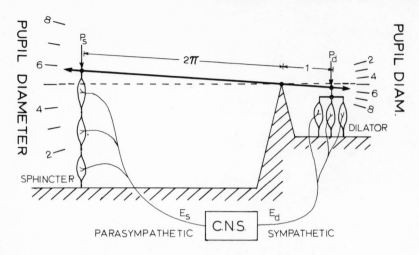

Figure 10. Another mechanical analogy to the sphincter-dilator muscle system. Here P_s and P_d are the "total" sphincter and dilator forces, respectively. E_s and E_d are the corresponding excitation levels.

teristic length of the intact push-pull system. In the case of the iris, x can be taken as the pupil diameter.

In summary, the steady state iris can be characterized by the following quantities.

ℓ_s, ℓ_d : characteristic lengths of the sphincter and dilator muscles

x : characteristic length of the push-pull system (pupil diameter)

P_s, P_d : total restoring tension of the sphincter and dilator muscles, respectively

E_s, E_d : excitation of the sphincter and dilator muscles, respectively

There is strong evidence that the excitation relationship is recripocal. Descartes originally described, and Sherrington (1894) was the first to show reciprocal innervation in the lateral and medial rectus muscles of the oculomotor system. Lowenstein and Loewenfeld (1970) showed that if light is momentarily interrupted in the two eyes of a cat, one of which is sympathectomized, dark- ness dilation is less in the abnormal eye. The conclusion was that dark dilation must be due to 1) sympathetic impulses which reach the normal eye only; and 2) relaxation of the pupillary sphincter which affects both pupils. That is, stated mathematically in terms of the models.

$$E_s = (1 - E_d) \qquad\qquad 17$$

where
$$E_s = E \qquad\qquad 18$$

Equations 15, 16a, 16b, 17, and 18 give us five equations for seven unknowns. What remains to be determined is the descriptive equations for the muscle tensions, P_s and P_d.

Nature of Muscle. The basic behavior of all muscle is essen- tially the same in form if not degree. Therefore, it seems appro- priate to review some of the general characteristics of contractile processes.

If a length of freshly excised muscle is placed in a tension- measuring device, it can be shown that below a minimum length the tissue is flaccid. However, as the muscle is stretched beyond this "rest length", which we will refer to as ℓ_r, there appears a resistive force $P_r(\ell)$, which is related to the thickness and type of the muscle as well as the amount of stretching. This relation- ship is termed the passive tension curve since it is a property of the passive parallel elements of the muscle (e.g., collagen and other connective elements). If we repeat the experiment but this time "activate" the muscle with an electrical stimulus we will find that, for any given length (isometric) the muscle will provide a tension greater than that measured in the passive case. This in- crease in tension (called the "active" tension) has been shown to be proportional to the magnitude of the nervous activation (Bahler 1967; Bigland and Lippold, 1954). The length corresponding to maximum active tension which we will call ℓ_o, is greater than ℓ_r in the gastroenemius muscle. This relationship between ℓ_o and ℓ_r appears to be characteristic of smooth muscle.

The shape of the active tension curve for striated muscle has been described by Carlson (1959) and Bahler (1968) as quadratic. For the case of maximal activation, the curve can be expressed mathematically as:

$$P_o(\ell) = P_o^* - K\left(\frac{\ell - \ell_o}{\ell_o}\right)^2 \qquad\qquad 19$$

where $P_o(\ell)$ = "active" tension at length, ℓ_o

             P_o^* = maximum active tension

             ℓ = muscle length

             K = constant

Since Carlson and Bahler worked with striated muscle at lengths less than ℓ_r, the influence of the passive parallel elasticity was not taken into consideration. Also, data taken by Meiss (1971) from multi-unit smooth muscle in cats shows an almost linear relationship observed by others for skeletal muscle.

Because of the variation between striated and smooth muscle characteristics and because muscle experiments had not mapped behavior over a large range of muscle lengths, the following two versions of the Carlson equation appeared applicable.

$$P_v(\ell, E) = EP_o - K(\xi)^n \qquad\qquad 20a$$

and $$P_f(\ell, E) = E(P_o - K\{\xi\})^n \qquad\qquad 20b$$

where $$\xi = (\ell - \ell_o)/\ell_o \qquad\qquad 21$$

and $$E = (0 < E < 1) \qquad\qquad 22$$

These approximations to the muscle active tension curve are illustrated in Figure 11. We refer to equations 20a and 20b as "variable structure" and "fixed structure" muscles as was suggested in the figure. The mechanical analogy to the two equations is a pure tension source in parallel with a nonlinear spring. We should remind ourselves, however, that this analogy is strictly a convenient means of generating the active tension curve-shape and probably has no physiological significance. The pseudo-spring constant, K, should not be confused with the passive parallel elastic component, $P_r(\ell)$ which was mentioned above.

A schematic representation of a simple active component push-pull system is drawn in Figure 12. As was determined in equations 16, ℓ_s and ℓ_d, the sphincter and dilator muscle lengths, are directly related to x and L - x respectively where x can be interpreted as pupil diameter and L is maximum extension (analogous to iris diameter = 10-12 mm). For convenience, all lengths were normalized by L when speaking of the two-muscle system, whereas ℓ_o was

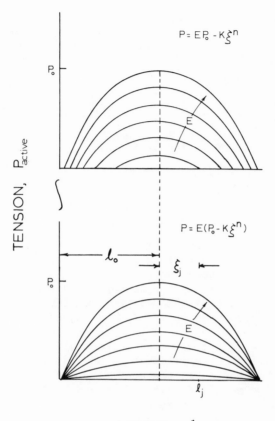

LENGTH, ℓ

Figure 11.   The variation of active tension with muscle length.
Upper figure: Variable structure muscle. A variation of Carlson's
equation which assumes that muscle length for zero active tension
varies with level of excitation, E. Lower figure: Fixed structure muscle. Assumes that muscle length for zero tension is independent of excitation level, E. Basic shape of curve is shown here
as a simple power law, Carlson (1959) and Semmlow (1970) use n =
2. ℓ_o equals muscle length at maximum active tension, P_o.

$$\left(\xi \;=\; \frac{\ell - \ell_o}{\ell_o} \right)$$

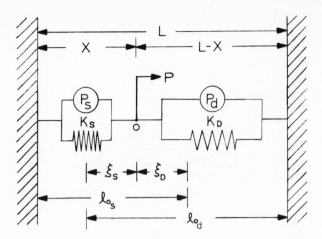

Figure 12.   A simple push-pull system.   Diagram represents two
contractile components linked in a push-pull arrangement.   Each
component consists of a pure tension source, P in parallel with a
nonlinear spring, K.   This spring is not to be confused with muscle
passive parallel elasticity which is not considered here, but,
rather, is a mechanical equivalent to the second term in the Carlson
equation for active contractile force.   L equals maximum system dimension (e.g., iris diameter); X equals normalized characteristic
length (e.g., pupil diameter); and ℓ_{os} and ℓ_{od} are the lengths
for maximum active tension of the sphincter and dilator respectively.
P is the sum of the muscle forces at "0" and is defined such that
positive force tends to increase X.

the normalization factor when speaking of one muscle.

    Summing the forces at point "0" in Figure 12 we have: (Here
P equals the tension of the combined push-pull system.)   For variable
structure

$$P = E_d P_{od} - E_s P_{os} + K_s (x - \ell_{os})^n - K_d (L - x - \ell_{od})^n \quad 23$$

For fixed structure

$$P = E_d(P_{od} - K_d(L - x - \ell_{od})^n - E_s(P_{os} - K_s\{x - \ell_{os}\}^n) \qquad 24$$

Assuming that $P_o = L = 1$, $K_s = K_d = K$ for both sphincter and dilator, and letting $n = 2$, we see that 23 reduces to

$$P = E_d - E_s + K(1 - 2x) \qquad\qquad\qquad 25$$

That is, the length-tension curve for a symmetrical, variable structure, quadratic, push-pull iris system is linear.

Model Characteristics - Range Nonlinearity

The analysis of iris movement becomes apparent when we observe that P, as defined by equation 25, is identically zero for steady state conditions (Newton's law). If we imbed the conditions for reciprocal innervation (equation 18) and solve equation 25 for x, we have

$$x = \frac{\alpha(1 - E) - E + K}{2K} \qquad\qquad 26$$

This is the static variation equation for the variable structure system, and it is seen to be linear. The gain is constant

$$\frac{dx}{dE} = \frac{\alpha + 1}{2K} \qquad\qquad\qquad 27$$

as illustrated in equation 27. The parameter α was introduced to provide a measure of the relative effectiveness of the sphincter and the dilator muscle. It is defined here as the ratio of maximum excitation levels

$$\alpha = \frac{E_d(max)}{E_s(max)} \qquad\qquad\qquad 28$$

It can also be interpreted as the ratio of maximum tensions.

If we now repeat the above analysis with equation 24 we can derive the static characteristics of the fixed structure, push-pull system. Imbedding the same constraints (equation 18) and setting $n = 2$, we find that the fixed structure system is considerably more realistic in terms of the experimental results described earlier. Figure 14a shows the length-tension curves for a fixed structure quadratic system as a function of E and simulated for an α- value of 0.25. Directing our attention to the steady state requirement of P = 0 we find that x is not a linear function of innervation level, E (Figure 13B) but assumes the classic "s" shape which we

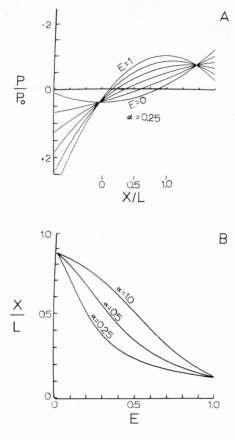

Figure 13. Static characteristics of the fixed structure quadratic system. (A) Length-tension as a function of excitiation. (B) Static X-E curve.

see in the actual pupil system. The influence of the dilator/ sphincter ratio, α, is also shown in Figure 13B as a progressive "bowing" of the static curve as dilator effectiveness is decreased.

The other parameter which had not been considered to this point was the active tension curve shape, defined by the exponent, n (equation 19 and 20). Carlson (1959) and Semmlow (1970) had assumed n = 2. The smooth muscle data from cat intestine Meiss (1971), however, indicated that the active tension curve is linear (n = 1) except around the point $\ell = \ell_o$. A compromise value of

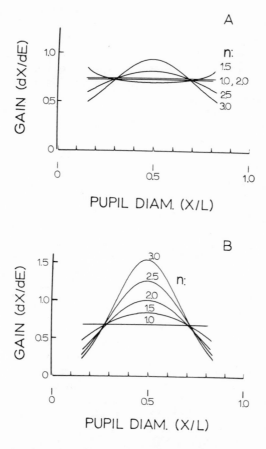

Figure 14.   Variation is shape of model range N.L. with change in characteristic muscle parameter, n.   Without PE means, of course, without parallel elasticity.   (A) Upper: Variable structure system.   (B) Lower: Fixed structure system.

n = 1.5 was chosen for the following reason: Figure 14B shows that the fixed structure model adequately models the pupil range nonlinearity with n = 1.5 Note that the variable structure model (Figure 14A) shows constant gain for n = 1 or 2 as predicted by equation 27 and does not show a nonlinearity of appropriate magnitude until n is equal to 2.5 or greater.

Model Characteristics: Response Asymmetry

Since response asymmetry is found in both light reflex and

near response it may be conjectured that the nonlinearity is produced by processes located in the motor system, and should be
represented in the model.   Yet other motor outputs of accommodative
stimulation, such as accommodative vergence, also show response
asymmetry suggesting sensory elements are involved.   As response
asymmetry is such a strong feature of pupillomotor output that
the element causing it must be a strong influence on system dynamics; particularly suspect in this regard would be a dynamic
muscle characteristic such as the nonlinear viscosity process defined in skeletal muscle by the well known force-velocity relationship.   If the nonlinear process responsible for response asymmetry
is a smooth muscle analog of skeletal muscle force-velocity characteristics we would expect asymmetrical behavior to be dependent on
response velocity.   That is, as response velocity switched from
positive (constricting) to negative (dilating) we would expect behavior to switch simultaneously from fast dynamics to slow dynamics.
Alternatively, if the asymmetry is premechanical, imbedded in the
controlling excitatory signal, the change in behavior would not
relate directly to movement velocity.   If the reversal of excitation
and velocity can be separated out in time, dynamical behavior as
velocity goes through zero should indicate the presence or absence
of asymmetrical mechanical elements.

Excitation and velocity may be separated out by applying steps
of excitation opposite to an ongoing, nonzero initial velocity.
Simulation of experiments involving steps from nonzero initial
velocities were used to confirm the foregoing assumptions, evaluate
the suitability of this stimulus pattern, and alert us to aberrant
modes of behavior.   Simulation results show that discontinuities
of the velocity trace, though small, are seen when the asymmetry
is velocity dependent (Figure 15A).   Similar experiments on human
iris showed generally continuous behavior about the zero axis
(Figure 15B), indicating a primary role for a premechanical process
in producing this nonlinearity.

Thus, we conclude that response asymmetry is not a result of
muscle mechanical characteristics, though other smooth muscle
features such as a nonlinear activation-deactivation process can
not be ruled out.   Other likely origins for the asymmetry nonlinearity include the motor nucleus and deep sensory processes.

In review, the model, as developed to this point, can be described as a rectilinear push-pull arrangement of two muscles, each
of which is composed of active and passive tension elements.   Under
the hypotheses that 1) the active tension element is a "fixed structure" Carlson muscle with an exponent, n equal to 1.5, and 2) that
the two muscles are reciprocally innervated, static gain curves
can be simulated which exhibit the same type of extended nonlinear
range behavior that is observed with actual experimental data
presented earlier.   We can further test the validity of the model

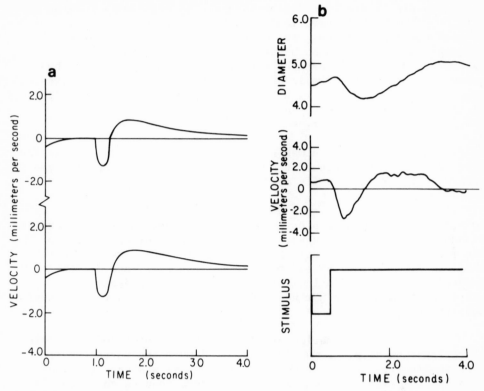

Figure 15. Double-step experiments. (a) Model responses to steps
applied while initial velocity was nonzero. Top: asymmetrical
mechanical; bottom: unequal excitation time constants. (b) Pupil
velocity characteristics from double-step experiment. Smooth trans-
ition across zero velocity indicates the absence of an asymmetrical
mechanical process. (Semmlow and Stark, 1971).

by examining its response to experiments for which it was not specifically tuned.

Model Predictions

Terdiman's experiments in cats (Terdiman, Smith and Stark, 1969);
(Terdiman, Smith and Stark, 1971) were designed to provide insight
into the nature of the pupil system from "inside the black box." By
artificially stimulating the parasympathetic and sympathetic pathways
he controlled what in our model has been labelled E_s and E_d, the

sphincter and dilator excitation inputs. E_s and E_d are related to E the pupil system innervation signal by equation 17 and 18. One of Terdiman's conclusions, based on analysis of dynamic responses to sinusoidal inputs in both the parasympathetic and sympathetic nervous pathways, was that the sphincter and dilator muscles have essentially the same dynamic characteristics. These data, however, seemed to be in conflict with his steady-state experiments, Figure 3, which revealed different static variation curves for the sphincter and the dilator.

To simulate the Terdiman experiments the model dilator excitation, E_s was held constant at different values (analogous to sympathetic stimulation) while sphincter excitation, E_d, was varied.

One is able to see that if appropriate model curves are selected, the composite plot in Figure 16 is not unlike the Terdiman steady-state variation curve, Figure 3. The important point to understand here is that all of the above simulation results were obtained from a model based on identical sphincter and dilator properties. This would indicate that the Terdiman dynamic and static experiments are not necessarily in conflict, but are mutually supportive.

As further confirmation of the suitability of fixed structure representation of pupil muscles was noted when the variable structure muscle (all other parameters being equal) was used to simulate the Terdiman experiments. Satisfactory results could not be obtained.

Another experiment showing promise as an interesting model test was the drug experiments of Miller and Stark (1964). Using at one time a sphincter inhibitor (Tropicamide), and at another time a dilator stimulant (neosynephrine), they measured pupil contraction amplitude (to a fixed light stimulus) as a function of pupil diameter. Both drugs dilate the pupil over a period of time. The Tropicamide appeared to induce a steady decrease in gain (slope) with increasing diameter (Figure 17) whereas the neosynephrine did not decrease gain until quite large diameters were reached. This behavior was originally used as support for the active-sphincter, passive-dilator theory of iris structure.

These drug experiments were simulated on our model (Figure 18) by: 1) decreasing the effectiveness of the sphincter to simulate Tropicamide infuence (A); and 2) increasing the effectiveness of the dilator to simulate neosynephrine effect (B). Since basic pupil system innervation level, E, is assumed to be constant throughout the experiment (shown here as E = 0.5) the pupil dilation is represented by a vertical migration along the indicated lines. The slopes of the various curves which are crossed as one travels upward are equivalent to the current gain of the system. It could be

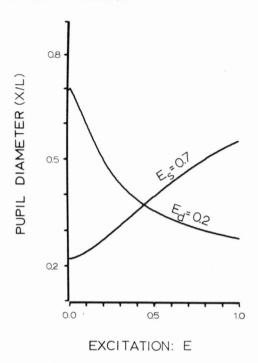

Figure 16. Model simulation of Terdiman experiment. Compare with Figure 3. $E_s = 0.7$ and $E_d = 0.2$ are the static antagonistic model excitation level. The antagonist levels may have an experimental counterpart in that Terdiman did vary these in order to get usable levels.

argued that, as pupil diameter increases in (A) -- the Tropicamide experiment -- system gain steadily decreases; while as diameter increases in (B) -- the neosynephrine experiments -- system gains does not decrease as rapidly. This is supported by the fact that the curves drawn in (B) each represent a 50% increase in effectiveness of the dilator. That is, the top curve represents a static variation curve for which dilator forces are four times normal. Since neosynephrine is probably not that influential, actual vertical displacement is (Figure 18b) likely to be restricted. In such a case, change in gain would be minimal, in agreement with Figure 17. However, the simulated final diameter would not be as large as that actually produced by tropicamide, in disagreement with Figure 17.

Finally, the relative pupil response to the two drugs is directly related to the background innervation level, E. For instance, it is not made clear in Figure 17 whether the subject was accommodating near or far, or what were the associated background light levels. These parameters would need to be systematically controlled

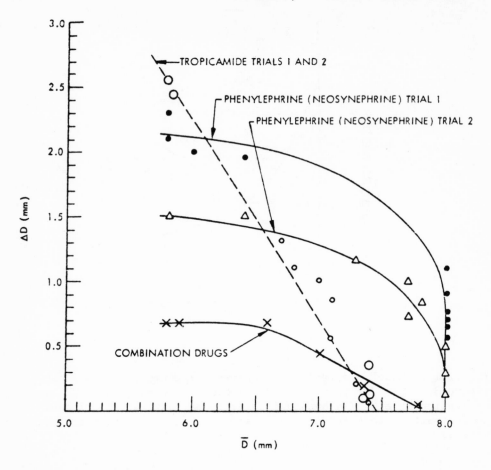

Figure 17.   Relationship of pupillary diameter $\bar{D}$ in mm to amplitude
of pupillary contraction ΔD in mm for trial 1 and trial 2 of the
dilator stimulating drug phenylphrine.   Trial 1 and Trial 2 of
the sphincter-paralyzing drug tropicamide, and an average of the
experiments in which the combination drugs homatrophine and phenylephrine and cyclopentolate and phenylephrine were used.

before a more meaningful comparison of actual response data and
model results could be made.

Summary of Model

A mathematical model of the human iris was derived based on
known muscle physiology and the mechanical features of the iris.
From comparison with actual experimental results a final model was

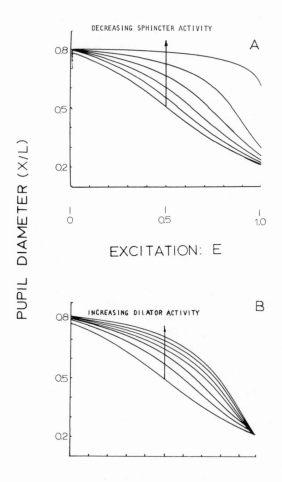

Figure 18. Model simulation of drug effects. (A) Inhibition of sphincter muscle (Tropicamide). Assuming that signal from the central nervous system remains constant at, say E = 0.5, drug effect is modeled as a decrease in sphincter excitation, E_s. If bottom curve represents normal sphincter activity, Eo_s, then subsequent curves represent E_s/Eo_s = 0.8, 0.6, 0.4, 0.2, and 0.0. (B) Stimulation of dilator (Neosynephrine). Bottom curve represents normal dilator activity Eo_d. Subsequent curves represent static pupil response for heightened dilator activity, E_d/Eo_d = 1.5, 2.0, 2.5, 3.0, 3.5, 4.0. It is doubtful that increased activity due to drug action would be of such large magnitudes.

selected which is characterized as follows:

1) Rectilinear symmetrical push-pull system.
2) Carlson fixed structure active tension element (n = 1.5).
3) Reciprocal innervation (α = 1).
4) Premechanical asymmetry.

These basic characteristics applied symmetrically to both sphincter
and dilator were sufficient to not only duplicate the extended
pupil range nonlinearity (static gain curve), but also the Terdiman
experiments and, to a lesser extent, the Miller-Stark experiments.

REFERENCES

Apter, J. T. Distribution of contractile forces in the iris of
cats and dogs. *American Journal of Physiology*, 1960, *199(2)*,
377-380.

Bahler, A. S. Series elastic component of mammalian skeletal
muscle. *American Journal of Physiology*, 1967, *213*, 1560-1564.

Bahler, A. S. Modeling of mammalian skeletal muscle. *Transactions
of Bio-medical Engineering*, BME, 1968, *15.4*, 249-257.

Bigland, B., and Lippold, O. W. The relation between force,
velocity and integrated electrical activity in human muscles.
Journal of Physiology, 1954, *123*, 214-224.

Carlson, F. D. Kinematic studies on mechanical properties. In
J. W. Remington (Ed.), *Tissue Elasticity*. Washington, D.C.:
American Physiological Society, 1959, 55-72.

Carlson, U. Individual pupillary reactions to certain centrally
acting drugs in man. *Journal of Pharmacology and Experimental
Therapeutics*, 1957, *121*, 501-506.

Cartevette, E., and Cole, M. Comparison of the receiver-operating
characteristics for messages received by ear and eye. *Journal
of the Acoustical Society of America*, 1962, *34*, 172-178.

Eijkmann, E., and Vendrile, A. Detection theory applied to the
absolute sensitivity of sensory systems. *Biophysics Journal*,
1963, *3*, 65-78.

Hansmann, D. R. Human Pupillary Mechanics: Physiology and Control,
Ph.D. Dissertation, University of California, Berkeley, Calif., 1972.

Hess, E. Attitude and pupil size. *Scientific American*, 1965, *212*,
46-54.

Loewenfeld, I. The iris as a pharmacologic indicator. *Archives of
Ophthalmology*, 1963, *70*, 42-51.

Loewenfeld, I., and Newsome, D. Iris mechanics influence of pupil
size and dynamics of pupillary movements. *American Journal of
Ophthalmology*, 1971.

Lowenstein, O., and Loewenfeld, I. The pupil. In H. Davson (Ed.),
The Eye. (Vol. 3). Academic Press, 1970.

Meiss, R. A. Some mechanical properties of cat intestinal muscle.
American Journal of Physiology, 1971, *220*, 2000.

Miller, D., and Stark, L. Effect of mydriatic drugs on pupillary dynamics. *Quarterly Progress Report*. Massachusetts Institute of Technology. No. 14, 1964, 265-269.

Morgan, M. W. Accommodation and vergence. *American Journal of Ophthalmology*, 1968, *45*, 417-454.

Newsome, P., and Loewenfeld, I. E. Iris mechanics II: influence of pupil size in details of iris structure. *American Journal of Ophthalmology*, 1971, *71*, 553-575.

Semmlow, J. Nonlinear pupil mechanisms. Ph.D. Dissertation, University of Illinois Medical Centre, Chicago, Illinois, 1970.

Semmlow, J., Hansmann, D., and Stark, L. Variation on pupillo-motor responsiveness with mean pupil size. Submitted for publication.

Semmlow, J., and Stark, L. Stimulation of a biomechanical model of the pupil. *Mathematical Bioscience*, 1971, *11*, 109-128.

Semmlow, J., and Stark, L. Pupil movements to light and accommodative stimulation: A comparative study. *Vision Research*, 1973, *13*, 1087-1100.

Sherrington, C. S. Experimental note on two movements of the eye. *Journal of Physiology* (London), 1894, *17*, 27-29.

Stanten, S. F., and Stark, L. A statistical analysis of pupil noise. *IEEE Transactions of Bio-medical Engineering*, 1960, *BME-B*, 140-152.

Stark, L. Nonlinear operator in the pupil system. *Quarterly Progress Report*. Massachusetts Institute of Technology, 1964, *72*, 258-260.

Stark, L. *Neurological Control Systems: Studies in bioengineering*. New York: Plenum Press, 1968.

Stark, L., and Cornsweet, T. N. Testing a servoanalytic hypothesis for pupil oscillations. *Science*, 1958, *127*, 588.

Terdiman, J., Smith, J. D., and Stark, L. Dynamic analysis of the pupil with light and electrical stimulation. *IEEE Transactions on Systems, Man and Cybernetics*, 1971, *SMC-1*, 239-251.

Terdiman, J., Smith, J., and Stark, L. Pupil response to light and electrical stimulation: static and dynamic characteristics. *Brain Research*, 1969, *16*, 288-292.

Usui, S., and Stark, L. Variations in pupillomotor noise as a function of mean pupil size. In preparation.

Wyber, K. C. Ocular manifestations of disseminated sclerosis. *Proceedings of the Royal Society of Medicine*, 1952, *45*, 315-320.

CHAPTER IV:

THE UTILIZATION OF PUPILLOMETRY IN THE DIFFERENTIAL DIAGNOSIS AND

TREATMENT OF PSYCHOTIC AND BEHAVIORAL DISORDERS

Leonard S. Rubin

Eastern Pennsylvania Psychiatric Institute

Philadelphia, Pennsylvania

"DRY" AND "WET" CONCOMITANTS OF THE FUNCTIONAL PSYCHOSES

A vast literature has accumulated over the last three decades implicating the central autonomic nervous system in the functional psychoses and other behavior disorders. Any attempt to crystallize conclusions from this prolific field of inquiry necessitates a categorization which hopefully possesses heuristic value. Laboratory parlance makes the distinction between "dry" and "wet" investigatory efforts. The first term generally refers to physiological investigations while the latter refers to chemical, pharmacological investigations of the juices of life-processes. Interestingly, these approaches to the problem of the role of autonomic mechanisms in psychoses have developed in a parallel fashion with little or no interaction. The following presentation attempts to converge these parallel modes of inquiry by demonstrating that pupillometry may serve as a useful transfer operator function.

Autonomic Dysfunction in Schizophrenia

Hoskins (1946) and his collaborators played a major role in establishing that central autonomic responses were aberrant in schizophrenia. Many peripheral components reflecting central autonomic activity were diminished in chronic schizophrenic patients as shown by studies on cardiovascular reactions, responses of blood sugar to stress, and temperature regulation on exposure to cold. Lesser reactivity of the hypothalamic-hypophyseal system was also noted, particularly under conditions of psychological stress. Shattock (1950) demonstrated that schizophrenics showed a lower skin temperature on exposure to cold than other psychotic

75

groups. The diurnal rhythm of body temperature was less than in
normals, and on exposure to cold some chronic schizophrenics
failed to show a fall in temperature while others showed paradoxical reactions (Buck, et al. 1950). Eysenck (1956) found that the
skin resistance of chronic schizophrenics was higher than that of
normals or neurotics at rest and after exposure to emotional
stimuli. Earle and Earle (1955) and Igersheimer (1953) found the
blood pressure rise in the cold pressor test to be less than in
the control group or absent. Freeman et al. (1944) reported that
the blood sugar curve in the glucose tolerance test ran higher in
chronic schizophrenics than in normals. Under the physical strain
of exposure to heat, Pincus and Elmadjian (1946) found that the
hypothalamic-hypophyseal response leading to the liberation of
ACTH and reduction of lymphocytes was less in chronic schizophrenics than in the control group. These observations led Hoskins to
propose that; a) there were systematic differences in autonomic
homeostasis between schizophrenics and normals as regards the
resting functional level which in schizophrenia is characterized
by "sluggish sympathetic reactivity"; b) schizophrenics were unable to "hold to the steady state" under ordinary conditions of
existence; c) schizophrenics were characterized by "defective
autonomic reactivity to stimulating agents"; and, d) their autonomic homeostatic process was dilatory in correcting imposed dis-
tortions. Thus, there is presumptive evidence of long standing
for the existence of central autonomic imbalance in schizophrenia.

These quantitative differences in autonomic reactions emphasized by Hoskins and his group were further elaborated by the
Mecholyl and noradrenaline tests employed by Gellhorn (1961) and
Funkenstein and his colleagues (1948, 1950). Mecholyl is an effective blood pressure lowering drug. The induced fall in blood
pressure reflexly releases the sympathetic centers and leads to
the restitution or even overshooting of the basal blood pressure
and an increased heart rate, depending on the sympathetic reactivity of the sympathetic division of the hypothalamus. By plotting
blood pressure and heart rate changes derivative measurements of
sympathetic responsiveness to Mecholyl are obtained. Similarly,
injections of noradrenaline have been employed as an index of
parasympathetic reactivity. For, following the initial increase
in blood pressure, there is an increase in parasympathetic outflow
accompanying reequilibration. Both research groups found statistically significant differences between normals and neuropsychiatric
patients in sympathetic activity as disclosed by the Mecholyl test
and in parasympathetic activity as revealed by the Noradrenaline
test. The tests for reactivity of each autonomic division demonstrated that the schizophrenic groups contained significantly more
hypo- and hyperreactors. These findings are not in accord with
Hoskins assertion that chronic schizophrenics are all characterized by sluggish sympathetic activity. The nature of autonomic

involvement is far more complicated. Heightened sympathetic
activity in schizophrenics had also been reported by Malmo and
Shagass (1949) and Malmo et al. (1951) who found high base-line
electromyogram profiles, with the highest resting levels being
characteristic of the most withdrawn patients. Faster heart
rates and higher systolic blood pressures have been reported among
schizophrenics than among non-schizophrenics.

An overview of the physiological evidence suggests that hypo-
or hyperreactivity of either the sympathetic or parasympathetic
divisions of the autonomic nervous system are, at least, concomitants of schizophrenia.

Neurotransmitters of the Autonomic Nervous System

Complementing the physiological studies that focus upon the
role of central autonomic dysfunction in the functional psychoses
are the chemical theories and pharmacological findings that implicate aberrant neurohumoral activity in the central representation
of the autonomic nervous system. There seems to be general agreement that compounds such as acetylcholine (ACh) and norepinephrine
(NE) which are neurotransmitters in the peripheral nervous system,
also serve as neurohumoral agents in the central nervous system
(CNS). Transmitter function has also been ascribed to dopamine
(DA), tryptamine, 5-hydroxytryptamine (serotonin, 5-HT), gamma
amino butyric acid (GABA) and glycine. The evidence suggests that
the central representations of the autonomic nervous system are
cholinergic for the parasympathetic division and noradrenergic
for the sympathetic division.

Vogt (1954) examined the concentration of sympathin (a combination of norepinephrine and epinephrine) in the different parts
of the central nervous system of the dog and found that sympathin,
like acetylcholine, possessed a specific pattern of distribution.
Two regions of the brain, the hypothalamus and the area postrema,
stood out above all others by their high concentrations of norepinephrine. This fact suggests, though it does not prove, that
these amines play a part in the specialized function of those
regions of the brain in which their concentration is high. Vogt's
conclusion regarding the correlation between sympathin content
and central representation of sympathetic functions was summarized
in the following statement: "With exception of the area postrema,
those regions which contain the highest concentration of sympathin
- the hypothalamus, parts of the midbrain and the floor of the
fourth ventricle - also contain the central representation of
sympathetic activity" (p. 473).

However, when Vogt attempted to localize the site of sympathin
within the hypothalamus, it was found that the anterior and

posterior hypothalamus did not show consistent differences in
sympathin content. This is of some interest because of the controversy over whether or not the anterior hypothalamus is the site
of parasympathetic, and the posterior hypothalamus is the site of
sympathetic centers. In this particular histochemical aspect, the
two regions resemble each other. When the hypothalamus was divided
into dorsal and ventral parts, however, a definite concentration
gradient was found. The ventral region contained more noradrenaline than the dorsal region. Based upon Vogt's findings, the position taken in this paper is that the central representation of
sympathetic function in the hypothalamus contains the highest concentration of the biogenic amines; norepinephrine, epinephrine,
and serotonin.

In attempting to ascertain whether the central representation
of the autonomic nervous system may be cholinergic for the parasympathetic division, the following facts must be considered. For
purposes of description, the hypothalamus in man may conveniently
be subdivided into four regions: the supraoptic middle region
located above the optic chiasm and rostral to it, the tuberal or
infundibular middle region, the mammillary middle region, and the
lateral region. For a purpose that will become clearer as the
discussion continues, the composition of the supraoptic middle
region will be described. It includes the nuclei supraopticus,
paraventricularis, suprachiasmaticus, supraopticus diffusus, and
the anterior hypothalamic area (Kuntz, 1953). Feldberg and Vogt
(1948) attempted to map out, in the central nervous system of the
dog, the distribution of the enzyme (or enzyme system) that syn-
thesizes acetylcholine. They found a very high value of enzymatic
activity in the region of the supraoptic nuclei. By their definition, this portion of the hypothalamic area may be considered
cholinergic. However, the high figures for the supraoptic nucleus
do not suggest that cholinergic fibers originate from cells in
this region, rather, such fibers terminate in synaptic connection
within these cells. Unfortunately, the enzymatic activity of the
anterior hypothalamus, the controversial site of parsympathetic
activity, was not determined.

It seems reasonable to conclude from the foregoing discussion
that specific areas within the hypothalamus cannot be viewed as
exclusively adrenergic or cholinergic. The evidence does suggest
that the hypothalamus contains large quantities of the biogenic
amines as well as components of the cholinergic system. Consequently, in the remainder of this paper, when describing the central adrenergic-cholinergic imbalance that characterizes the
functional psychoses, I do not necessarily implicate specific
sympathetic and parasympathetic central structures as such.

Catecholamines and Schizophrenia

Several astute formulations of aberrant biogenic amine metabolism in schizophrenia have been made. Osmond and Smythies
(1952) noted the similarity between mescaline and norepinephrine
and postulated that an alteration in the biochemical transmethylation of norepinephrine might produce hallucinogenic endogenous
methylated amines which would be responsible for some forms of
schizophrenia. The enzyme necessary for methylating hydroxyl
groups (O- methylation) has been shown to be present in human
brain. With regards to the methylation of indoles (serontin)
Axelrod demonstrated its presence in rabbit lung and Mandell and
Morgan (1970) reported the presence in human brain of an enzyme
that N-methylates indole ethyl amines. Thus, by inference, chemical agents that increase the total amount of endogenous methylated
hallucinogenic compounds should exacerbate schizophrenia, whereas
a reduction in available quantities of hallucinogenic derivatives
should improve or eliminate schizophrenia. Unfortunately, the
administration of precursor substances i.e., L-dopa, and phenyla-
nine for norepinephrine, and L-tryptophan, the precursor for
serotonin, have not been conspicuously successful in the production
of augmented psychotic symptomatology.

Frequently, it has been found that a methyl donor (methionine),
in combination with a monoamine oxidase inhibitor intensifies
psychotic symptoms (Polin, et al. 1961; Brune and Himwich, 1962),
however, it is extremely difficult to differentiate conclusively
between drug toxicity and a true exacerbation of schizophrenic
psychosis. Marked clouding of the sensorium, the frequency of
confusion and wide-spread autonomic manifestations with methionine
administration are highly suggestive of toxicity.

As nicotinic acid and nicotinamide are potent methyl acceptors
which decrease the amount of methyl donor substances available for
transmethylation, Hoffer and Osmond (1964) treated schizophrenics
with these substances and reported them to be effective. The results of other chemical investigations have not been as sanguine
(Ashby, et al., 1960; Ban and Lehmann, 1970).

Osmond and Smythies (1952) also hypothesized that abnormal
methylation of dopamine, the precursor of NE, might play a role in
psychoses and in 1962 Friedhoff and Van Winkle actually demonstrated that 3, 4 dimethoxyphenylethylamine (DMPEA) was found in the
urine of 15 of 19 acute schizophrenics but not in the urine samples
of 14 normal controls. A summary of the abundant literature on
this topic suggests: DMPEA does not produce schizophrenic-like
symptoms when given to humans either in the presence or absence of
monoamine oxidase inhibitors; well-controlled studies do not sug-
stantiate the earlier findings that it is more common in the urine

of schizophrenics than in that of normals; moreover, tea consumption may be a very important source of DMPEA in urine.

This brief overview of some contemporary chemical theories of psychotic behavior suggests that the major thrust of the current research effort revolves about the transmethylation of the catechol amines (norepinephrine and its precursor dopamine), the neurotransmitters of the sympathetic autonomic nervous system.

Indoleamines and Schizophrenia

It has been demonstrated that there are both parasympathetic and sympathetic areas in the brainstem. In the hypothalamus, one of the principle foci of integration of the entire autonomic system, one finds primarily parasympathetic representation in the forepart and sympathetic in the posterior part. Brodie and Shore (1957) have postulated that the posterior hypothalamus, the sympathetic center, is controlled by nerve fibers that release norepinephrine following innervation. It may be recalled that Vogt suggested that from its uneven distribution and its localization in the parts of the brainstem that control the sympathetic centers, norepinephrine might have a transmitter role in the brain. As serotonin concentration closely matches the distribution of norepinephrine, being highest in the brainstem, especially the hypothalamus, Brodie and Shore proposed that serotonin is the chemical transmitter of nerve impulses to the centers of the parasympathetic division of the autonomic nervous system. He labelled these fibers that innervate this parasympathetic center, "serotonergic". Serotonergic activation should produce parasympathetic activation with concomitant cholinergic outflow whereas blockade should activate the opposing central sympathetic system with concomitant increases in noradrenergic outflow.

Although the hypothesis has been fruitful, no current evidence has established beyond doubt that serotonin plays a transmitter role or is auxiliary to the action of other transmitters. Woolley and Shaw (1954) accepted the presumptive evidence for serotonin as a central neural transmitter substance and went on to postulate that the hallucinogenic effect of LSD (lysergic acid diethylamide) might be due to its interference with the action of serotonin in the brain. According to these authors, the action of LSD as well as other alkaloids, can be ascribed to the indole moiety in the structures of LSD and serotonin. Consequently, compounds containing the indole ring may act as antimetabolites to serotonin. This suggested to them that mental aberrations were produced by endogenously produced indole compounds that competed for serotonin receptor sites in the brain. This attractive theory has been challenged by at least two observations. Cerletti and Rothlin (1955) found that a close analogue of LSD,

2-bromo-D-lysergic acid diethylamide, was as effective as LSD in antagonizing several peripheral actions of serotonin, yet this antagonist of serotonin was found to be devoid of hallucinogenic action in humans. It should be noted that chlorpromazine is also a potent antiserotonin and, instead of being hallucinogenic, is a powerful antihallucinogen employed in the treatment of psychotics.

The abnormal methylation of serotonin with the production of bufotenine has also been invoked as the pathogenetic mechanism underlying psychosis. The interest in bufotenine was elicited by the following observations: it had been shown to be capable of producing a schizophrenic-like syndrome when administered to humans; several authors claimed the presence of bufotenine or a bufotenine-like substance in urine from schizophrenics, or, have found it in lower concentrations, in normal urine. Other investigators were unable to induce hallucinations with bufotenine despite profound EEG changes, loss of consciousness, and intense peripheral action of a serotonin character. Furthermore, those investigators who used blind analyses and a plant-and-cheese free diet found no evidence for a bufotenine-like substance in urine from either schizophrenics or non-schizophrenics, with or without monoamine oxidase inhibitors. Interestingly, most studies that reported a differential incidence of these substances in schizophrenics and normals did not use a blind method of analysis.

That ubiquitous neurotransmitter, acetylcholine, (ACh) has also been coupled with a pathogenic mechanism for the production of psychoses. Feldberg and Sherwood (1954) initiated interest in this area by reporting that cats given ACh intraventricularly became agitated and catatonic. Compounds that increase central cholinergic activity and compounds that decrease it, have both been invoked to describe the production of psychotic behavior. They will be described shortly.

The chemical theories reviewed appear to reinforce the leads provided by the earlier physiological studies. They too suggest that psychoses are somehow related to central autonomic dysfunction. But, whereas the earlier workers examined objectively observable physiological variables mediated by sympathetic and parasympathetic activity, the chemists have focused their efforts on the neuro-humoral mediators of autonomic activity. Unfortunately, some chemical investigators have focused upon mediators of sympathetic activity to the exclusion of parasympathetic mediators and others have confined their studies to the role of acetylcholine mechanisms to the exclusion of sympathetic mediators. Thus, the dynamic aspects of autonomic interaction which may be etiologic for psychotic behavior have been virtually ignored. Furthermore, by restricting their efforts to either one or the other transmitter system apparently paradoxical findings surface. In the following section evidence

will be presented which suggests that neurohumoral dysfunction in
psychotics may be characterized by either an excessive or deficient sympathetic noradrenergic mechanism.

A DISORDERED ADRENERGIC RESPONSE MECHANISM IN THE
FUNCTIONAL PSYCHOSES

Iproniazid (Marsilid) an amine oxidase antagonist that inhi-
bits the oxidative deamination of epinephrine, had been used ex-
tensivley in the treatment of mental depression. In vivo studies
on animals treated with this agent indicate that it can produce a
relatively rapid and large (threefold) rise in brain serotonin
(Zeller, et al., 1955). Shore (1958) found that it increased the
concentration of norepinephrine in the brain and other organs of
small animals. Numerous other monoamine oxidase inhibitors have
also been reported to be effective in the treatment of depression.
Spector (1963) and his co-workers were able to demonstrate that
behavioral excitation was correlated with increased brain levels
of norepinephrine and not with serotonin. Parenthetically, it
should be noted that there is some controversy concerning the
relative chemical effectiveness of some of the monoamine oxidase
inhibitors and the specific subgroups of depressed patients for
whom these drugs are most indicated (Cole, 1964). Imipramine and
other tricyclic antidepressants have also been found to be clinically effective for some types of depression. Presumably, this
beneficial effect results from a decrease of the cell membrane or
storage-granule membrane permeability to norepinephrine. By inhi-
biting norepinephrine uptake in the brain, the tricyclics exert
their antidepressant action through potentiation of catecholamines
at adrenergic receptor sites.

In recent years, lithium salts have been used in the treatment of abnormal elations, i.e., hypomania and mania. Schildkraut
et al. (1966) have proposed that lithium may increase the intracellular deamination of norepinephrine and decrease the norepinephrine available at adrenergic receptor sites.

From these findings. Schildkraut (1965) proferred a formulation designated the catecholamine hypothesis of affective disorders which states "that some, if not all, depressions may be
associated with a relative deficiency of norepinephrine at functionally important adrenergic receptor sites in the brain, whereas elations may be associated with an excess of such amines."

The heuristic value of this formulation cannot be under estimated. However, it seems to focus upon variations in the biochemical anlage of norepinephrine as related to discrete, isolable,
unique states or traits of either depression or mania devoid of

the personality matrix in which level of activity is embedded. Klerman et al (1972) have emphasized that "depression" may refer to a symptom, syndrome or diagnostic entity. The diagnostic and symptom designation are inadequate for they have not been fully validated nor standardized. Furthermore, there is as yet no clear, direct relationship between treatment and diagnosis or symptom of depression. Although the clinician proceeds pragmatically in his treatment of depression viewed as a syndrome, treatment practices lack firm foundation in theoretical concepts and scientific rationale. The same criticisms may be made of the ambiguous term "mania".

A simpler formulation, in a logical sense, was offered by Rubin in 1960. The implication was drawn that *some* psychotics who are benefitted by agents that increase levels of brain amines may be defective in some brain catecholamines or in central adrenergic stimulation. *Some* other functionally psychotic patients for whom norepinephrine depletion therapy is efficacious may be characterized by excessive adrenergic activity in subcortical centers. This latter formulation was promulgated after reviewing the results of treating schizophrenia with reserpine and the phenothiazines.

Hyperemotional responses mediated by sympathetic centers in the hypothalamus are markedly depressed by the action of reserpine. Peripherally, the syndrome produced by reserpine is marked by bradycardia, slight lowering of the blood pressure, stimulation of peristalsis, and gastric hypersecretion. Brodie and Shore (1957) proposed that reserpine prevented serotonin binding and thereby caused constant activation of the vegetative, parasympathetic centers with resultant cholinergic outlfow. In addition, reserpine was found to deplete the store of biogenic catecholamines in the body as determined by the increased excretion of 5-hydroxy-indole-acetic acid, a metabolite of serotonin. Evidence has been presented in Truitt (1958) which favors a role for serotonin as a central excitatory agent at least in subcortical centers. The hyperactivity of serotonin, rather than its deficiency, therefore, may play a dominant role in mediating uncontrolled emotional responses in acute psychoses. Thus, the mechanism of reserpine action may be by depletion of brain concentration of serotonin and other catecholamines rather than through the sedative action of released serotonin. These observations therefore suggest that some functionally psychotic patients for whom reserpine therapy is efficacious may be characterized by excessive adrenergic activity in subcortical centers. This same conclusion is also applicable when chlorpromazine is considered, for, in addition to its peripheral antihistaminic and anticholinergic effects, it has been shown to have a central adrenergic blocking action.

In summary, it is postulated that the neurohumoral dysfunction that characterizes some psychotics may be due to either: (a)
a neurohumoral deficiency of some sympathomimetic amine or to some
enzyme disorder such as monoamine oxidase overactivity in the
adrenergic excitatory mechanism of the brain; or, (b) a neurohumoral overabundance of some sympathomimetic amine or to some
enzyme disorder such as monoamine oxidase underactivity in the
adrenergic mechanism of the brain.

A DISORDERED CHOLINERGIC RESPONSE MECHANISM IN
THE FUNCTIONAL PSYCHOSES

There are suggestions that the cholinergic component of generalized autonomic activity is also an important parameter of the
functional psychoses. Feldberg and Sherwood (1954) found that cats
given acetylcholine intraventricularly became agitated and catatonic. Goodman and Gilman (1965) reported that myasthenic patients
refused to continue anticholinesterase therapy with DFP (diisopropyl-
fluorophosphate) because of severe central nervous system side effects
produced presumably by increased central acetylcholine levels. On
the other hand, Stevens (1967) has reported that anticholinergic
anti-Parkinson drugs have a potential for producing psychotic disorders. Abood (1968) classified one of these, Ditran, as a psychotomimetic which was shown to produce disturbances similar to the
acute alcohol psychoses (Alpert, et al. 1970). Forrer (1956) has
recommended the use of large doses of the anticholinergic atropine
(tertiary) in the treatment of manic-depressives in the manic
phase. He claimed that these patients responded remarkably well
and immediately to this chemotherapy but he offered no mechanism
which could possibly account for the effectiveness of this drug.
As the pharmacological action of atropine is that of a cholinergic
blocking agent, it may be inferred that excessive brain acetylcholine or deficient acetylcholinesterase with manifest excessive
cholinergic outflow is important to the understanding of the chemical fundament in some psychotics. A strong theoretical statement
which in part supports this inferred mechanism as to the efficacy
of atropine therapy has been offered by Hoffer et al. (1954). He
has claimed that excessive parasympathetic activity, with concomitant increases in the concentration of acetylcholine, is an essential feature of the schizophrenic process. In contrast to Forrer,
however, Hoffer believes that cholinergic blocking agents as well
as cholinergic compounds should aggravate the schizophrenic process
and perhaps make psychotics worse.

Paradoxically, Pfeiffer, et al. (1957) have reported that
some schizophrenics respond with a lucid interval to cholinergic
stimulants such as pilocarpine, arecoline, and 2-dimethylamine
ethanol. The implication of this report is that some psychotics

are characterized by <u>defective</u> cholinergic responsiveness. Rubin
(1958a, 1958b) has reported that a functionally psychotic sample
of patients was significantly differentiable from normals by
virtue of the rate of hydrolysis of acetylcholine chloride by
erythrocyte cholinesterase. All of the patients employed in the
study manifested a defect in rate of hydrolysis. Some subjects
hydrolyzed the substrate too rapidly and others too slowly. The
inference made, on the basis of the kinetics of the enzymatic
reactions, was that some psychotics may be deficient in cholinergic activity while others may be characterized by excessive
cholinergic activity.

PATTERNS OF DISORDERED ADRENERGIC-CHOLINERGIC STEADY STATES IN PSYCHOTIC DISORDERS

A hurried review of the evidence presented seems replete with
paradoxical facts and theories. At first it appears that an effective chemotherapy for some psychotics should counteract deficient
adrenergic activity. Then, it seems that more effective drugs
which decrease adrenergic activity should be developed. Additional
conflict and confusion is raised by assertions of efficacy for
cholinergic as well as anticholinergic drugs. These apparent con-
tradictions, it was proposed, may be resolved by regarding the
population of functional psychotics as consisting of a specifiable
number of discrete patterns of disordered adrenergic-cholinergic
levels of reactivity. From the preceding review of the pharmacological action of certain drugs on the neurohumoral components of
the autonomic nervous system, it was assumed that in the population of psychotics there existed three levels of adrenergic activity: overreactivity, deficiency, and a normal level from which
directional deviations were measurable. The cholinergic outflow
was also described as consisting of three levels: excessive or
deficient cholinergic levels as measured by reference to a level
characteristic of the unstressed normal. The matrix of adrenergic-
cholinergic steady states derivable from such a paradigm is presented in Figure 1. In this figure, A represents central adrenergic
activity and C central cholinergic activity. The levels of activity of each dimension are symbolized by +, 0 and -. The positive
sign represents excessive activity, the zero, normal activity, and
the negative sign, deficient activity. The combination of AoCo
represents the levels of adrenergic and cholinergic activity that
characterize the normal human adult at rest. The eight other combinations represent hypothetical adrenergic-cholinergic levels of
interaction. Previously, the hypothesis had been developed that
a normal, ordered response to stress consisted of maximal generalized sympathetic activity that was attained when cholinergic stimulation was decreased (C-), while adrenergic stimulation continued

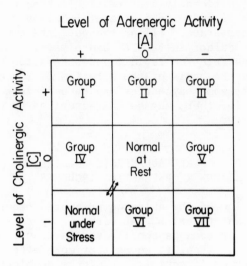

Figure 1. Patterns of adrenergic-cholinergic interaction for normals and psychotics.

to increase (A+) up to that maximal level which characterized the individual. This characteristic adjustment is contained in Figure 1, and may be represented as A+C-. It is now further hypothesized, within the framework of the general theory, that the remaining seven interactions between the adrenergic-cholinergic activity represent the discrete patterns which comprise the population of functional psychotics. To recapitulate, the major hypotheses elaborated from the above considerations are: (a) Effective autonomic adjustment to emergency situations requires a maximal generalized adrenergic response; (b) To attain a maximal level of sympathetic activity, it is not only necessary that increased levels of adrenergic activity follow the emergency but that the level of cholinergic activity decrease; (c) The functional psychoses are characterized by patterns of neurohumoral dysfunction that deviate significantly from the pattern of the normal, healthy individual at rest, as well as from the adrenergic increase and cholinergic decrease that characterizes the normal individual during stress; and (d) The varieties of neurohumoral dysfunction represent discrete levels of activity of interacting adrenergic

and cholinergic mechanisms. That is, each pattern of neurohumoral
dysfunction represents an impairment of function of either the
adrenergic or cholinergic mechanism or both.

PUPILLARY REACTIVITY AS A METHOD FOR INVESTIGATING PATTERNS
OF DISORDERED ADRENERGIC-CHOLINERGIC STEADY
STATES IN PSYCHOTIC DISORDERS

The hypotheses elucidated would remain interesting speculations unless a method was employed which could systematically
measure the relevant parameters. To this end pupillometry was
selected for investigating the patterns of disordered autonomic
steady states in psychotic disorders. The miotic response of the
pupil to light (constriction) and the mydriasis ensuing from the
absence of light (dilatation) were employed to measure cholinergic
and adrenergic mechanisms, respectively.

The rationale underlying the efficacy of the procedure is
buttressed by pharmacological and physiological considerations.
The cholinergic nature of the activity of the oculomotor nerve
under the influence of light has been proved by the positive assay
for acetylcholine in the anterior chamber of the eye, (Engelhart,
1931) and by the disappearance of the light reflex after the injec-
tion of cholinesterase (Mendel & Hawkins, 1943). Conversely, the
anticholinesterases induce miosis, presumably by interfering with
the hydrolysis of acetylcholine by acetylcholinesterase. The
adrenergic nature of the dilatory response of the pupil is suggested by the work of Poos (1939), Hess and Koella (1950), and Hess,
Koella, and Szabo (1950) on isolated radial preparations of the
iris. These studies demonstrated that the iris muscle contracted
in response to small concentrations of adrenalin and noradrenalin.
Since these substances are responsible for neurohumoral transmission
in sympathetically innervated structures, they believed it reasonable to assume that a dilator muscle existed that responded to
sympathetic excitation. In addition, Frohlich and Loewi (1910)
had shown that the mydriasis induced by adrenalin is intensified
by cocaine, a monoamine oxidase inhibitor. Since pupillary constriction had been shown to be dependent upon the liberation of
acetylcholine and dilatation upon an adrenergic mediator, the
rate of dilatation was considered to represent the kinetics of a
general adrenergic mechanism, while the rate of constriction was
considered indicative of the kinetics of the cholinergic mechanism.

The physiological and anatomical evidence establishing the
internal validity of pupillometry as a measure of autonomic nervous
system activity has been summarized by Loewenfeld (1958). A brief
review of the evidence seems in order. The arc of the pupillary
light reflex starts with stimulation of the retinal rods and cones.

These impulses pass through the optic nerves, with partial decus-
sation at the chiasm, and into the optic tract. The afferent
pupillary fibers leave the optic tract just before they reach the
lateral geniculate body, and they pass through the brachium of
the superior colliculus to reach the pretectum. There the fibers
synapse. Half of the post synaptic fibers go to the homolateral
Edinger-Westphal (EW) nucleus and the other half pass through the
posterior commissure and enter the opposite EW nucleus. From each EW
nucleus, efferent fibers to the sphincter muscle of the iris pass
with other third nerve fibers through the midbrain and cerebral
peduncles into the interpeduncular space and along the base of
the brain into the orbit. These parasympathetic fibers form a
short motor root to the ciliary ganglion. Beyond a synapse in the
ganglion, the postsynaptic fibers comprise the short ciliary nerves
which run to the sphincter muscle.

    The innervation of the dilator muscle is from the sympathetic
nervous system. The sympathetic pupillary fibers originate in
the sympathetic centers of the ventral hypothalamus and descend
along the ventrolateral part of the stem and spinal cord to enter
the center of Budge in the cervico thoracic region, where they
synapse. The preganglionic fibers leave the cord through the
ventral roots of the first and second thoracic segments, enter the
first thoracic sympathetic ganglion, and then go up the sympathetic chain to synapse in the superior cervical ganglion. The post-
ganglionic fibers accompany the carotid artery and its branches,
traverse the tympanic cavity, re-enter the cranial cavity, and
join the Gasserion ganglion. The fibers run via the ophthalmic
branch of the fifth cranial nerve into the orbit. Some fibers go
directly to the long ciliary nerves and some go through the
ciliary ganglion and to the long ciliary nerves which innervate
the dilator pupillae.

    Thus constriction of the pupil may be produced (1) by active
contraction of the sphincter muscle through parasympathetic third
nerve fibers; (2) by lessening of the inhibitory influences on
the EW nucleus, i.e., sleep, fatigue, narcosis, organic injury.
And, dilatation of the pupil may be brought about (1) by active
contraction of the dilator muscle through sympathetic stimulation;
(2) by increased inhibition of the EW nucleus by impulses arising
from the cerebral cortex, thalamus, hypothalamus, or peripheral
sensory pathways. In their classic investigation of the role of
sympathetic and parasympathetic systems on reflex dilatation of
the pupil, Lowenstein and Loewenfeld (1950) reported that the
active sympathetic reflex dilatation of the pupil accounts for
from four fifths up to nine tenths of the total extent of dilatation, while less than one fifth of the total amount of dilatation
is due to influences of the third nerve. The dilatation due to
relaxation of the third nerve was found to be a practically negli-

gible quantity. If the varieties of disordered neurohumoral function that characterize the functional psychoses do represent discrete levels of activity of interacting parasympathetic-cholinergic
and sympathetic-adrenergic mechanisms that differ significantly
from the patterns manifested by normals at rest and under stress,
then different patterns of constriction and dilatation should be
observable. That is, it was assumed that peripheral cholinergic
and adrenergic imbalances, respectively, mirror central cholinergic
and adrenergic imbalances.

PATTERNS OF ADRENERGIC-CHOLINERGIC ACTIVITY OF THE NORMAL ADULT UNDER STRESS

The details of the apparatus and procedures employed to
measure and record pupillary dilatation and constriction have been
reported in the author's publications over the last decade and
references will be cited in the remainder of the paper. Essentially,
two measuring devices were employed: A Grass Kymograph with a
135 mm. lens that employed infra-red film; and a binocular infrared electronic pupillograph that was designed by Lowenstein and
Loewenfeld (1958). Electronic timers were employed to regulate the
durations of light and darkness by interrupting the output of a
R1131C, Sylvania Glow Modulator Tube. A two-channel Texas Instrument Servo-recorder was used in conjunction with the infra-red
pupillograph. The infra-red pupillograph photographic procedure
necessitated 11x enlargement of each photograph with a Traid Corp.
projector and the use of a linear transducer calibrated to digi-
tally record pupillary diameter.

To test the hypothesis that normal adult subjects react to
emergencies with an increased adrenergic response and decreased
cholinergic response, measurements of pupillary dilatation and
constriction were obtained on six normal, healthy adults between
the ages of 19-40 (Rubin, 1960b). Due to the variety of perceptual responses that are elicited in humans to the same stimulus,
it is difficult to define a stimulus situation that is realizable
in a laboratory as an "emergency" or as a "threat". Consequently,
following the control measurements obtained when the subjects
were at rest, each subject was required to immerse the right hand
and forearm in a cold water bath maintained at 5°C. while measurements were made of either dilatation or constriction. When the
rate of pupillary dilatation at rest was compared to the rate
obtained during the stress condition, it was found that the slopes
of the curves were equal (parallel) but that the absolute level
of dilatation under the cold pressor condition was significantly
greater (Fig. 2).

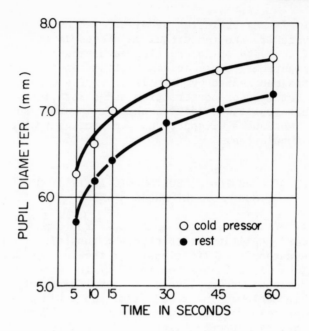

Figure 2.   Pupillary dilatation in normal subjects exposed to the cold pressor test.

When the rates of pupillary constriction over a period of 5 seconds for the normal individuals at rest and under the condition of the cold pressor were compared a significant difference was obtained (Fig. 3). As opposed to the relationship observed during dilatation, the level of constriction of the pupil under the condition of the cold pressor test was decreased.

These human results demonstrating the reciprocity of the relationship between the sympathetic-parasympathetic divisions of the autonomic nervous system during stress are entirely concordant with the animal findings of Loewenfeld (1958), Bonvallet and Zbrozyna (1963), and Zbrosyna and Bonvallet (1963). The latter authors recorded action potentials simultaneously from the cortex, the cervical sympathetic nerve and the short ciliary nerves (para-sympathetic) of one eye, and observed the pupil of the opposite eye. They found that electrical stimulation of peripheral sensory nerves or the ponto-mesencephalic reticular activating substance evoked an arousal pattern in the cortex, inhibition of the short ciliary nerves and an increase in activity of the cervical sympa-thetic nerve. These results support the interpretation of the experimental findings that under a condition of stress, the normal

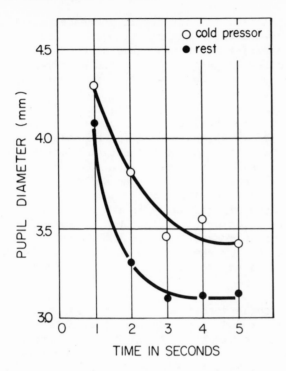

Figure 3.   Pupillary constriction in normal subjects exposed to the cold pressor test.

human adult responds with an increased sympathetic-adrenergic out-flow and a decreased parasympathetic-cholinergic outflow. This reciprocal balance between the system insures maximal mobilization of the resources of the organism required for "fight, flight or fright".

ADRENERGIC-CHOLINERGIC REACTIVITY LEVELS OF FUNCTIONAL PSYCHOTICS

Several additional experiments were performed by the author (Rubin, 1961a, 1961b) in order to test two additional hypotheses. The first hypothesis tested was that the population of psychotics exhibited three distinct levels of sympathetic activity and three distinct levels of parasympathetic activity. The second hypothesis tested was that psychotics manifest patterns of neurohumoral dys-function that deviate significantly from the pattern of normals

at rest as well as from the adrenergic increase and cholinergic
decrease that characterizes the normal person during stress.
Furthermore, the varieties of neurohumoral dysfunction could be
represented by discrete patterns of levels of adrenergic-cholinergic interaction, as described previously in Figure 1.

To test these hypotheses, measurements of dilatation and constriction at rest were obtained on 23 healthy control subjects
between the ages of 19-40 years. Ratios representing the amount
of dilatation or constriction as a function of time were obtained
for each subject. And after appropriate tests for normality of
distribution of these ratios (Bliss and Calhoun, 1954), the sample
mean was employed to determine the likelihood of obtaining ratio
values that deviated significantly in the direction of excessive
or deficient dilatation or constriction. The probability of obtaining dilatation or constriction ratios significantly greater
than or less than the extreme values in each distribution was then
employed to evaluate the measurements obtained from psychotic
samples.

The results to be described were obtained on two samples of
patients who were tested at two different psychiatric institutions.
As the results of the first experiment were confirmed by the
second experiment, the following description pertains to 71 patients
who had been diagnosed as functionally psychotic (Rubin, 1961b).
Employing the probability limits obtained for the distribution of
the dilatation ratios in the sample of normal individuals, it was
found that 21 of 71 patients manifested excessive dilatation, 26
of 71 patients manifested deficient dilatation, and 24 of 71
patients manifested normal dilatation. These relationships are
presented in Figure 4 where the mean dilatation ratio for each of
the three groups at each time interval is presented as a function
of the amount of time spent in darkness.

Inspection of the figure clearly indicates that there are
three levels of dilatation that characterize the sample of patients
employed in the experiment. The hypothesized three distinct levels
of adrenergic activity, as measured by pupillary reactivity, seem
to have been confirmed. That is, if it is assumed that the magnitude of pupillary dilatation is proportional to sympathetic-noradrenergic outflow, then it may be concluded that: some of the
patients responded in a manner characteristic of normals at rest;
others showed excessive sympathetic-noradrenergic outflow; and
still others manifested deficient sympathetic-noradrenergic outflow.

Employing the probability limits obtained from the distribution of the constriction ratio in the sample of normal individuals,
it was found that 36 of 71 patients manifested excessive constric-

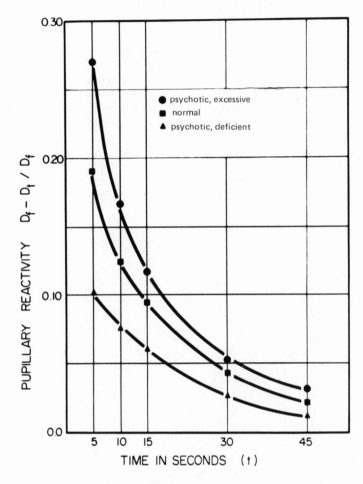

Figure 4.   Reactivity levels of pupillary dilatation in psychotic
patients.   (The values of the ordinate, D_f-D_i/D_f, consist of the
final level of dilatation, mm., after 60 seconds of dark adaptation,
D_f, minus the level of dilatation at each interval in darkness,
D_t, divided by the final level of dilatation, D_t.   The abscissa
represents the intervals of darkness in seconds, t, preceding
photographing of the pupil.)

tion, 7 of 71 patients manifested deficient constriction, and 28
of 71 patients showed normal constriction. These relationships
are presented in Figure 5 where the average constriction ratio for
each of the three groups at each interval is represented as a
function of length of time of exposure to a constant intensity
light source. When the curve for those showing defective constriction is compared to the curve representing normal constriction, it
is seen that the amount of change in pupil size for the deficient
group remains smaller than for normal constriction. For the group
manifesting excessive constriction, it is apparent that the amount
of constriction per unit time is much greater than that of the
normal or defective group. With respect to constriction, therefore, three levels, each significantly different from the other,
were found in the sample of patients employed in the studies.
Assuming that the tendency toward constriction of the sphincter
pupillae is proportional to parasympathetic-cholinergic outflow,
the demonstration of three levels of constriction suggests that:
(a) in one group of patients, either excessive quantities of

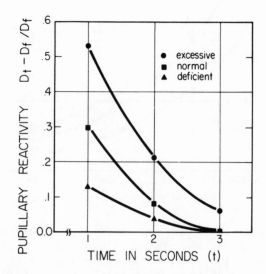

Figure 5. Reactivity levels of pupillary constriction in psychotic
patients. (The values on the ordinate, D_i-D_f/D_f, consist of the
average diameter - mm. -- of the constricted pupil at each interval,
D_t, minus the diameter of the maximally constricted pupil after 5
seconds of light adaptation, D_f, divided by D_f. The abscissa
represents the duration of light adaptation in seconds, t.)

acetylcholine were liberated or there was deficient acetylcholinesterase activity accompanying hyper-parasympathetic outflow; (b) in
a second group of patients, insufficient quantities of the neuro-
humor were liberated or enzyme activity was excessive during hypo-
parasympathetic outflow; (c) the third group manifested that level
of parasympathetic-cholinergic activity that was equivalent to the
level of normal subjects. These observations on the kinetics of
adrenergic and cholinergic activity confirmed two hypotheses
deduced from the theory; that is, the existence of three distinct
levels of adrenergic activity and three distinct levels of cholinergic activity.

     In order to establish that there are varieties of neurohumoral
dysfunction that comprise the population of functional psychotics,
it remained necessary to show that the disorders consisted of an
impairment of function of either the adrenergic or cholinergic
mechanism, or both. The demonstration of these patterns of interaction was derived from the following considerations. Twenty-four
out of 71 psychotic patients, it will be recalled, showed no impairment in the extent of dilatation. However, all of the members
in this group manifested aberrant constriction. Twenty of the 24
manifested excessive constriction, while 4 patients were deficient
in constriction. Conversely, of the 28 psychotic patients out of
71 who showed no impairment in constriction, all were aberrant in
the extent of dilatation; 12 showed excessive dilatation and 16
manifested deficient dilatation. In confirmation of the major
hypothesis, it may be stated that all of the 71 patients employed
in the studies showed a significant impairment in either the
tendency to dilatation or to constriction or both. Furthermore,
if the magnitude of dilatation is considered to be proportional
to the quantity of adrenergic mediator liberated, and the amount
of constriction of the sphincter pupillae proportional to the
quantity of acetylcholine liberated, then it may be concluded that
all of the psychotics employed in these studies were differentiable
into seven discrete patterns of adrenergic-cholinergic imbalance.

     The varieties of adrenergic-cholinergic dysfunction elucidated
indicate that the population of functionally psychotic individuals
is heterogeneous. Thus, the current quests for a chemical panacea
that affects only one of the components of the autonomic nervous
system unidirectionally do not seem promising. Instead, the results of these studies suggest that each pattern of adrenergic-
cholinergic activity may require a specific combination of drugs
which differentially affect the level of activity of either or
both components (Table 1). The value of the present study is that
it seems to provide a rationale for the selection of patients who
require distinct chemotherapies as determined by their specific
pattern of adrenergic-cholinergic imbalance.

TABLE 1

A CLASSIFICATION OF FUNCTIONAL PSYCHOSES INTO DISCRETE
LEVELS OF ADRENERGIC-CHOLINERGIC INTERACTION
AND THE DERIVED CHEMOTHERAPIES

	Adrenergic-Cholinergic Reactivity Pattern	Suggested Chemotherapy
I	A+C+	Adrenolytic agent in addition to an anticholinergic compound
II	AoC+	Anticholinergic compound
III	A-C+	Adrenergic stimulant in addition to an anticholinergic compound
IV	A+Co	Adrenolytic agent
V	A-Co	Adrenergic stimulant
VI	AoC-	Cholinergic stimulant
VII	A-C-	Adrenergic stimulant in addition to cholinergic stimulant

At the time this paper was in preparation, a theoretical article by Friedhoff (1973) appeared that focused attention upon the interaction of a dopaminergic-cholinergic mechanism in the production of psychotic symptoms. He proposed that an increase in dopaminergic activity or a decrease in cholinergic activity produces psychotic symptoms. As dopamine is the in vivo precursor of nora-drenaline, Friedhoff's hypothesis may be subsumed under Rubin's Theory if certain assumptions are made. If the normal enzymatic action of beta-hydroxylase is unimpaired, then the concentrations of DA and NE covary, therefore, as DA levels increase so should NE levels. Then, it may be affirmed that Friedhoff asserts that psychosis is characterized by increased NE levels or decreased cholinergic levels. The author's theory would consider this rela-tionship to obtain normally when an adult is under stress.

An obvious but unwarranted implication that may be drawn by the reader of the foregoing exposition is that the author believes with warrantable assertability that these patterns of autonomic dysfunction are etiological factors in the functional psychoses.

Admittedly, it is difficult to conceive of an environmental process that could produce central neurohumoral dysfunction. However,
the experiments described in this report were not designed to
answer the question, "Is central neurohumoral dysfunction the in-
variable antecedent of psychotic behavior or the effect of dynamic,
environmental variables?" Although the answer to the question may
be of academic interest, it would be more fruitful to accept the
attitude of a pragmatist and insist that truth is preeminently to
be tested by the practical consequences of belief.

ADRENERGIC-CHOLINERGIC DYSFUNCTION IN PSYCHOTIC CHILDREN

The technique of employing pupillary measurements to determine
adrenergic-cholinergic steady-states that characterize adult psychotics was also applied to ascertain whether autistic, psychotic
children were significantly differentiable from normal children.
An additional comparison could readily be made between those
steady-states that characterized normal children and the adrenergic-
cholinergic responsivity of normal adults. Thus an opportunity
was also afforded to contribute to an understanding of the development of autonomic reactivity in normal individuals. The data on
dilatation and constriction was obtained on four normal, healthy
children between the ages of 7-9.5 years, and five autistic
children between the ages of 7-12 years. A statistical analysis
of the rate of dilatation between these groups indicated that the
slopes were equal and parallel but separated significantly by a
constant (Fig. 6). Assuming that the magnitude of the response of
the dilator pupillae is an increasing monotonic function of the
amount of adrenergic mediator liberated by sympathetic outflow at
the effector site, then the absolute level of sympathetic-adrenergic
outflow for the normal children is greater than that for the psychotic children. This suggests that normal children have a significantly greater capacity for increased adrenergic outflow than autistic children.

When the two groups of children were compared with respect to
constriction, it was found that the rate was significantly faster
for the normal children, although no significant differences were
obtained when the asymptotic levels were compared (Fig. 7). This
result was interpreted as indicating that the rate of cholinergic
activity was more rapid for normal children.

Juxtaposing these findings it may be concluded that normal
children have a greater capacity for sympathetic-adrenergic outflow,
and, of equal importance, a greater manifest capacity to reestab-
lish more quickly the vegetative functions mediated by the parasympathetic-cholinergic system. Clearly, autistic children demonstrate a pattern of autonomic dysfunction, however, the limited

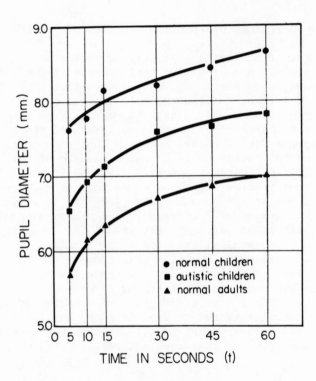

Figure 6. Change in pupillary dilatation as a function of the amount of time spent in darkness for normal adults, normal children, and autistic, psychotic children.

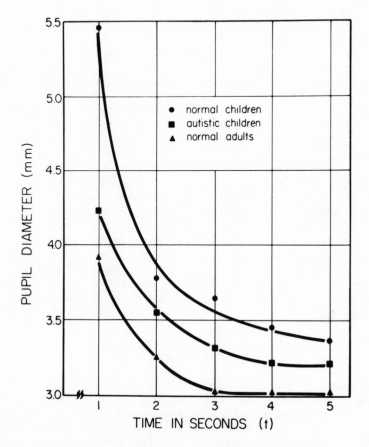

Figure 7. Change in pupillary constriction as a function of duration of light adaptation for normal adults, normal children, and autistic, psychotic children.

sample sizes employed in this experiment precluded the utilization
of appropriate statistical techniques for the elucidation of discrete patterns of neurohumoral dysfunction as performed with adults.

Reference to Fig. 6 provides another experimental comparison
that may throw some light upon the ontogeny of adrenergic responsivity. When the course of dilatation for normal children was
compared to that of normal adults, it was found that the mean
pupil diameter at each interval for the children was significantly
greater than that of normal adults. Again, if it is assumed that
the amount of dilatation is proportional to sympathetic-adrenergic
outflow, then it may be concluded that normal children have a
significantly greater capacity for increased adrenergic outflow.
An interesting difference in cholinergic reactivity was revealed
when the course of constriction in normal adults was compared to
that of normal children. A statistical analysis of the results
presented in Fig. 7 revealed that normal adults manifested significantly greater constriction than normal children. However, although
the absolute level of cholinergic activity was found to be consistently greater for the normal adult, the rate of cholinergic activity was found to be significantly greater for the normal child.
These results suggest that normal children and normal adults are
significantly different with respect to autonomic responsivity.
Furthermore, although the intermediate biochemical (genetic?)
factors that are responsible for the change in neurohumoral activity
are not as yet known, it would seem that the normal child, as he
develops into a normal adult, undergoes changes that reduce the
level of adrenergic outflow, decrease the rate of cholinergic
activity, and increase the absolute level of cholinergic outflow.

SUMMARY

The results of the studies described up to this point confirmed several hypotheses derived from a theoretical formulation
of the role of adrenergic and cholinergic mechanisms in psychotic
disorders. The salient features of the theory are: effective
adjustments to emergency situations require a maximal, generalized
sympathetic response; to attain a maximal level of sympathetic
activity, it is not only necessary that increased levels of adrenergic outflow follow the emergency but that the level of cholinergic activity decrease; the neurohumoral dysfunctions that characterize the psychoses represent significant departures from the
adrenergic-cholinergic states that characterize the normal individual at rest and during stress; and, the varieties of dysfunction
represent discrete levels of activity of interacting adrenergic
and cholinergic mechanism. That is, each pattern of neurohumoral
imbalance represents an impairment of function of either the adrenergic or cholinergic mechanism or both.

The nature of the adrenergic impairment that characterizes some psychotics it is suggested may be a neurohumoral deficiency of some biogenic amine or some enzyme disorder such as monoamine oxidase or catechol orthomethyl transferase (COMT) overactivity in the adrenergic centers of the brain. Other psychotics manifest adrenergic impairment by a neurohumoral excess of some sympathomimetic amine that may be the result of some enzyme disorder such as monoamine oxidase or COMT underactivity in central adrenergic centers. Similarly, the cholinergic impairment of some psychotics may be characterized by excessive concentrations of brain acetylcholine or deficient acetylcholinesterase while other psychotics may possess an inadequate level of acetylcholine or excessive acetylcholinesterase activity. A theoretical matrix of neurohumoral steady states, derived from considerations of the interaction of the levels of the two systems, characterized the population of functional psychotics as well as the normal individual at rest and under stress.

The application of measurements of pupillary reactivity to the study of autonomic dysfunction in autistic, psychotic children demonstrated that adrenergic-cholinergic imbalance clearly differentiated these children from normal children. The significance of this obtained difference was evaluated with respect to the pattern of autonomic function manifested by normal adults.

That the adult psychotic may be classified into any one of seven discrete categories of adrenergic-cholinergic activity levels throws reasonable doubt upon the current quest for a single chemical panacea. Instead, the elucidation of these discrete patterns of adrenergic-cholinergic activity suggests a rational approach to chemotherapy. Each pattern of adrenergic-cholinergic dysfunction requires a specific combination of drugs that differentially affect the levels of activity of either or both components of the autonomic nervous system.

PSYCHOTICS IN REMISSION

In view of the ambiguities inherent within the concept of clinical remission or recovery, several experiments were designed to determine whether the reactivity of the iris muscles could effectively contribute to an understanding of the autonomic concomitants of schizophrenics in remission. Working with psychotics in remission also offered an opportunity to attenuate the confounding effects of psychotropic drugs on pupillary reactivity (Rubin and Barry, 1972, a,b.).

The need for greater accuracy and precision of the term clinical remission has been made most urgent in view of the sweeping changes that have taken place in the treatment and control of

schizophrenic psychosis over the past 15 years. Today much
shorter periods of hospitalization are required before patients
are discharged. However, the fact that patients are discharged
in a matter of weeks certainly does not mean that a specific cure
has been found or that anything more is known or understood about
the etiology of the process. More likely it suggests a growing,
self-fulfilling belief in psychiatric circles that hospitalization
is "bad" for the patient and that his recovery will be hastened
and perhaps insured by his speedy return to the community. Recent
follow-up studies cast serious doubt on the validity of these
current convictions. According to these studies (Catterson, et al.
1963; Mandelbrote & Folkard, 1961; Wing, 1966) the adjustments of
many of the patients living in the community is rather poor or
marginal at best. Many of them suffer from symptoms which are
quite indistinguishable from hospitalized patients. Families are
often under considerable stress, and while the population of
hospitalized patients has fallen, the number who are dependent on
the community and its various agencies has increased. It is difficult to continue thinking in terms of recovery or significant remission when reports continue to appear which claim that only 10
per cent of 500 schizophrenic patients did not relapse 5 years
after discharge from the hospital (Kerbikov, 1962). Insofar as
the prospect of full and permanent recovery is concerned there
would seem to be little agreement as to what these terms mean and
even less empirical, valid evidence to conclude that it actually
ever occurs.

As the concept of clinical remission is logically dependent
upon one's understanding of the nature of the process diagnosed,
and as it had been shown that measurements of pupillary reactivity
were significantly related to the disease process, it seemed de-
sirable to employ these measurements as an index of autonomic
dysfunction in clinically remitted schizophrenics.

In the first experiment, three groups of subjects were
examined pupillographically, at rest. The results obtained for
26 normal subjects were compared to those obtained from 27 active
psychotics and 16 psychotics evaluated as clinically remitted by
the professional staff at Haverford State Hospital.

Measurements of dilatation and constriction at rest were obtained on 26 normal subjects, 14 males and 12 females, who ranged
in age between 20 and 51 years and whose mean age was 30. Twenty-
one of the subjects were Caucasian, 4 were Negro, and 1 subject
was Oriental. Each subject was required to complete the Cornell
Medical Index-Health Questionnaire (Weider, et al. 1946) a 4-page
letter-sized sheet on which are printed 195 questions corresponding closely to those usually asked in a detailed and comprehensive
medical interview including many on the psychological aspects of
illness. No follow-up medical examination or psychiatric inter-

view was deemed necessary on the basis of the responses given by
these subjects. Several additional questions were asked of each
subject to eliminate those on _any_ medication.

The 43 psychotic patients employed in the experiment had all
been diagnosed as schizophrenic. The 27 patients who were judged
to be actively psychotic by the psychiatric staff were free of
other significant medical and neurological illness. Sixteen of
these patients were diagnosed schizophrenic reaction, paranoid
type; 9 had been diagnosed schizophrenic reaction, chronic undifferentiated; 1 had been diagnosed as schizophrenia, schizoaffective
type; and, another as schizo reaction, acute undifferentiated.
The median duration of the illness, 4 years, was loosely determined
from the date of the first hospitalization. The patients had all
received a variety of chemotherapies and 5 of them had also received electric shock therapy. Their average age was 30 years and
the age range was 20 to 49 years. Twenty-two of the patients were
males and 5 were females. Twenty-two were Caucasian, 4 were Negro,
and 1 was Oriental. Prior to pupillographic examination, all
medication was terminated. Thereafter, at 24-hour intervals, early
morning urine specimens were examined for the presence of phenothiazines and their metabolites by means of the Forrest tests.
Only after a negative urine finding was pupillographic examination
conducted.

The 16 psychotics evaluated by the staff as clinically remitted ranged in age from 23 to 41 years, and the average age was
33 years. All of the subjects were males. Fourteen were Caucasian
and 2 were Negro. Medical and neurological findings were negative.
Ten of the patients had been diagnosed schizophrenic reaction,
paranoid type; 5 as schizophrenic reaction, chronic undifferentiated; and 1 as schizophrenic reaction, acute hebephrenic type. All
of the patients had received a variety of psychological and drug
therapies and 1 had also received electric shock therapy. These
patients were examined just prior to discharge. Eight of the
patients were on maintenance doses of medication and 8 were off all
medication for a considerable period at the time of the pupillographic examination. The urine specimens of the eight patients off
medication were nevertheless examined by means of the Forrest test
and found to be negative prior to pupillographic examination.

The mean change in pupil diameter at 1 sec. intervals from
1-10 secs. in darkness along with the range and standard deviation
at each interval were obtained for 26 normal subjects. The 95
per cent confidence limits were calculated for each interval and
were employed to evaluate the significance of the changes in
dilatation for active psychotics and psychotics in remission, as
a function of time in darkness. The results of this evaluation
suggested the existence of two quantitatively distinct aberrant

patterns of dilatation among the active psychotics. The mean
change in diameter at each interval for each group and the 95 per
cent confidence limits at each interval are plotted in Fig. 8 as
a function of the amount of time in darkness. Group A, consisting of 13 patients, manifested uniformly smaller increments in
pupillary dilatation than the normals throughout the period of
dark-adaptation. Another group of active psychotics, Group B, N=8,
also manifested significantly less pupillary dilatation than normals
but the magnitude of dilatation was greater for this group than
that of Group A. Of the 27 active psychotics, 21 (78 per cent)

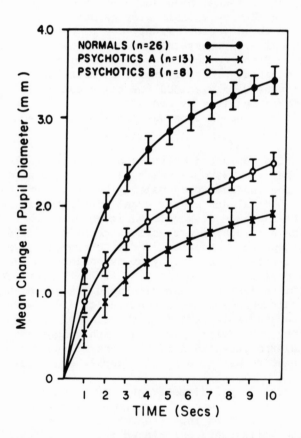

Figure 8. Active schizophrenics, dilatation. The mean change in
pupil diameter (mm) as a function of the time in darkness (sec.).
The 95 per cent confidence limits of each mean at each interval of
time for each group are represented by the vertical lines.

were found to be aberrant with respect to dilatation at rest, while the remainder were found to dilate normally.

The change in pupil diameter as a function of the duration of darkness for each of the 16 patients in remission was also evaluated with respect to the 95 per cent confidence limits previously calculated for the normal group. It was found that the psychotics in remission were also distributed into quantitatively distinct groups. Group A in Fig. 9, N=7, was found to be comparable to Group A of the active psychotics. A smaller group of patients,

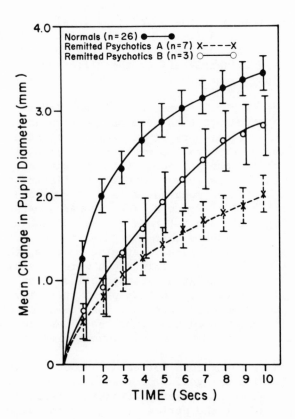

Figure 9. Schizophrenic patients in remission, dilatation. The mean change in pupil diameter (mm) as a function of the time in darkness (sec). The 95 per cent confidence limits of each mean at each interval of time for each group are represented by the vertical lines.

Group B, N=3, was found to dilate in essentially the same manner
as Group B of the active psychotics. Ten of the 16 psychotics in
remission (63 per cent) were aberrant with respect to dilatation
while the remainder were normal.

As 8 of the patients in remission were on a small maintenance
dose of a phenothiazine at the time of testing, and 8 were not on
any medication, it was necessary to determine whether the significant differences in dilatation response observed were a function
of this state of affairs. To test the hypothesis that differences
in pupillary dilatation were the result of the drug condition, a
chi-square test was performed. Six of the 8 patients on medication showed abnormal pupillary reactivity while 4 of the 8 who
were off medication also manifested abnormal pupillary reactivity.
As the resulting chi-square was found to be far below the value
required for significance at the 5 per cent level of confidence,
it was concluded that the different patterns of dilatation were
independent of the drug condition, or that the doses of medication
employed did not significantly affect the differences in observed
pupillary dilatation.

The mean change in pupil diameter at 1-sec. intervals from
1-10 sec. of light stimulation as well as the standard deviation
range and 95 per cent confidence limits were calculated for the
26 normal subjects and employed to evaluate the significance of
changes in constriction manifested by the actively psychotic
patients and the psychotics in remission. Two distinct patterns
of constriction were found among the 27 actively psychotic patients
as represented in Fig. 10. Group A, N=4, showed a markedly attenuated response to light at each interval throughout the period of
stimulation. If it is assumed that the extent of constriction is
proportional to the level of parasympathetic outflow, then it may
be concluded that the members of this group were parasympatheti-
cally hyporeactive. Another group of psychotics, Group B, N=6,
showed a very rapid constriction of the pupil initially, comparable
to that shown by normals, which was soon abnormally attenuated and
followed by redilation. In total, 10 of the 27 psychotics (37 per
cent) manifested aberrant constriction, as measured at rest.

The evaluation of the record for each psychotic in remission
generated the following categories of response. Four patients
designated Group A showed a markedly attenuated response to the
light stimulus throughout the period of light stimulation that was
qualitatively similar to that shown by the actively psychotic
patients of Group A. The subjects in Group B, N=3, all showed a
prompt, normal response to light initially which was quickly
followed by abnormal attenuation of constriction and an abnormal
rapid redilatation. This pattern of response is similar to that
of Group B for the active psychotics. The mean changes in pupil
diameter as a function of duration of light stimulation for these

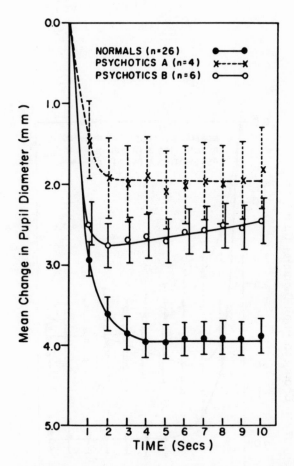

Figure 10. Active Schizophrenics, constriction. The mean change in pupil diameter (mm) as a function of duration of light stimulation (sec.). The 95 per cent confidence limits of each mean at each interval of time for each group are represented by the vertical lines.

groups are plotted in Fig. 11. Thus, 7 out of 16 (44 per cent)
clinically remitted psychotics were aberrant during constriction.

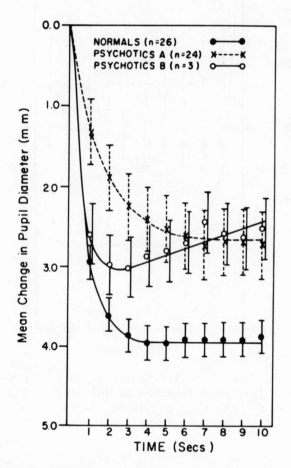

Figure 11. Schizophrenics in remission, constriction. The mean
change in pupil diameter (mm) as a function of duration of light
stimulation (sec.). The 95 per cent confidence limits of each
mean at each interval of time for each group are represented by
the vertical lines.

In order to determine whether the different patterns of constriction were independent of the drug condition, a chi-square
test was performed. Of the 7 patients manifesting a pattern of
abnormal constriction of either type A or B, 5 were on medication
and 2 were not. The 9 patients who constricted normally consisted
of 6 patients who were not on medication and 3 who were. The
calculated chi-square corrected for continuity for these frequen-
cies was 1.10 for 1 df, far below the value required to reject the
hypothesis. Based upon this evaluation it was concluded that the
abnormal patterns of constriction found to prevail among psychotics
in remission were independent of the drug condition, or the medication at the doses administered did not significantly affect the
observed differences in pupillary constriction.

Another parameter of the records that was employed to differentiate the patient groups from the normal group was the variability of the asymptote manifest during constriction. The invar-
iable response of the pupil of normal subjects to the intense
light stimulus employed in the experiment could be characterized
by a) a decreasing monotonic function for the first 3 to 4 seconds
of light stimulation; i.e., the diameter of the constricting pupil
decreased regularly and rapidly; and, b) little variation in the
diameter of the maximally constricted pupil for the remaining period the light was on; the absolute difference in pupil diameter
between adjacent intervals of time never exceeded 0.20 mm with an
average deviation of ±0.10 mm following maximal constriction.
These relationships are depicted in Fig. 12.

An analysis of the distribution of the magnitude of the absolute differences between adjacent intervals revealed that many of
the actively psychotic patients as well as patients in remission
showed significant departure from the well-modulated variations
about the asymptotic level that characterized the normals. Of the
27 actively psychotic patients, 16 of them (59 per cent) were
demonstrably aberrant with respect to the ability to maintain an
asymptotic steady state. Five of the 16 patients in remission
(33 per cent) were also aberrant in their ability to maintain an
asymptotic steady state. Chi-square tests performed to determine
whether significant departures from the asymptote were independent
of the medication - no medication condition showed that the medication did not significantly affect the aberrant departures from
the constriction asymptote.

When the results on pupillary dilatation, pupillary constriction, and asymptotic variability were combined for the psychotic
groups examined at rest, the following conclusions emerged. *Of the 27
patients who were actively psychotic, 25 were found to be aberrant
on one or more of the variables while 12 of the 16 psychotics in
remission were found to deviate significantly. The utilization of*

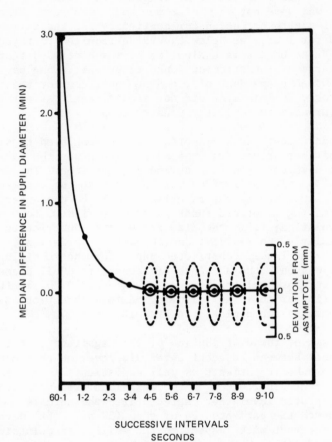

Figure 12. Asymptotic variability during constriction for normals, active schizophrenics, and schizophrenics in remission. The median differences in pupil diameter (mm) plotted as a function of successive intervals of light stimulation (sec.) _____, Normal subjects; ___ ____ median, value of the differences that exceed 0.20 mm.

*pupillography as an index of autonomic dysfunction successfully
identified 93 per cent of a sample of actively schizophrenic
patients. More importantly, 75 per cent of a sample of schizophrenics in remission, about to return to their families and
communities, were found to be characterized by states of autonomic dysfunction comparable to those manifested by actively psychotic patients.* This finding tends to support the position articu-
lated by Slater (1968) after reviewing the earlier evidence on
genetic factors in schizophrenia: "Schizophrenia is an illness
affecting the mind and the personality of the patient in a way
which is seldom completely resolved; after an attack of illness
there is nearly always some degree of permanent change of personality, and if there are several attacks this change will become
more and more marked" (p. 15).

In any consideration of autonomic function, reference per-
force must be made to the monumental work of Gellhorn (1956, 1957).
His concept of "tuning" of autonomic mechanisms is especially
relevant to the results of this experiment. Sympathetic "tuning"
Gellhorn described as a tendency to increased sympathetic responsiveness of the hypothalamus attendant upon diminished parasympathetic outflow. Conversely, parasympathetic tuning refers to an
increased tendency to parasympathetic responsiveness following
diminished sympathetic outflow. Applied to the results of this
study, the diminished sympathetic outflow of the psychotic groups,
as evidenced by marked attenuation of dilatation in darkness, would
suggest a tonic state of parasympathetic tuning that would eventu-
ate in increased pupillary constriction in response to light. However, the psychotic groups showed an obviously attenuated response
to light. If viewed from the standpoint of sympathetic tuning,
the diminished constriction of the psychotic groups would suggest
that they were sympathetically tuned. Contrary to the prediction
from this premise, the active and remitted psychotics did not
respond to darkness with increased sympathetic outflow. These
interpretations suggest that physiological tuning as a characteristic feature of normal autonomic homeostatic balance is aberrant
in schizophrenia. This conclusion is congruent with that of
Gellhorn as well as with some generalizations regarding autonomic
dysfunction in schizophrenia proposed by Hoskins more than a
quarter of a century ago. He maintained that there were several
systematic differences in homeostasis between schizophrenics and
normals as regards the resting functional level and that schizophrenics were also unable to "hold to the steady state" under ordinary conditions of existence.

The significance of these findings must be evaluated within
the framework of current deficiencies in the criteria for the
diagnosis of schizophrenia and the standards for clinical judgments
of remission or recovery. It would appear to be advisable to
complement the phenomenological evaluations of the course of the

illness with more objective criteria that have internal validity.

PUPILLARY RESPONSES OF SCHIZOPHRENICS IN REMISSION TO STRESS

In order to further elucidate the role of autonomic mechanisms in schizophrenics, active and clinically remitted, another study was performed to determine the adequacy of sympathetic-parasympathetic mechanisms in response to stress (cold pressor test) and the characteristics of homeostatic mechanisms in both groups following the termination of the stress, as measured pupillographically (Rubin and Barry, 1972).

Measurements of dilatation and constriction in response to the cold pressor test and following the termination of stress were obtained on eight normal subjects. Four of the subjects were males whose average age was 29 years and four were females whose average age was 32 years.

The five male patients who were judged to be actively psychotic by the psychiatric staff were free of other significant medical and neurological illness. The average age of these patients was 28 years. Prior to pupillographic examination, all medication was terminated. Thereafter, at 24-hr intervals, early morning urine specimens were examined for the presence of phenothiazines and metabolites by means of the Forrest Tests (Forrest et al., 1961). Only after a negative finding was the patient examined pupillographically.

The 16 psychotics evaluated by the staff as clinically remitted ranged in age from 23-41 years, and the average age was 33 years. All of the subjects were males. Medical and neurological findings were negative. The median duration of the illness, as determined, was 5 years. All of the patients had received a variety of psychological and drug therapies, and one had also received electric shock therapy. These patients were tested in the pupillography laboratory just prior to discharge. Eight of the patients were on maintenance doses of medication and eight were off all medication for a considerable period at the time of the examination. The urine specimens of the eight patients purportedly off medication were nevertheless examined by means of the Forrest Test and found to be negative prior to pupillographic examination.

Each subject in this experiment was comfortably positioned in the headrest mounted in front of the electronic pupillograph. After several minutes were spent in darkness, the recorder was started and continuous binocular tracings of the maximally dilated pupils were obtained for 1 min. At the termination of this interval of darkness, a constant intensity light source came on and illuminated the right eye for 10 sec. during which time binocular continuous recordings of the constricting pupils were obtained. The ensuing pupillary dilatation following the termination of the light stimulus was recorded for 60 sec. Another cycle of light and darkness with the same intervals was then presented without interruption. The third presentation of the 10-sec. light stimulus was followed by exactly 45 sec. of pupillary dilatation in darkness. At that moment, an assistant helped place the left arm of the subject into a cold water bath maintained at $5°C \pm 2°C$. Continuous recordings of the dark-adapted pupil were obtained for the remaining 15 sec. of the dark-adaptation portion of the cycle. The constant intensity light source then went on for 10 sec. was followed by 1-min. darkness and another 10-sec. period of light stimulation. At the termination of this interval, the arm was quickly removed from the bath by the assistant and dried, with the subject's head still properly positioned. Without interruption, the cycle of light and dark stimulation continued for approximately six additional minutes (six cycles). This period following termination of stress will henceforth be referred to as the period of homeostatic recovery.

The amount of change in maximal pupil diameter as a function of time (min.) for each normal subject is plotted in Fig. 13. The interval S_1 represents 15 sec. of stress, S_2 represents an additional minute of stress, and H_1, through H_6 represent 1-min. intervals following the termination of stress. Several outstanding characteristics common to all the normal subjects were noted. During the period of stress there was an increase in the diameter of the dark-adapted pupil corresponding to increased sympathetic outflow occasioned by the cold pressor test. Following the termination of stress at S_2, there was a rapid decrement in pupil diameter, and within 2-3 min. the diameter of the pupil approximately equalled the control diameter. Individual differences were then observed in the extent of the subnormal period and subsequent rebound.

The individual graphs for schizophrenics in remission employing the same units on the ordinate and abscissa are presented in Fig. 14. A perusal of these individual graphs indicated significant departures from the typical normal response to stress and significant aberrations during restitution following the termination of stress. Similar abnormal responses to stress and during homeostatic recovery for the active schizophrenics may be observed in Fig. 15.

After determining the 95 per cent confidence limits of the mean at each interval for the normals, it was possible to categorize the results obtained by the psychotics in remission into

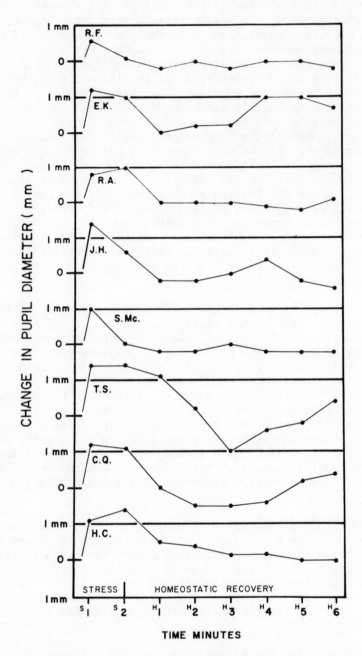

Figure 13. Pupillary dilatation, stress, and homeostatic recovery; normal subjects.

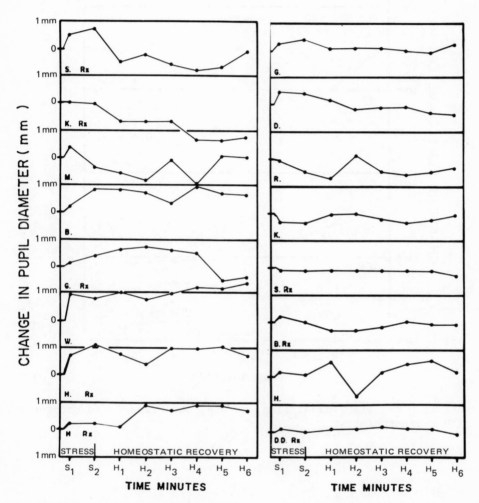

Figure 14. Pupillary dilatation, stress, and homeostatic recovery:
schizophrenic patients in remission.

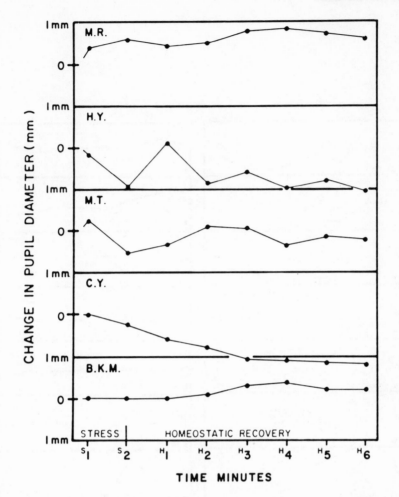

Figure 15. Pupillary dilatation, stress, and homeostatic recovery; active schizophrenics.

groups. Because of the marked divergence in responses within the smaller sample of active psychotics no attempt at grouping was made. However, a visual comparison between the data generated by the active psychotics and the psychotics in remission revealed that the actively psychotic patterns of dilatation coincided with the patterns exhibited by the psychotics in remission. In this way, the patterns of aberrant pupillary dilatation could be cate-

gorized into three groups. These categories of response are presented in Fig. 16.

In the normal curve, the 95 per cent confidence limits are
symmetrically placed about the mean. The patients in remission
comprising Group A (N=8) manifested little or no response to the
condition of the experiment. The cold pressor test barely elicited
any dilatation and consequently there were no significant changes

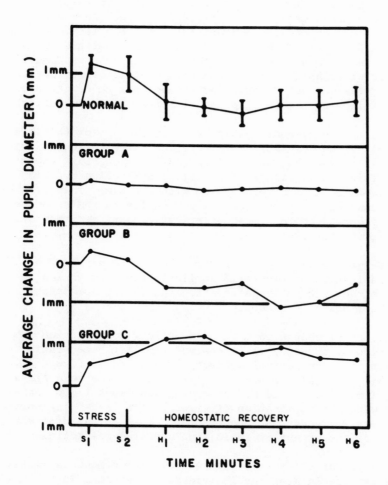

Figure 16. Dilatation, stress and homeostasis; normals and schizophrenics in remission.

in the size of the dark-adapted pupil during homeostatic recovery.
The patients in this group showed no sympathetic outflow in response
to stress and no changes in sympathetic activity during the homeostatic recovery period. The clinically remitted patients in Group
B (N=3), although minimally responsive to stress, (no patient in
this group showed an increase in pupil size that equalled the lowest increase among the normals) were manifestly aberrant with respect to the observations made during the period of homeostatic
recovery. Following the termination of the cold pressor test there
was a marked decrement in the diameter of the pupil which continued to increase in magnitude throughout the period measurements
were made. The extent of the sympathetic subnormal period was extreme and of long duration for these patients.

In contradistinction to the minimal dilatation response to
stress by the above groups, the remitted patients in Group C (N=5)
showed a normal response. However, following the termination of
stress, the diameter of the dark-adapted pupil remained as large
or larger than it had been during the time the hand was immersed
in the cold water bath. The increased sympathetic outflow occasioned by stress was not reversed by an appropriate compensatory
mechanism following the termination of stress in these patients.

Whereas in a previously cited study by the author (Rubin and
Barry, 1971) 75 per cent of schizophrenics in remission, examined
at rest, manifested aberrant pupillary dilatation, this experiment, utilizing measurements of pupillary dilatation occasioned by
stress and following its termination with the same group of subjects, demonstrated that all of the psychotics in remission were
abnormal with respect to sympathetic outflow during either stress,
homeostatic recovery, or both.

No attempt was made to categorize the active psychotics. However, reexamination of Figure 15 similarly revealed marked aberr-
ancies of either the response to stress or during homeostatic recovery in all of the patients.

The amount of change in maximal pupillary constriction (mm)
as a function of duration of stress and time for homeostatic recovery (min) for each normal subject, is plotted in Figure 17. The
interval S_1, represents a duration of 25 sec of the cold pressor
test, S_2, 1 min later, and H_1 through H_6 represent 1-min intervals following the termination of stress. The descending portions
of the curves represent the amount of increase in the diameter of
the pupil, or the extent of inhibition of parasympathetic outflow.

Examination of the normal figures revealed common characteristics as well as interesting individual differences in the maximally constricted values obtained during and after stress. Each
normal individual reacted to stress with an immediate increase in

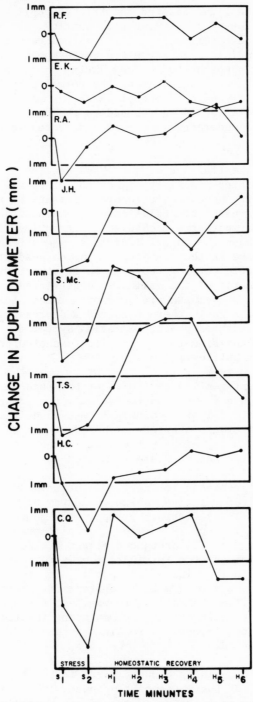

Figure 17. Pupillary constriction, stress, and homeostatic re-covery; normal subjects.

the diameter of the light-adapted constricted pupil which represents an attenuation of parasympathetic outflow. At the termination of stress, there followed a rapid, marked decrease in pupil
diameter corresponding to an increased parasympathetic outflow.
The amount of parasympathetic rebound during the remaining period
of homeostatic recovery varied among the normal subjects. Some
normals rebounded beyond the control value initially and then returned, while others seemed to rebound to the control level rapidly and then showed moderated increases and decreases about the
control level.

     Juxtaposing the findings of the above section to those of
the section describing pupillary dilatation of normals in response
to stress and during homeostatic recovery results in a vivid description of the synergistic relationship obtaining between sympathetic and parasympathetic mechanisms. Comparing Figs. 13 and
17 revealed that when the normal individual was stressed, there
followed an increase in the diameter of the dark-adapted pupil,
increased sympathetic outflow; concomitantly, there was an increase in the diameter of the maximally constricted pupil representing decreased parasympathetic outflow. Immediately following
the termination of stress, there occurred a decrease in the diameter of the dark-adapted pupil, decreased sympathetic outflow;
and a decrease in the diameter of the light-adapted pupil, increased parasympathetic outflow.

     The 95 per cent confidence limits of the mean at each interval
was then determined and employed to evaluate the constriction of
each of the psychotics in remission. It was found that 10 out of
16 of these patients were aberrant with respect to their pupillary
response to light during either stress or homeostasis. The graphs
for each of these ten patients are presented in Fig. 18.

     The abnormal responses to light adaptation shown in the figure
were then categorized relative to the standards calculated for the
normal sample into three distinct groups. The remitted patients
comprising Group A in Fig. 19 showed a normal increase in the size
of the light-adapted pupil throughout stress but no subject in this
group (N=3) responded to the termination of stress with the characteristic decrease in the size of the pupil. In other words these
patients responded to stress with an appropriate decrement in
parasympathetic outflow but failed to manifest the appropriate increase in parasympathetic outflow accompanying the termination of
stress. Parasympathetic outflow remained attenuated throughout
the restitution period.

     The patients comprising Group B (N=3) in the figure responded
differently. Each of the patients responded with a markedly
attenuated increase in the size of the light-adapted pupil but
then showed a characteristic decrease in pupil diameter at the

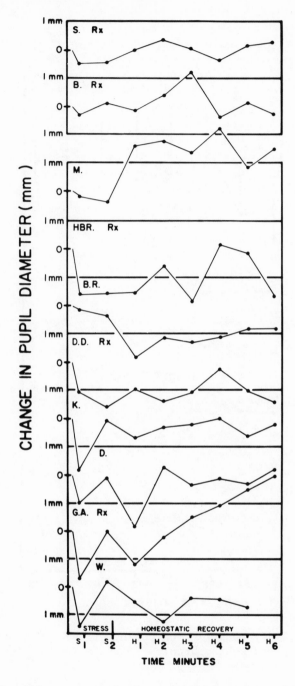

Figure 18. Pupillary constriction, during stress and homeostasis; schizophrenics in remission.

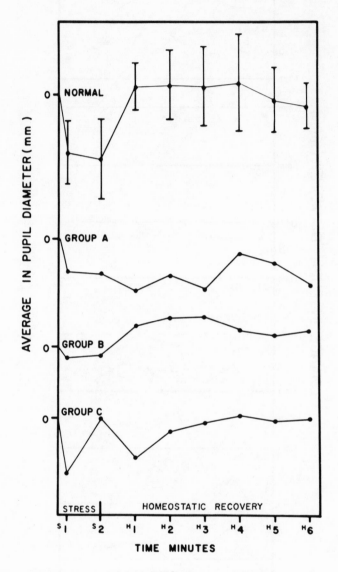

Figure 19.   Pupillary constriction during stress and homeostatic recovery; normals and schizophrenics in remission.

termination of the cold pressor test. The individuals in this
group were therefore defective with respect to the magnitude of
attenuation of the parasympathetic outflow during stress but were
normal with respect to the level of increased parasympathetic outflow concomitant with the termination of stress. Finally, the remitted patients in Group C (N=4) all showed still another significant deviation from the normal pattern of constriction elicited by
stress. Each patient in this group showed a normal increase in
the size of the light-adapted pupil after the first 25 sec. of
stress but then quite dramatically, while the arm was still in the
cold water bath, they manifested a rapid, unusual decrease in the
size of the pupil. Furthermore, following the termination of
stress, each of these patients showed a marked increase in the
diameter of the pupil. It may be said that the patients in Group
C responded to stress initially with a normal attenuation of parasympathetic outflow, but that increased parasympathetic outflow
was elicited prematurely, while the patient was still being
stressed. Compounding the dysfunction of the members of this group
was the sudden, aberrant increase in the size of the light-adapted
pupil when the stress was terminated. Instead of manifesting recovery by a sharp increase in parasympathetic outflow, these
patients showed a marked attenuation of outflow.

     Fewer analyses were required to be performed on the data of
the five patients who were actively psychotic. The changes in
pupil diameter (mm) as a function of the duration of stress and
homeostatic recovery (min) for each of these patients was compared
to the standards derived for the normal group. The reactivity of
the maximally constricted light-adapted pupil for each subject
under stress and homeostatic recovery is presented in Fig. 20. A
visual comparison of these figures to that of the normal group in
Fig. 19 was then made. Patient MR responded to stress with an
adequate inhibition of parasympathetic outflow and an appropriate,
rapid increase in outflow at the termination of stress. However,
the other four patients showed marked aberrations. Patient HY
responded to stress with insufficient parasympathetic outflow,
with an inappropriate decrease in outflow, while the hand was still
immersed in the cold water bath. Similar aberrant responses were
manifested by patients BKm and Cy. Patient Mt responded in a most
unusual fashion. During stress he responded with an increased
parasympathetic outflow. This dysfunction was further compounded
by a decreased outflow during recovery.

     In summary, measurements of pupillary dilatation and constric-
tion were employed as indices of sympathetic-adrenergic and parasympathetic-cholinergic activity, respectively, to study autonomic
dysfunction in active and in remitted schizophrenic patients during
stress and following the termination of stress. The integrated
reciprocal relationships between the sympathetic and parasympathe-

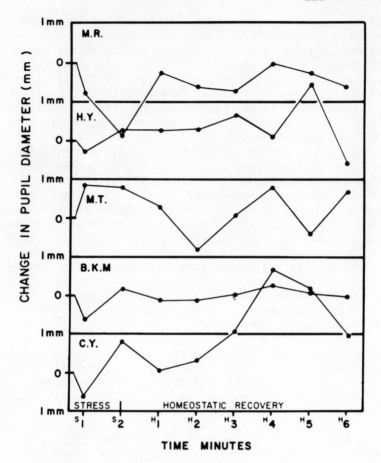

Figure 20. Pupillary constriction during stress and homeostatic recovery; active schizophrenics.

tic systems that characterized normal individuals during stress and homeostatic recovery were not found in any of the patients. Instead, *all* actively psychotic as well as remitted patients showed distinct, discrete varieties of disorganized, unintegrated autonomic responses to stress and during homeostatic recovery. The results of the study suggest that the schizophrenics are characterized by a persisting, possibly irreversible, defect of central autonomic origin, and that the non-integrative autonomic mechanisms are unrelated to the patient's clinical picture, the course of illness, or the state of clinical recovery.

To recapitulate, all of the schizophrenic patients in remission as well as those who were actively psychotic manifested
non-integrative autonomic activity in response to stress and
during the interval of restitution. The adaptive, synergistic
relationship between sympathetic and parasympathetic mechanisms
was not found in schizophrenic patients.

AUTONOMIC DYSFUNCTION IN NEUROTIC BEHAVIOR

What of neurotic disorders? Do they also show characteristic
patterns of autonomic dysfunction? Are these dysfunctions qualitatively or quantitatively different from those that characterize
the psychoses and can they be differentially diagnosed with the
aid of pupillography? Three previously published papers by the
author (1964, 1965a, 1965b) provide the basis for the following
discussion and contain some of the details of the experiments.

Infra-red photography was employed to record pupillary responses to darkness and to light during rest, 1 min. of cold-
pressor stress, and throughout the 20 min. of homeostatic recovery.
The 11 neurotic patients who participated in the study were obtained from the outpatient department of the Eastern Pennsylvania
Psychiatric Institute and were free of any significant medical or
neurological problems. Seventy-two hours prior to the examination,
all chemotherapeutic regimens were discontinued on those few patients who had been on medication. The 11 normal subjects were
matched for age and sex and screened by means of the Cornell Medical
Index.

The diameter of the pupil following each interval of darkness
was obtained for each control subject and patient at rest. The
results of an analysis of variance indicated that the normal and
neurotic groups manifested similar patterns of dilatation to darkness at rest. A similar analysis was performed upon the diameters
of the pupil in response to light and no significant differences
were found. On the basis of the results of the analyses for dilatation and constriction, it was concluded that there was no significant difference in autonomic responsivity between normals and
neurotics at rest.

Similarly, under the cold stress normals and neurotics responded to darkness with a significant increase, at each interval,
in the level of pupillary dilatation. Also for both groups, there
was less pupillary constriction initially under stress than there
was at rest. In general, in contrast to the psychotics who manifested aberrant pupillary reactivity in response to light and dark-

ness at rest, *none* of the neurotics were significantly different
from the normals at rest.   The diagnostic implication of these
findings is that if a subject manifests aberrant pupillary constriction or dilatation at rest, the overwhelming likelihood is
that he is psychotic.   On the other hand, if a subject's pupillary
light and dark reflexes are normal at rest, he may still be either
normal or neurotic.

Comparisons were also made between normals and neurotics of
the difference in diameter between the 1-min dark-adapted pupil
during cold stress and its diameter at each 1 min. interval throughout 20 min. following cessation of the stress.   An analysis of
variance revealed a significant difference between the groups.   The
curves are presented in Figure 21.   The average decrease in dila-

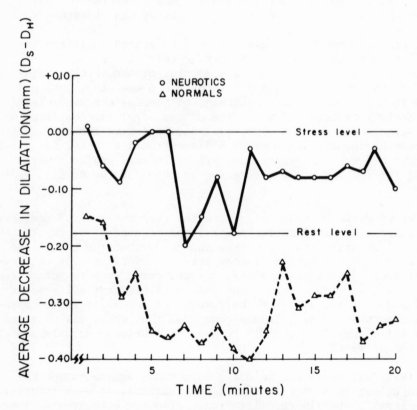

Figure 21.   Homeostatic response curves during darkness in normals
and neurotics.   Note how sharply the normals have descended from
the stress level 1 min. after the end of the stress, in contrast
to the neurotics.

tation (mm) was obtained for each group at each interval by sub-
tracting the diameter of each subject's pupil at each interval
during homeostasis (D_h) from the maximally dilated 1-min. dark
adapted pupil during the cold stress (D_s). As normals and neurotics did not differ significantly at rest or under stress, the
average diameter of the 1-min. dark-adapted pupil was obtained
for both groups under each condition. The average difference in
diameter between rest and stress was found to be 0.18 mm. In
Figure 21, the average difference is represented by the horizontal
lines labelled "stress level" and "rest level".

Following the cessation of noxious stimulation, neurotics
continued to manifest heightened adrenergic outflow characteristic
of stress for 7 min. before returning to the level characteristic
of rest. This level of activity was maintained for approximately
3 min. and then there was again an increase in dilatation typical
of subjects under stress. In the normals, by contrast, the
cessation of stress was followed by an almost immediate change in
the pupillary response in the direction of the rest level. A
marked subnormal period ensued which after 10 mins. was replaced
by a gradual return to the rest level.

When the pupillary responses of the two groups were measured
at 1 min. intervals for a period of 20 min. starting immediately
after the termination of the cold pressor test while the constant
intensity light remained on, an analysis of variance revealed
that the homeostatic response curves were non-linear and significantly different from each other. The curves for the groups are
presented in Figure 22. The diameter of the light-adapted pupil
at each interval during homeostasis was subtracted from the equivalent diameter of the pupil at rest. The diameter of the constricting pupil of the normal individuals during recovery became gradually smaller throughout the recovery period, while that of the
neurotics became rapidly smaller at first, and then, more gradually,
smaller still.

In summary, it may be said that while there are differences
during homeostatic recovery between normals and neurotics, the
differences appear to be quantitative rather than qualitative.

DIAGNOSTIC APPLICATIONS OF THE EXPERIMENTAL FINDINGS

The various experiments described above clearly indicate the
potential value of pupillographic measurements for the differential
diagnosis of neurosis and schizophrenia. The following procedure
is suggested.

If, after examining the pupillary light and dark reflexes at
rest, the record of a subject demonstrates marked aberrations of

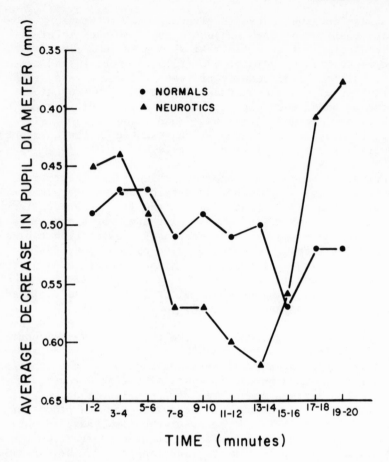

Figure 22.   Response curves in normals and neurotics to light during
homeostasis.

either or both, then it is extremely likely that the subject is
schizophrenic. On the other hand, if a subject's pupillary light
and dark reflexes are normal at rest, then he is likely to be
either normal or neurotic; but these reflexes are also normal in
7 per cent of active schizophrenics and 25 per cent of those in
remission. It is then necessary to administer a cold stress. The
normal individual and the neurotic will respond to stress with increased dilatation to darkness and decreased constriction to light;
though following the termination of stress, the neurotic will require a great deal more time to regain equilibrium. The schizophrenics will be identified by deviations in their response to

light and darkness either during stress, or during homeostatic
recovery, or both.

PROSPECTUS

Currently, two major areas are being investigated with the
invaluable aid of pupillometry. From the material considered in
this paper it may be obvious that one of the investigative areas
is the proposed rational approach to chemotherapy. Studies are
in progress to determine the effects of a variety of psychotropic
agents on the activity of the iris muscles.

An effort is also being made to elucidate the genetic contribution to psychotic disorders by investigating childhood vulnera-
bility to schizophrenia. We intend to examine large numbers of
normal children, low-risk children, high-risk children and psychotic children, pupillographically. Follow-up studies will then be
initiated to identify pre-morbid patterns. These studies hopefully will contribute to the resolution of the vexing etiological
problem.

REFERENCES

Abood, L. G. The psychotomimetic glycolate esters and related
    drugs. In D. H. Efron (Ed.), *Psychopharmacology*. Public Health
    Service Publication 1836, United States Government Printing
    Office, Washington, D.C., 683-692.
Alpert, M., Angrist, B., Diamond, F., and Gershon, S. Comparison
    of Ditran intoxication and acute alcohol psychoses. In W. Keup
    (Ed.), *Origins and Mechanisms of Hallucinations*. New York:
    Plenum Press, 245-259.
Ashby, W. R., Collins, G. H., and Bassett, M. The effects of nico-
    tinic acid, nicotinamide, and placebo on the chronic schizo-
    phrenic. *Journal of Mental Science*, 1960, *106(445)*, 1555-1559.
Axelrod, J. Enzymatic formations of psychomimetic metabolites
    from normally occurring compounds. *Science*, 1961, *134(3475)*, 343.
Ban, T. A., and Lehmann, H.E. Nicotinic acid in the treatment of
    schizophrenia. *Canadian Psychiatric Association Journal*, 1970,
    15, 499-500.
Bliss, C. L., and Calhoun, D. W. *An Outline of Biometry*. New Haven:
    Yale Cooperative Corporation, 1954.
Bonvallet, M., and Zbrozyna, A. Les commandes reticularies du sys-
    teme autonoma et en perticulier de l'innervation sympathique et
    parasympathique de la pupille. *Archives Italiennes de Biologie*,
    1963, *101*, 174-207.

Brodie, B. B., and Shore, P. A.   A concept for a role of serotonin and norepinephrine as chemical mediators in the brain.   *Annals of the New York Academy of Science*, 1957, *66*, 631-642.

Brune, G. G., and Himwich, H. E.   Effects of methionine loading on the behavior of schizophrenic patients.   *Journal of Nervous and Mental Diseases*, 1962, *134(5)*, 447-450.

Buck, C. W., Carscallen, H. B., and Hobbs, G.E.   Temperature regulation in schizophrenia.   *Archives of Neurology and Psychiatry*, 1950, *64*, 828-842.

Catterson, A. G., Bennet, D. H., and Freudenberg, R. C.   A survey of long stay schizophrenic patients.   *British Journal of Psychiatry*, 1963, *109*, 750-758.

Cerletti, A., and Rothlin, E.   Role of 5-hydroxytryptamine in mental diseases and its antagonism to lysergic acid derivates.   *Nature*, 1955, *176*, 785-786.

Cole, J. O.   Therapeutic efficacy of antidepressant drugs: A review.   *Journal of the American Medical Association*, 1964, *190*, 448-455.

Earle, A., and Earle, B. V.   The blood pressure response to pain and emotion in schizophrenia.   *Journal of Nervous and Mental Diseases*, 1955, *121*, 132-139.

Englehart, E.   Der humorale Wirkungsmechanismus der Okulomotoriusreizung.   *Archiv. für die Gesamte Physiologie des menschen und der tiere*, 1931, *227*, 220-234.

Eysenck, S. B. G.   An experimental study of psychogalvanic reflex responses of normal, neurotic and psychotic subjects.   *Journal of Psychosomatic Research*, 1956, *1*, 258-272.

Feldberg, W., and Sherwood, S. L.   Behavior of cats after intraventricular injections of eserine and DFP.   *Journal of Physiology*, 1954, *125*, 488-500.

Feldberg, W., and Vogt, M.   Acetylcholine synthesis in different regions of the central nervous system.   *Journal of Physiology*, 1948, *107*, 372-381.

Forrer, G. R.   Symposium on atropine toxicity therapy: history and future research.   *Journal of Nervous and Mental Diseases*, 1956, *124*, 256-259.

Forrest, F. M., Forrest, I. S., and Mason, A. S.   Review of rapid urine tests for phenothiazine and related drugs.   *American Journal of Psychiatry*, 1961, *118*, 300-307.

Freeman, H., Rodnick, E. H., Shakow, D., and Lebeaux, T.   Carbohydrate tolerance of mentally disturbed soldiers.   *Psychosomatic Medicine*, 1944, *6*, 311-317.

Friedhoff, A.J.   A dopamine-cholinergic mechanism in production of psychotic symptoms.   *Biological Psychiatry*, 1973, *6*, 165-169.

Frohlich, A., and Loewi, E.   Uber eine Steigerung der adrenalin empfindlichkeit durch cocain.   *Archiv. für Experimentelle Pathologie und Pharmakologie*, 1910, *62*, 159-169.

Funkenstein, D. H., Greenblatt, M., and Solomon, H.C.   Autonomic nervous system changes following electric shock treatment.   *Journal of Nervous and Mental Diseases*, 1948, *108*, 409-422.

Funkenstein, D. H., Greenblatt, M., and Solomon, H.C. A test which
   predicts the clinical effects of electric shock treatment on
   schizophrenic patients. *American Journal of Psychiatry*, 1950,
   106, 889-901.
Gellhorn, E. *Physiological Foundations of Neurology and Psychiatry*.
   Minneapolis: University of Minnesota Press, 1956.
Gellhorn, E. *Autonomic Imbalance and the Hypothalamus*. Minneapolis:
   University of Minnesota Press, 1957.
Gellhorn, E., and Miller, A.D. Methacoline and noradrenaline tests.
   Archives of General Psychiatry, 1961, *4*, 371-380.
Goodman, L. S., and Gilman, A. *The Pharmacological Basis of Thera-
   peutics* (3rd ed.). New York: Macmillan Company, 1965, p. 460.
Hess, W. R., and Koella, W. Experimentelle Studien uber die
   antagonistische Innervation. *Zeitschrift für die Gesamte experimentelle medizin einschliesslich experimentelle chirurgie*, 1950,
   116, 431-443.
Hess, W. R., Koella, W., and Szabo, T. Experimentelle Studien uber
   die antagonistische Innervation. *Zeitschrift für die Gesamte
   experimentelle medizin einchliesslich experimentelle chirurgie*,
   1950, *115*, 481-490.
Hoffer, A., and Osmond, H. Treatment of schizophrenia with nicotinic acid: a 10 year follow-up. *Acta Psychiatrica Scandinavica*,
   1964, *40(2)*, 171-189.
Hoffer, A., Osmond, H., and Smythies, J. Schizophrenia, new approach;
   result of year's research. *Journal of Mental Science*, 1954, *100*,
   29-54.
Hoskins, R. G. *The Biology of Schizophrenia*. New York: Norton,
   1946.
Igersheimer, W. W. Cold pressor test in functional psychotic synd-
   dromes. *Archives of Neurology and Psychiatry*, 1953, *70*, 794-801
Kerbikov, O. V. Schizophrenia as a nosological problem. In,
   Symposium Schizophrenia. Vopr. Nozologii, Patogenaza, Klinikii,
   Anatomii, 1962, *1*, 5-18.
Klerman, G. L., Paykel, E. S., and Prusoff, B. In J. O. Cole, A.
   M. Freedman, and A. J. Friedhoff (Eds.), *Psychopathology and
   Psychopharmacology*. Baltimore: Johns Hopkins University Press,
   1972.
Kuntz, A. *The Autonomic Nervous System*. (4th Ed.). Philadelphia:
   Lea and Febinger, 1953.
Loewenfeld, I. E. Mechanisms of reflex dilatation of the pupil:
   Historical review and experimental analysis. *Documenta Ophthal-
   mologica*, 1958, *12*, 185-448.
Lowenstein, O., and Loewenfeld, I. E. Role of sympathetic and para-
   sympathetic systems in reflex dilatation of the pupil. *Archives
   of Neurology and Psychiatry*, 1950, *64*, 313-340.
Lowenstein, O., and Loewenfeld, I. E. Electronic pupillography:
   a new instrument and some clinical applications. *Archives of
   Ophthalmology*, 1958, *59*, 352-363.

Malmo, R. B., and Shagass, C. Physiologic studies of reaction to
  stress in anxiety and early schizophrenia. *Psychosomatic Medicine*,
  1949, *11*, 9-24.
Malmo, R. B., Shagass, C., and Smith, A. A. Responsiveness in
  chronic schizophrenia. *Journal of Personality*, 1951, *19*,
  359-375.
Mandell, A. J., and Morgan, M. Human brain enzyme makes indole
  hallucinogens. (Abstract). *Proceedings of the 1970 American
  Psychological Association Meeting*. 228.
Mandelbrote, B., and Folkard, S. Some factors related to outcome
  and social adjustment in schizophrenia. *Acta Psychiatrica
  Scandinavica*, 1961, *37*, 223-235.
Mendel, B., and Hawkins, R.D. Removal of acetylcholine by cholin-
  esterase injections and effect thereof on nerve impulse trans-
  mission. *Journal of Neurophysiology*, 1943, *6*, 431-438.
Osmond, H., and Smythies, J. Schizophrenia: a new approach.
  Journal of Mental Science, 1952, *98(411)*, 309-315.
Pfeiffer, C. C., Jenney, E. H., Gallagher, W., Smith, R. P., Bevan,
  W., Killam, K. F., Killam, E. E., and Blackmore, W. Stimulant
  effect of 2-dimethyl aminoethanol. *Science*, 1957, *126*, 610-611.
Pincus, G., and Elmadjian, F. The lymphocyte responses to heat
  stress in normal and psychotic subjects. *Journal of Clinical
  Endocrinology and Metabolism*, 1946, *6*, 295-300.
Polin, W., Cardon, P. V., and Kety, S. S. Effects of amino acid
  feedings in schizophrenic patients treated with iproniazid.
  Science, 1961, *133(3446)*, 104-105.
Poos, F. "Uber die Eignung der Pupillae als Testoojekt fur" pharma-
  cologische Reaktionen und Pharmakodiagnostik an Auge. *Ergebnisse
  der Physiologie, Biologische, Chemie, and Experimentellen Pharmakologie*, 1939, *41*, 883-916.
Rubin, L. S. Acetylcholine hydrolysis in psychiatric patients.
  Science, 1958, *128*, 254-255 (a).
Rubin, L. S. Cholinesterase activity. *Science*, 1958, *128*, 1176-
  1178 (b).
Rubin, L.S. Pupillary reactivity as a measure of autonomic balance
  in the study of psychotic behavior: a rational approach to chemotherapy. *Transactions of the New York Academy of Science*, 1960,
  22, 509-518 (a).
Rubin, L. S. Pupillary reactivity as a measure of adrenergic-
  cholinergic mechanisms in the study of psychotic behavior.
  Journal of Nervous and Mental Diseases, 1960, *130*, 386-400 (b).
Rubin, L. S. Autonomic dysfunction in psychotic adults and autistic
  children. *Archives of General Psychiatry*, 1961, *7*, 1-14 (a).
Rubin, L. S. Patterns of pupillary dilatation and constriction in
  psychotic adults and autistic children. *Journal of Nervous and
  Mental Disease*, 1961, *133*, 130-142 (b).
Rubin, L. S. Autonomic dysfunction as a concomitant of neurotic
  behavior. *Journal of Nervous and Mental Diseases*, 1964. *138*,
  558-574.

Rubin, L. S. An organic basis for neurotic behavior. *Psycho-somatics*, 1965, *6*, 220-228 (a).

Rubin, L. S. Autonomic dysfunction in neurotic behavior *Archives of General Psychiatry*, 1965, *12*, 572-585 (b).

Rubin, L. S., and Barry, T. J. The reactivity of the iris muscles as an index of autonomic dysfunction in schizophrenic remission. *Journal of Nervous and Mental Diseases*, 1972, *155*, 265-276 (a).

Rubin, L. S., and Barry, T. J. The effect of the cold pressor test on pupillary reactivity of schizophrenics in remission. *Biological Psychiatry*, 1972, *5*, 181-197 (b).

Schildkraut, J. J. The catecholamine hypothesis of affective dis-orders: a review of supporting evidence. *American Journal of Psychiatry*, 1965, *122*, 509-522.

Schildkraut, J. J., Schanberg, S. M., and Kopin, I. J. The effect of lithium on H3-norepinephrine metabolism in brain. *Life Sciences*, 1966, *5*, 1479-1483.

Shattock, F. M. The somatic manifestations of schizophrenia: a clinical study of their significance. *Journal of Mental Science*, 1950, *96*, 132-142.

Shore, P. A. Possible mechanism of antidepressant action of Marsilid. *Journal of Clinical and Experimental Psychopathology*, 1958, *19*, 56-60.

Slater, E. A review of earlier evidence on genetic factors in schizophrenia. In D. Rosenthal and S. S. Kety (Eds.), *Transmission of Schizophrenia*. New York: Pergamon Press, 1968.

Spector, S., Hirsch, C. W., and Brodie, B. B. Association of be-havioral effects of pargyline, a non-hydracide MAO inhibitor with increase in brain norepinephrine. *International Journal of Neuro-pharmacology*, 1963, *2*, 81-93.

Stephens, D. A. Psychotoxic effects of benzhexol hydrochloride (Artane). *British Journal of Psychiatry*, 1967, *113*, 213-218.

Truitt, E. B. Some pharmacologic correlations of the chemotherapy of mental disease. *Journal of Nervous and Mental Diseases*, 1958, *216*, 184-210.

Vogt, M. The concentration of sympathin in different parts of the central nervous system under normal conditions and after the administration of drugs. *Journal of Physiology*, 1954, *123*, 451-481.

Weider, A., Brodman, K., Mittelman, B., Wechsler, D., and Wolff, H. G. The Cornell Index: a method for quickly assaying personality and psychosomatic disturbances, to be used as an adjunct to interview. *Psychosomatic Medicine*, 1946, *8*, 411-413.

Wing, J. K. Five years outcome in early schizophrenia. *Proceedings of the Royal Society of Medicine*, 1966, *59*, 17-18.

Woolley, D. W., and Shaw, E. A biochemical and pharmacological suggestion about certain mental disorders. *Science*, 1954, *119*, 587-588.

Zbrozyna, A., and Bonvallet, M.   Influence tonique inhibitrice du
    bulbe sur a'activite du noyau d'Edinger-Westphal. *Archives
    Italiennes de Biologie*, 1963, *101*, 208-222.
Zeller, E. A., Barsky, J., and Berman, E. R.   Amine oxidases inhi-
    bition of monoamine oxidase by 1-isonicotinyl-2-isoprophlylhydra-
    zine. *Journal of Biological Chemistry*, 1955, *214*, 267-274.

CHAPTER V:

CONCEPTUAL STIMULI, PUPILLARY DILATION AND EVOKED CORTICAL

POTENTIALS: A REVIEW OF RECENT ADVANCES

Gad Hakerem

Department of Psychology, Queens College of CUNY and
Biometrics Unit of New York State Department of Mental
Hygiene

I am combining in this paper the two presentations I gave at
the symposium. The first part deals with the problem of instrumentation in the measurement of the pupil.

When Dr. Janisse called me just before my departure from New
York and asked whether we could substitute a panel presentation on
instrumentation for Dr. Loewenfeld's paper, who was prevented
by illness from attending, I wholeheartedly agreed.

I have often been criticized for being more concerned with the
problems of data acquisition and data analysis than with the
experiments and the data themselves. It is true that at times I
have spent extraordinary amounts of time on improving my experimental apparatus and data analysis systems, but I hope the second
part of my presentation will convince you that I have not completely gone astray as a gadgeteer and computer man but have kept on the
straight road of experimentation and data interpretation.

In my chapter in the "Manual of Psychophysiological Methods"
edited by Venables and Martin (1967), I have reviewed the history
of how we came to where we are now in instrumentation and why.
The history of pupillography is a very old one. Even Archimedes
had tried his hand on constructing an apparatus to measure the
pupil diameter. It is interesting to note that whenever a new
technology had evolved, someone tried to apply it to a device to
measure pupil diameter. For diverse reasons, there has always been
in history an interest in this small piece of muscular tissue and
much ingenuity was spent in studying its anatomy, its neuronal
connections, its dynamics and its relation to functions and

disorders of the mind and body.

A strong impetus to do something about pupil measurements
arose when a specific abnormality of pupillary reactions was found
to exist as an important diagnostic indicator in General Paresis.
This was the Argyll-Robertson pupil syndrome. Psychiatrists
speculated that other psychiatric disorders might be diagnosed by
the presence of pupil abnormalities. Bumke (1904) especially was
very much interested in this aspect. The first really objective,
"hard copy", type of measurement of the pupil was described by
Bellarminow in 1885. He used a photographic device, utilizing a
slit camera directed over the middle of the pupil. Light sensitive
paper placed behind the slit moved at a constant speed and recorded
the changing diameter as a black band. The diameter could then be
measured from the width of this band. This method was later used
again by a number of pupil researchers. Some people even re-
invented the method. I myself have used Bellarminow's basic idea
to develop a device to measure the pupil. We used infrared film
to record the pupil in darkness and monitored the position of the
camera slit and the pupil position through a modified infrared
sniperscope. It is still a useable method but requires considerable
training of both subject and experimenter, not to mention the
laborious procedure of later measurement. A device to speed up
this part of data analysis is described in the Manual of Psychophysiological Methods (Hakerem, 1967).

Lowenstein, in 1920, built on the then available technology
of cinephotography to measure the pupil first in dim blue light and
later in complete darkness under infrared illumination. The
development of infrared technology was probably the single most
important element in the design of present day devices to measure
the diameter or area of the pupil. In order to measure the pupil
or see the pupil, one needs light, but if the eye is exposed to
visible light, the pupil does things that one would not necessarily
want it to do. It dilates and constricts in diameter and therefore
it would be difficult to determine a base line diameter. The ideal
condition is to measure the base line pupil diameter in the absence
of all visible light. In that condition, the system is not
"loaded". Infrared technology provides us with this optimal
condition. Once this hurdle was scaled, it was all uphill for
pupillography.

Lowenstein used cinephotography at ten exposures per second.
The film records were measured by hand or semi-automatic devices
and the diameter plotted against time. These plots were called
pupillographs.

I mentioned the semi-automatic devices. One such device was
developed by Dr. Otto Lowenstein. I don't think that it has been

described in the literature. Since this was a rather ingenious
contraption and reflects the enormous drive and inventiveness of
Dr. Lowenstein to make pupillography a practical procedure in
research and clinical work, I will briefly describe it here. I
should mention that it worked adequately only under the luckiest
confluence of many complex variables and conditions. But when
these conditions confluenced, it indeed worked quite well. More
important, however, once electronic technology had advanced, its
basic design ideas led to the development of an extremely stable,
accurate and easy to operate device.

     Dr. Lowenstein's system used the 35 millimeter infrared film
records as the base. Lowenstein's camera used a dual lens system
which photographed both eyes at each frame. This dual lens system
allowed for a better utilization of the available space on the
film and thereby produced larger and sharper images of the pupil.
The developed film was then put into a special projector. The
image of each exposure was projected on to a rotating mirror. This
mirror rotated at a constant speed and projected the light and dark
areas of the picture across a sensitive photo-electric cell. Since
the images of both eyes, left and right, were on each exposure, the
mirror first projected the right eye and then the left eye across
the photoelectric cell. This photoelectric cell would output a
pulse, the duration of which depended on the length of time the
light part of the picture would be on the cell. It should be noted
that the film was negative, i.e. the pupil was light. Thus, the
larger the pupil the longer it would take the rotating mirror to
transmit the image across the cell.

     Naturally, the original film record had to be of high contrast
and good focus. The generated electric pulse was then transmitted
to an oscilloscope. The scope was set to trigger a sweep at the
onset of the pulse. The offset of the pulse (end of pupil diameter)
was then visible on the scope as a vertical line. The position of
this line in the sweep across the scope face was proportional to
the pupil diameter.

     A special camera was synchronized with the scope sweep and set
to photograph the position of the negative going end of the pulse
on lineograph paper. Also photographed on to the paper were time
lines, so that the recorded pupil diameter could be put into its
proper time sequence. Additional refinements of this method
allowed for differentiation between the right pupil and the left
pupil by using a neutral density filter. This filter snapped in
front of the lineograph camera lens whenever the pulse from the
left pupil would appear on the oscilloscope. The resulting line
would then be slightly dimmer than the line from the right pupil.
It was also possible to identify the stimulus onset and other
important aspects of the experimental procedures.

The lineograph paper was then developed and a rather good record of pupil motility of both eyes was obtained. Dr. Lowenstein was kind enough to let me use this device in the early stages of my research. Though this often proved to be a frustrating experience, considering that everything that can go wrong will go wrong, I am glad that I had the opportunity to participate in this stage of the development of apparatus for pupil measurement.

One other method which is frequently used should be mentioned here. This method is based on the use of infrared sensitive photoelectric cells. The eye is illuminated with infrared light and the total reflection of this light from the eye is intercepted by a photo cell. The amount of intercepted light is inversely proportional to the pupil area, i.e. the more iris area reflects infrared light, the smaller is the pupil and vice versa. The apparatus is rather simple and straightforward. There is however a large error factor when absolute measurements are attempted. One then has to calibrate the electrical output against photographs for each subject and even then the error factor remains large. If, however, the experiment involves an approximation of relative diameter changes or latency measurement, then this method is quite sufficient and adequate. Cueppers (1951) has described this method and Stark has also developed an adequately functioning device. The Alexandridis pupillometer is also based on the principle of the photoelectric cell. One advantage of this method is that the apparatus is rather small and can be built into a helmet or a head band and thus allows for freer movement of the subject.

The devices used by Hess and his students are essentially variations of the photography method of Lowenstein.

The next generation of pupillometers was the electronic scanning pupillometer described by Lowenstein and Loewenfeld (1958). This device was not only sound in principle but the engineer, Mr. George King (1960), who translated Lowenstein and Loewenfeld's ideas into contemporary technology was so conservative that he indeed over-designed its components. Only ten instruments were built but they were put together so solidly that they held up without any major breakdown in active research and clinical situations for 15 years. There are shortcomings in its design but one can live with them.

However, science and technology do not stand still and the latest developments are pupillometers based on vidicon and image disectortube technology. Several manufacturers are producing these instruments and it seems to me that they will bring with them an increase in the laboratories and clinics who will use pupil-lography in various research and diagnostic procedures. I think that we can look forward to an ever increasing number of participants in our biannual "Colloquium on the Pupil." Last year's international meeting in Germany (Dodt and Schrader, 1973) and this meeting in Winnipeg indicate that pupillographers from different disciplines want to get together and exchange ideas and experiences.

I would like to talk briefly about one further development in the field of pupillography. This too fits into the notion that pupillographers at all times were trying to make use of the latest technological developments. I refer here to the use of computer technology or, more specifically, the use of computers in the analysis of the pupil records.

In our own work we realized several years ago that the techniques for averaging biological signal-response curves would be applicable to pupillography. These techniques had been developed for biological data where a high noise level was present. They made it possible to extract from the noise the inbedded small signals. Fluctuations in pupil diameter unrelated to the experimental situation had made control of experiments and interpretation of data rather difficult. We used at first a Mnemotron-TMC CAT computer. We were rather surprised to find that we could detect diameter changes of the order of .02 millimeter or better. The method of averaging is a powerful one and we have been able to increase the sensitivity of pupil measurement by at least a factor of 10. As always when there is an increase in the sensitivity of measurement by such an order of magnitude, one encounters a whole new set of phenomena.

The use of magnetic tape decks allowed us to analyze the data off-line. We could play the data back into the computer in any combination or sequence of trials. The addition of a calibration pulse to each individual trial allowed us to make a precise determination of the absolute pupil size.

The addition of sophisticated timing equipment enabled us to execute rather complex experimental designs.

We have gone one step further and have developed a data analysis system for large digital computers. This step has again opened new vistas and we can now develop experiments of great complexities and still hope to interpret the results in a meaningful way.

These are some of the programs that we have developed so far:

1. *Analog to digital conversion.* The purpose of this program is self explanatory. The program samples pupil diameter 100 times per second from the analog curves.

2. *Scaling digital data to calibration.* This program seeks
out the digital equivalent of the calibration pulse. A point
on the lower leg of the pulse is assumed to be zero millimeter
and a point on the upper leg is assumed to be eight millimeter. The program then scales all data points proportionally.

3. *Grouping program.* In the A-D program step each trial is
given a sequential number. Simultaneously a clock is run
which deposits its position each time a trial onset is
recognized. The arbitrary time difference between each
consecutive trial is computed and deposited. The time difference allows us, by comparing them to the experimental log, to
designate properly the stimulus condition of each specific
trial. This is of extreme importance when conditions are
randomly distributed among trials. By coding the condition
to the trial number the program provides a base for grouping.
This program then combines trials into condition groups for
further analysis. I should state that this program will soon
be obsolete when we will be able to read the condition code
directly from the analog tape.

3. *Analysis program.* This program analyzes the groups or
combinations of groups and computes:

   a. the mean of each data point
   b. the standard deviation of each data point
   c. the median of each data point
   d. the quartiles and the inter-quartile range of each
       data point
   e. the skewness and kurtosis of the distributions around
       each data point
   f. the mean-median difference at each data point

There are additional computations available depending on the
specific nature of the experiment. I should mention that we
sample the analog curve one hundred times per second in real
time and thus have 100 data points per second. This program
outputs the results in digital form on the line-printer, on
analog graphs, and on punched cards.

5. *Combining program.* This program combines the results of
several experiments or several subjects and produces a new
master tape with the selected information from the result of
the Analysis program. It allows for the computation of
correlations between subjects and comparison between
similarities and dissimilarities in a given period. We have
provided for the possibilities of additional not yet
explored procedures and statistics.

The use of these programs has already yielded some very
interesting findings; we found, for example, that the distributions around the means of each data points were Gaussian distributions. When we used the CAT computer which is essentially an
adder and did not give us a measurement of central tendency at
each data point, we were not quite sure whether the mean was the
appropriate statistic. The use of separate odd-even trial
computations gave us some assurance of the propriety of mean
computation. However, we always felt that the computation of the
variance would be essential. When this problem was finally solved
by our digital computer program we found that the variances across
the experimental epoch formed nearly a straight line parallel to
the time axis. This means that the variability is normally distributed at each data point. A further confirmation of this finding
was the small mean-median differences and the skewness and kurtosis
computation which indicated the presence of normal Gaussian distributions around the mean data.

In our experiments the standard deviation of the pupil was
found to be on the order of .2 to .5 millimeter. Eventually this
could be an important measure in its own right. There seems to be
an indication that there is some correlation with the age of the
subject.

I understand that in Dr. Stark's laboratory rather sophisticated programs have been developed which allow comparisons between
averaged pupillograms obtained in experiments and pupillograms
simulated on the basis of an experimental hypothesis or model.

There is then no doubt that we are keeping on top of the
available technology like our predecessors in the field of
pupillography have done. Our goal, however, remains a better
understanding of the mechanisms and systems which together are
effecting the pupil motility.

As my major topic I choose to present at this meeting a
narrative of the efforts in my laboratory to solve some of the
procedural and conceptual problems in designing experiments where
conceptual or cognitive variables could be controlled, quantified
and experimentally manipulated.

Two factors influenced the direction of the work in my
laboratory which was mainly concerned with the study of the
parameters of pupillary constrictions to light. One factor was an
incidental finding of pupillary dilation in a light threshold
experiment (Hakerem, 1967). We found that in those trials where
the subject reported "seeing" the stimulus at threshold intensity,
there was a pupillary dilation instead of a constriction. Further

investigation showed clearly that the dilation was concommitant
to some cognitive element in the subject's performance of the
detection task.

The other factor was an attempt to get to the "kernel of
truth," in the experiments by Eckhard Hess and his students. In a
recent paper (Hakerem, 1973), I wrote:

> It was however Eckhard Hess, who for better
> or worse left an indelible imprint (pun
> intended) on the research on pupillary
> motility by some rather striking demonstra-
> tions of the pupillary dilations as a
> correlate of strong emotions. It was the
> right demonstration performed at the right
> time in an age where the general public and
> psychologists were looking for objective
> indicators of emotions, fear, eye detection,
> etc. The pupil as "a window to the soul"
> appeared to be a welcome addition to our
> research arsenal in the area of public
> opinion, consumer research, lie detection,
> personality research, sexual behavior and
> social attitudes. Hess' experiments
> generated an enormous interest in all of
> these areas. But as so often in psycho-
> logical research, after a strong beginning
> things turned out to be not quite as simple
> as they appeared at first. Contradictory
> and inconclusive results by other research-
> ers led to controversies and polemics which
> were at times rather vitriolic.

I had several objections to Hess' experimental methods (1965)
and the often indiscriminate and unwarranted use of his procedures
in applied problems. Nevertheless, there was no doubt that the
pupil dilated to some stimuli presented in some of these experiments and demonstrations. I want to mention here two major
objections to Hess' procedure. There was first our observation
of considerable pupillary unrest, especially under dim illumination, on which the recorded dilations seemed to ride. This tended
to make a quantitative analysis very difficult or even impossible.
A second objection was that the operative element in the stimulus
situation, the "emotionality" of the subject vis a vis the
stimulus, could not be adequately established or identified. It
became clear to us that "much more research was needed" before any
use of this method could be made in the applied field. We also
realized that if appropriate experimental procedures could be
developed which would satisfy the before mentioned objections, plus

some additional minor ones, a new field of psychological research
would open up.

The problems concerning the amplitude of the pupillary unrest
and the relatively small size of the signal which appeared buried
in it found an easy solution by the use of the average response
curve procedures. I am still amazed at the power of this method.
We often run into disbelievers who do not deem it possible to
reliably indentify pupillary changes of the order of one hundredth
of a millimeter.

Average procedures, however, require certain assumptions. One
such assumption is that in each of the N trials, which are entered
into the average curve, the experimental situation is the same.
Such an assumption cannot be made if we use as a stimulus, for
example, a picture of a nude woman and present to male subjects.
After two or three presentations, the emotionality and the con-
comittant pupillary dilation is reduced. I remind you of the
immortal words of the ex vice-president of the United States who
said, "If you have seen one, you have seen them all." Therefore,
it was necessary to find an experimental paradigm in which there
was no adaptation or habituation to the stimulus content and where
the attention of the subject could be kept constant. In addition,
the paradigm should allow for an experimental manipulation of the
attentional and emotional elements in the stimulus situation.

We found such a paradigm in the betting and guessing procedures which for years now have been the bread and butter of our
laboratory. It seems that there is something in the motivational
make-up of homo sapiens which compels him to "play the probabilities." It is an interesting philosophical question to ask why
this probability game is so attractive to us. In all these years
of work with betting and guessing paradigms we have not found a
single subject, young or old, male or female, normal or psychotic,
who would not play the probability game with us. Furthermore, not
a single subject did his betting consistently the "safe way," as
any self-respecting monkey or rat would do. Even in an 80:20
probability situation the subject would bet or guess the long
shots. Hyperkinetic children have eagerly played this game. They
sat still and quiet long enough so that we could obtain good pupil
and evoked potential recordings. As a matter of fact, we had the
greatest problem in the so-called "certain" conditions where the
subject was told what the next stimulus would be and was not
allowed to guess. At times we do see in the certain conditions
small dilations. They are probably the results of an illegal or
unallowed guess which the subject makes to himself. Some subjects
complained that they tended to fall asleep during these "certain"
conditions. On the other hand, we had students, who, when acting
as experimenters, would make bets on how the subject in the booth

would bet.   I mention this here because all these observations
indicate that betting and guessing, and playing the probabilities
is an extremely strong human drive.

A few words about the experimental apparatus. We measured the
pupils with a Lowenstein-Loewenfeld pupillometer. The analog
voltage output of the pupillometer was recorded on a seven channel
Sangamo tape deck. Appropriate timing and scheduling equipment
was used. The stimuli were auditory clicks at about 60 dB above
threshold intensity. The data were analyzed from the magnetic
tape with a CAT computer and on a XDS-Sigma 7 digital computer.
A rectangular calibration pulse was added into each trial and
indicated the voltage equivalent of an 8 millimeter pupil or the
equivalent of 30 microvolts in the evoked cortical potential
recording. This enabled us then to determine the absolute pupil
diameter and express the level of electrical brain activity in
microvolts with respect to ground.

The electrical activity of the brain was recorded with Beckman
electrodes positioned over the vertex (C_Z position) and referred
to the right ear lobe. A neck electrode served as a ground
reference. The amplifiers had been developed to our specifications.
Their main characteristic was a very low noise level. The lower
frequency cutoff point was .01 cycles per second and the upper
cutoff point was 100 cycles per second. Thus, the lower end was
practically open to DC.

Let me first review some of our earlier work. The subjects
in these experiments were asked to guess the configuration of a
stimulus pattern. The choices were single click, double click, or
triple click. The temporal configurations of these stimulus
patterns are shown in Figure 1. Figure 2 shows the results of a
typical experiment in this series. It is quite clear that the
pupillary dilation occurs only if some meaning is attached to the
stimulus pattern by means of the instructions. The mere fact that
attention is required to perform the task according to instructions
could produce a dilation of the pupils. However, control of the
attention factor showed that this by itself could not account for
the full extent of this dilation. Figure 3 shows the results of an
experiment in which we attempted to isolate the attention factor
from other psychological variables.

In trying to identify the psychological processes and
variables in these experiments, one can easily get lost in seman-
tics. How could one describe the psychological components which
clearly exist in betting, above and beyond the attention factor.
Betting and guessing are extremely complex cognitive processes.
A knowledge of the probabilities of occurrence of a stimulus
pattern is necessary. A strategy has to be developed and
implemented. The subject has to keep track of several preceding

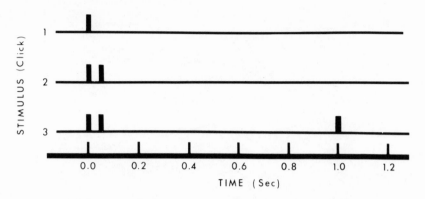

Figure 1. Temporal configuration of stimulus pattern. First two
clicks are separated by 20 msec. Third click occurs at 1000 msec
after first click.

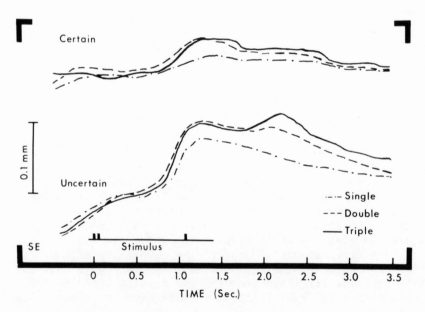

Figure 2. Averaged pupillary response curves from "certain" or
"told" and "uncertain" or "guess" condition for single, double and
triple click pattern. Note difference in dilation between the two
conditions. (Levine experiment)

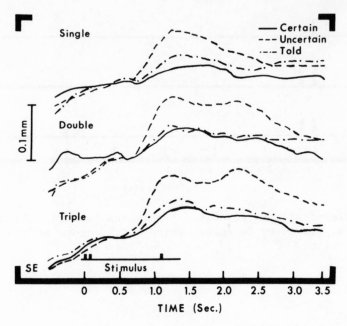

Figure 3. Averaged pupillary response curves from "certain",
"uncertain" and "told" conditions for single, double and triple
click problems. In all cases the rank order of dilation (certain-
told-uncertain) is maintained. (Levine experiment)

trials in order to adjust his strategy to the formulation of the
next guess. Then there is the subjective feeling about having
guessed right or wrong. If betting for money is part of the
experimental situation, then the amount of gain or loss is of
importance and gives an indication of the value the subject
attaches to a given amount of money. The complexity of the
situation can be varied and manipulated in so many ways that it
resembles life itself. This guessing and betting paradigm has
close resemblance to "real life" human cognitive processes.

The results of our first series of relatively simple
experiments encouraged us to add more complexity to the situation.
We tried, however, to vary the basic experimental procedure only in

such a way and in such small steps that, in our own minds at least, we could keep track of the added psychological components.

If we assume that the pupil motility is indeed an indicator of the status of the autonomic nervous system, it was logical to look for some other "proven" indicators of neuronal activity.

One of my colleagues, Dr. Samuel Sutton (1965), had been working with similar experimental designs. The dependent variable in his experiments was the vertex evoked potential. The data from these experiments followed such similar trends though with much longer latencies in the pupil responses that it became of great interest to record both pupil and vertex evoked potential simul-taneously in our experiments. The trouble was that we knew neither the neuronal and autonomic mechanisms which produce the pupil dilation, nor do we have much knowledge of the meaning of the complex wave forms which we record from the vertex electrodes. We only know that the pupillary motility and the vertex evoked potential exist in all people, that they are highly stable, and that they vary with the manipulation of certain psychological variables. These variables can be interpreted in terms of an *a priori* knowledge of human performance and by introspection.

Let me now present some of our more recent experiments. I was rather fortunate in being able to gather enthusiastic students and co-workers who shared with me the interest in the pupil dilation phenomenon and evoked potentials. They developed their own series of experiments designed to disentangle these complex cognitive processes.

Steven Levine (1969) demonstrated in his experiments the qualitative characteristics of the pupillary dilations in the guessing situation. His experiments included three sets of instructions to the physical stimulus situation (click pattern) which was the same in all conditions. The subject (1) was told what the next stimulus pattern (single, double or triple click) would be; (2) he was instructed to report after the stimulus pre-sentation what the stimulus had been; and (3) he was asked to guess before the stimulus presentation what the click pattern would be and report after the stimulus presentation what click pattern he had heard.

Condition or instruction (1) was the "certain" or "told" condition, (2) was the "report" condition, and (3) was the "guess-report" condition. Condition (2) and (3) were both "uncertain" conditions but in condition (2) no guessing or predicting the stimulus pattern was involved. (See Figures 1, 2 and 3.)

In addition to the recording of the pupil diameter, Levine also recorded the evoked vertex potential. The components of this

evoked potential have been described in the literatrue in numerous
publications. The specific components of the evoked potential we
were concerned with in these experiments were the N_1, N_2, N_3, P_2
and P_3 components. The P_3 component was of special interest. It
is a late (300 msec after stimulus onset) component. Sutton (1965)
has shown that this component is related to uncertainty and some
other psychological variables. Levine (1969) found that the P_3
component of the evoked potential and the extent of pupil dilation
were similarly related to the stimulus condition.

David Friedman (1973) manipulated the degree of uncertainty
by varying the probability at which a given stimulus pattern would
be presented. The subjects were asked to guess whether the next
stimulus would be a single or a double click. Both stimulus
patterns were actually double clicks, but in one case they were so
close together that they were perceived by all subjects as a single
click. The time differences between the clicks were 4 milliseconds
for the "single click" and 8 milliseconds for the "double click."
The subjects were told the probability at which either the single
or the double click would occur in a series of presentations. The
probabilities were 60:40, 80:20, 40:60, and 20:80 for the single
and double clicks respectively.

These data showed very clearly that the extent of the dilation
and the amplitude of the P_3 component varied monotonically with
stimulus probabilities. The lower the probability of the stimulus,
the larger the dilation and N_1-P_3 amplitude in the evoked potential. It should be noted that for the misses, i.e., those trials
where the subject guessed wrong, the curve was not monotonic. I
will come back to this phenomenon later.

I also should mention that Dr. Tueting (1971) had used a
similar design in her evoked potential study. Friedman confirmed
essentially Tueting's results and added the information on pupil
motility.

In all our work it became clear that both the vertex evoked
potential and pupillograms were strikingly stable and repeatable
measures of whatever we were recording. This repeatability
extended over many months. Subjects would always give us the same
individually characteristic curves. The questions arose then
whether these characteristics of the recordings from a given
individual were the result of learning in its broadest sense or
whether they represented inherited characteristics of the sequence
in which neuronal aggregates fired.

We attempted to approach this question by studying twins.
The hypothesis was that if pupillograms and the vertical evoked
potential curves to a given stimulus situation were characteristics

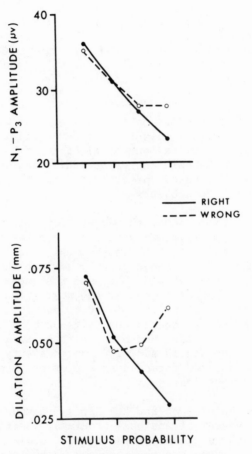

Figure 4. Mean N_1-P_3 and peak dilation amplitudes for right and wrong outcomes plotted as a function of stimulus probability. (Friedman experiment)

of the inherited neuronal hook-up of an individual, then monozygotic twins should have identical curves and dizygotic twins and
siblings should differ.

There are studies in the literature which show both for pupil
and evoked potential that indeed there seems to be a greater
similarity in the monozygotic twins than in the dizygotic twins or
in siblings. Two recent evoked potential studies on twins by
Dustman (1965) and by Lewis (1972) dealt with sensory stimuli
(light, sound and somato sensory) only. Their results show the
highest correlation between the monozygotic twins. One could argue
that the physical characteristics of the stimulus would be regis-
tered in the same way by the identical twins because of the
identity of the sense organs.

The pupillographic studies on twins also dealt only with
responses to sensory stimuli (light). In our studies, however, we
were dealing with more complex conceptual or cognitive situations
and the recordings thus should represent indications of the way in
which information is processed and evaluated in the context of the
instructions given to the subjects.

The result of a pilot study showed striking similarities for
the monozygotes and some similarity in the dizygotes in nearly all
conditions of our experiment, both in the pupil and in the evoked
potential recordings. Ms. Frances Bock is now embarked in a more
extensive study of this question. She used the guessing paradigm
asking the subjects to predict whether the next stimulus pattern
would be a single or a double click in 60:40 and 70:30 probability
situations. So far she has tested ten pairs of monozygotic twins,
nine pairs of dizygotic twins, and nine pairs of siblings, a total
of 56 individuals. She has in addition paired twenty of our
subjects by age and sex and formed a sample of pairs of individuals
without family relationships.

The data were analyzed on the XDS Sigma 7 computer. We used
the rather complex system of analysis programs, described earlier,
which includes the computation of mean curves, median curves,
standard deviation curves, and skewness and kurtosis curves. We
are not quite sure how we will eventually evaluate and further
reduce this enormous amount of output, but by using eyeballing
techniques, we saw that the recordings from the monozygotic twins
were nearly superimposable in all stimulus conditions. Siblings
and dizygotic twins were less alike, though one pair of siblings
showed quite similar curves.

At the 8th Colloquium on the Pupil, in Detroit, I indicated
that I would present at this meeting a full account of the twin
experiment. However, the development of proper statistics and

computer programs has taken more time than we expected and the analysis has not yet been completed. In view of the fact that this study might yield data of great importance and implications, we want to be absolutely sure of the correctness of our interpretations.

So far we have computed some Pearson r correlations over given periods or epochs in these curves. We found all correlations to be very high. This expresses the fact that all subjects had a dilation time-locked to the onset of the stimulus. These correlations, however, were in the .92 to .98 range for the monozygotic twins and in the .86 to .94 range for the dizygotic twins and siblings. The range of unrelated subjects was from .58 to .76.

Some caution is necessary in the use of correlations. We have seen cases where the eyeballing technique indicated considerable differences in amplitude and other characteristics of the curve in a pair while the computed correlation was relatively high. In other cases the curves looked very much alike but had a latency difference of 10 or 20 milliseconds. This then resulted in a relatively low correlation. We have now programmed a "distance measure" and a t-test at each data point. It seems now that these three statistical measures together will confirm what we already could deduce from inspections of our data.

It might be premature to speculate on the possible implications of this study. However, sometimes one is tempted to extrapolate and hypothesize beyond the data. All the material from our pilot studies and the presently available data from Ms. Bock's more systematic experiments show striking similarities in the curves of the monozygotic twins. One cannot assume that this is a chance occurrence.

At the present time we know only that the pupillary motility curves and the evoked potential recordings in our guessing and betting experiments are characteristic for any given individual. They are highly stable and repeatable and they reflect manipulations of cognitive variations in the parameters of the experiments.

We also assume that we record some activity of the nervous system in the pupillograms and in the evoked potentials. Since the experimental variables and parameters in our experiments change the pupil motility curves and certain specific characteristics of the evoked potentials in a predictable and probably lawful way, we can draw, at least tentatively, the further conclusion that the obtained curves express or are correlates of the neuronal activity generated in response to the different stimulus situations. Again, we have found these curves to be highly individualistic in amplitude and temporal characteristics.

We also found the curves from the monozygotic twins, who are
biologically identical, to be highly similar. Can we now go one
step further on this dangerous trail and conclude that our data
indeed are expressions of an inherited cognitive and evaluative
process in the nervous system?

At this point of the argument we have to leave science temporarily and ask a perhaps more philosophical question: What control
do we have over these "neuronal processes" or are they our
"control mechanisms", *ergo:* our personality?

The evidence is quite convincing that these processes, which
might be the result of sequential firing of neuronal aggregates,
are genetically determined. Is it then that this genetically
determined "neuronal hook-up" governs our behavior? I will leave
you at this point to your own speculations, conclusions and
phantasies. I will only state that the data from our laboratory
as well as from many other laboratories doing similar work, will
inevitably force us to pursue research to pose and answer these
questions.

In a very recent experiment we have pursued a phenomenon which
we had seen in some of our previous data. Figure 5 shows separately the average response curves for the "right" guesses and the
"wrong" guesses superimposed at the point of maximum dilation. It
is quite clear that the recovery slope in the "wrong" trials is
steeper than in the "right" trials. We have examined the records
of many subjects and this phenomenon was found in all of them.
There seems to be something in the neuronal processing of the
interpretation of difference between right and wrong guesses that
expresses itself in the recovery slope. I would like to point out
here that the term "recovery slope" is probably not accurate. The
term constriction might indicate that we deal here with an active
process to a given stimulus situation. I have no information as to
what produces this specific slope characteristic or what neuronal
elements are involved. Lacking a better name, we are using the
term recovery slope at the present time. Friedman's (1973) data
showed the same trend, though we never analyzed his data with
respect to recovery slope and stimulus probability.

We found in our files a number of pilot experiments where we
had manipulated some of the parameters which we in retrospect
consider operative in such a situation. One such parameter was
the difference between two amounts of payoff. In a pilot study we
gave the subjects the choice to bet either 5 cents or 25 cents or
put no cash at all on the line. The rules of the game stated that
a single click would represent wins and a double click would
represent losses. The probability of any of the click patterns to
occur in this experiment was not known to the subject. Actually

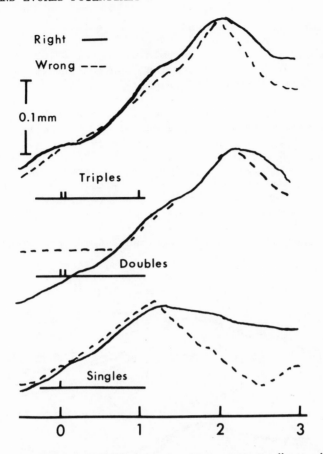

Figure 5. Averaged pupillary response curves in "guess" condition for all three click problems separately averaged by right and wrong guesses. The curves are superimposed at point of largest dilation. In all cases recovery slopes are steeper for wrong guesses. (Levine experiment)

we presented a computer generated 50:50 probability sequence.
What surprised us was that the constriction slope was least steep
in a condition where the subject had put no money on his bet and
the stimulus pattern indicated "lose." This appeared paradoxical
since the less steep slopes usually were found in a winning condition. The routine post-experiment interview revealed that the
subject thought the game was stacked against his winning. He
indicated that in his estimate the chance of winning was 80:20

rather than the actual 50:50 chance. Thus, each time he had not
bet on a "lose" trial, he considered it a win. One subject said,
"never mind winning but I want to hold on to the $5.00 of the
initial stake." In her interpretation "the getting rid of doubles"
without losing money was really a winner.

Mr. Stuart Steinhauer, one of my graduate students, is now
studying this right-wrong, win-lose problem in a more systematic
way. The stimuli in his series of experiments are again auditory
clicks, singles and doubles. The subject is instructed to bet
either 5 cents or 10 cents or to "pass" (bet zero). On a given day
single clicks win and on another day double clicks win. Thus,
characteristics of the winning stimulus was reversed. Again, pupil
and vertex evoked potentials are recorded.

Figure 6 shows the data from one subject in this experiment.

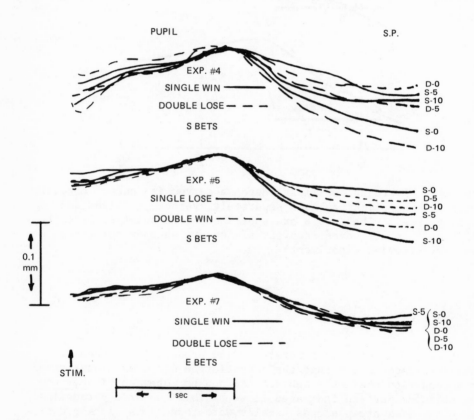

Figure 6. Averaged pupillary response curves in betting experiment. Upper two sets are from "Subject bet" experiments; lower
set from "Experimenter bet" experiment. (Steinhauer experiment)

Note that the slope is always steeper for the losing trials. The
zero bet trials in a "single wins" condition have a steeper slope.
It is as if the subject argues, "Gee, if I had bet money on this
one I would have won, I missed the opportunity." The least steep
slope in Figure 6 is for the "lose, bet zero" situation. Here the
argument would be "Thank God I didn't bet money on this one, I
would have lost. Thus, I really won." When the significance of
the click was reversed (single lose, double win), the results were
the same, the steeper slopes were the loser slopes. Figure 7 is a
summary of the data in the form of a graph. On the y axis are the
diameter differences between the point of maximal dilation and a
point 1600 milliseconds later.

Another condition was added: the subject was told before the
trial how much money (5¢, 10¢ or pass) was riding on the trial.

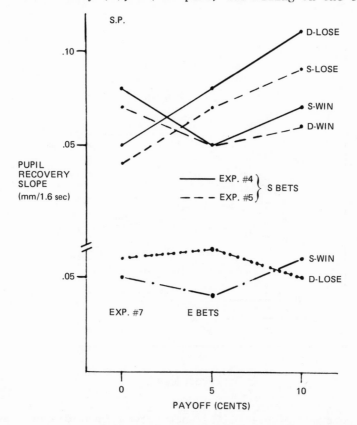

Figure 7. Recovery slopes (difference between peak diameter and
diameter 1600 msec later) plotted against amount of money bet.
These are the values derived from curves in Figure 6. Note difference between "Subject bet" and "Experimenter bet" data.
(Steinhauer experiment)

If the stimulus was a single click, the subject would be credited
with an amount of money indicated to him by the experimenter; if
the stimulus was a double click the subject would lose that amount
(experimenter bet). The subjects were told that the sequence of
the bets and the sequence of stimuli were generated randomly by
computer. In other words, the experimenter would make no adjustment to deprive the subject of his well earned winnings. The
results are shown in Figures 6 and 7 (bottom). There is much less
dilation and no slope difference between the "win and lose." One
could interpret this to mean that the subject showed little involvement in the whole procedure since he had no control over the
situation. We have not yet been able to identify in the evoked
potential any specific wave form or amplitude characteristic which
seems to correspond to the information carried in the pupil changes.
There is some indication that the N_1-P_3 amplitude was larger in the

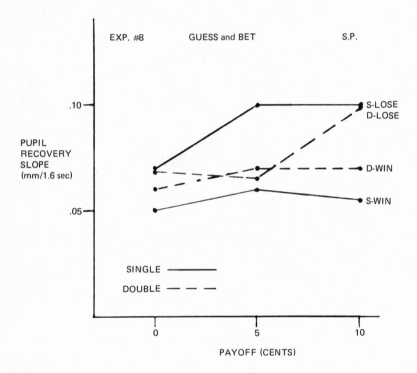

Figure 8. Recovery slopes (difference between peak diameter and
diameter 1600 msec later) from "guess and bet" experiment. Note
that pass (0 pay-off) condition no longer shows difference
between "would have won" and "would have lost" situation. (Figures
6, 7 and 8 represent data from same subject.) (Steinhauer experiment)

"lose" trials.   There appears to be no quantitative difference in terms of how much money was bet nor is there any difference in the "bet zero" condition between "win" and "lose."

    In another modification of this procedure, the subject was asked to bet 5 cents, 10 cents or pass. He then pressed one of two buttons. The pressing of one button indicated that the subject guessed the stimulus will be a single click. If he was right in this guess he got the amount of money he had bet, if he was wrong he lost it. Thus he both guesses and bets. Naturally, these two are not unrelated but there are substantial conceptual differences between the simple bet situation and this more complex situation. Figure 8 shows a graph of the slopes in this experiment. With the exception of one reversal, there are the same quantitative differences between the wins and losses, but the "bet zero" has lost its importance. Again, the *post hoc* explanation could be that the subject puts a greater emphasis on his guess than on his bet, expecially since there is only 5 cents or 10 cents involved. In the present day inflation this is not very much and does not outweigh his concern over "being right." Or what other explanation is there?

    In conclusion then, we have shown data which demonstrate more ways in which the pupil and vertex evoked potential can be used as indicators or correlates of ongoing conceptual and cognitive processes in the nervous system. We have also shown that the characteristics of these curves appear to be expressions of inherited neuronal hook-ups and sequential utilization of neuronal aggregates. Can we go one step further in our interpretation and say that an individual's personality and destiny lies in the structure and function of his specific model of the nervous system? But to ask that question and infer all the implications might lead to unpleasant consequences in the present social climate.

ACKNOWLEDGEMENTS

    The research described in this paper was in part supported by Grant 14580 from the National Institute for Mental Health and by a grant from the General Motors Corporation.

    The author wishes to thank and give full credit to his students, Dr. David Friedman, Mr. Steven Levine, Ms. Frances Bock and Mr. Stuart Steinhauer.

REFERENCES

Bellarminow, L. Anwendung der graphischen Methoden bei Untersuchungen der Pupillenbewegungen: Photograph. *Arch. Ges. Physiol.*, 1885, 19.

Bumke, O. *Die Pupillenstoerungen in Geisteskrankheiten.* Jena: Fischer Verlag, 1904.

Cueppers, C. Eine neue Methode zur stetigen Registrierung der konsensuellen Pupillenreaktion. *Klinische Monatsblatter fur Augenheilkunde*, 1951, *119*, 411.

Dodt, E. and Schrader, K. E. (Eds.) *Die Normaleund die Gestoerte Pupillenbewegung.* Muenchen: J. F. Bergman Verlag, 1973.

Dustman, R. E. The visual evoked potential in twins. *EEG*, 1965, *19*, 570–575.

Friedman, D., Hakerem, G., Sutton, S. and Fleiss, J. Effect of stimulus uncertainty on the pupillary dilation response and the vertex evoked potential. *Electroencephalography and Clinical Neurophysiology*, 1973, *34*, 475–484.

Hakerem, G. The effect of cognitive manipulation on pupillary diameter and evoked cortical potentials. In, E. Dodt and K. E. Schrader (Eds.) *Die Normale und die Gestoerte Pupillenbewegung.* Muenchen: J. F. Bergman Verlag, 1973.

Hakerem, G. Pupillography. In, P. Venables and I. Martin (Eds.) *A Manual of Psychophysiological Methods.* Amsterdam: North Holland Publishing Company, 1967.

Hakerem, G. and Sutton, S. Pupillary response at visual threshold. *Nature*, 1966, *212*, 485–486.

Hess, E. H. Attitude and pupil size. *Scientific American*, 1965, *212*, 46–54.

King, G. An improved electronic pupillograph for clinical use. *Proceedings of the National Electronics Conference*, 1960, *16*.

Levine, S. Pupillary dilation as a function of stimulus uncertainty. Unpublished Master's Thesis, Queens College of CUNY, 1969.

Lewis, E. G., Dustman, R. E. and Sebek, E. Evoked response similarities in monozygotic, dizygotic and unrelated individuals: a comparative study. *Electroencephalography and Clinical Neurophysiology*, 1972, *23*, 309–316.

Lowenstein, O. and Loewenfeld, I. E. Electronic pupillography. *Archives of Ophthalmology*, 1958, *59*, 353–363.

Sutton, S., Braren, M., Zubin, J. and John, E. R. Evoked potential correlates to stimulus uncertainty. *Science*, 1965, *150*, 1187–1188.

Tueting, P., Sutton, S. and Zubin, J. Quantitative evoked potential correlates of the probability event. *Psychophysiology*, 1971, *7*, 385–394.

Venables, P. H. and Martin, I. *A Manual of Psychophysiological Methods.* Amsterdam: North Holland Publishing Company, 1967.

CHAPTER VI:

INDIVIDUAL DIFFERENCES IN PUPIL SIZE AND PERFORMANCE

W. Scott Peavler

Human Performance Technology Center
Bell Laboratories
New Brunswick, New Jersey

Individual differences in pupil size are not surprising since they have been well documented by ocular scientists for years, although emphasis has typically been on abnormalities. What may be surprising, however, is the possibility that some of these presumably inherent differences may be related to performance characteristics of the individuals. I would like to discuss some research which suggests that certain pupillary measurements may be useful as performance predictors of individual capabilities, and/or group behavior. Before describing the first study (Peavler, in press), a brief review of some of the previous pupillary research seems appropriate.

The use of pupillary response patterns in psychological research has flourished during the last decade (Goldwater, 1972), as a result of the initial work of Hess and Polt (1960, 1964). The primary areas of investigation involve the response as a measure of affect (Hess, 1972; however see also Janisse, 1973) and as a measure of mental effort. Data resulting from structured tasks requiring information processing are characterized by consistent and reliable dilation patterns. Kahneman and Beatty (1966) reported a linear relationship between pupil dilation and the amount of information processed in a short-term memory task. Another study (Beatty and Kahneman, 1966) demonstrated that information retrieval from long-term memory storage, which presumably requires greater effort, produced more dilation than retrieval of a like amount of information from short-term memory storage. Similar relationships between task difficulty and pupil dilation were obtained by Bradshaw (1967, 1968) who employed a variety of problem solving information processing tasks.

The magnitude of the dilation response has been shown to be related to the apparent processing effort rather than the absolute amount of information processed (Kahneman, Onuska, and Wolman, 1968) and the concept of "processing load" has been offered by Kahneman (1967) to describe the momentary demands placed on a subject by a particular task. Thus, increasingly difficult pitch-discrimination tasks produce a greater demand on the organism which is accompanied by increased dilation (Kahneman and Beatty, 1967). These attentional demands may be imposed by the intrinsic nature of the task or they may be produced voluntarily by the subject relative to an existing payoff matrix (Kahneman, Peavler, and Onuska, 1968). Differences in incentive value for learning digit-noun pairs had an effect of improving behavioral performance, and apparent selective learning effort, as measured by pupil dilation, for high-reward items (Kahneman and Peavler, 1969).

Because of the complexities of the autonomic system, the pupil is also sensitive to a number of factors which are not necessarily related to attention or processing load. Some of these variables include influences from motor responses (Simpson and Paivio, 1966; Simpson, 1967), induced muscle tension (Nunnally, Knott, Duchnowski, and Parker, 1967), verbal response requirements (Bernick and Oberlander, 1968; Hakerem and Sutton, 1966; Simpson and Paivio, 1968), sensory stimulation (Loewenfeld, 1958; Shakhnovich, 1965), anxiety (Simpson and Molloy, 1971), and fatigue (Geacintov and Peavler, in press; Lowenstein and Loewenfeld, 1964).

It therefore becomes critical to exercise caution in ascribing changes in pupil diameter to processing efforts or attentiveness when alternative interpretations have not been eliminated. Carver (1971) and Johnson (1971) have suggested that mental tasks may be accompanied by emotional influences (anxiety associated with task performance) in proportion to task difficulty, which are also mirrored by dilation. Such an explanation might be particularly probable when the subject has prior knowledge of the difficulty level of the task (Kahneman and Beatty, 1966). The first study was designed to assess the contribution of presumed anxiety associated with task difficulty to the pupil dilation response produced by information overload.

Sixteen female college students served as subjects. Ages ranged from 18 to 21 years and each subject was compensated $4.00 for her participation.

Pupillary response records were obtained with equipment similar to that described by Hess (1972). The cabinet, measuring 93 x 51 x 45 cm, contained a translucent rear projection screen at one end and a binocular viewing aperture with a cushioned head frame and adjustable chin rest at the other end. A constant visual fixation point was provided by a slide containing seven typed Xs projected onto the translucent screen from a projector positioned 118 cm behind the screen. The screen image of the fixation slide was 29.5 x 20.5 cm which subtended a visual angle of approximately 18° for the subject seated 93 cm away. A Kodak Wratten neutral density filter was used in the projector lens to reduce the fixation slide to 0.2 footcandles as measured from the viewing aperture with a Gossen TRI-LUX footcandle meter. An additional 5.8 footcandles was provided by a 25-watt red bulb with aluminum reflector, located on the center of the cabinet floor, 30 cm in front of the viewing aperture. This resulted in a total of 6.0 footcandles necessary to achieve median pupil sizes between 4 and 4.5 millimeters.

Infrared photographs of the subject's left eye were made with a 16 mm Bolex camera mounted on the side of the cabinet and focused onto a small mirror positioned in the subject's peripheral field of view within the cabinet. This arrangement afforded the subject an unobstructed, binocular view of the screen. Camera speed was regulated to a constant rate of two frames per second by an external motor. A small pin light, mounted inside the upper portion of the viewing aperture and out of the subject's view, provided a controlled method of signaling stimulus events on the photographic records.

Stimulus material was prerecorded with the aid of an electronic metronome. Sound level was controlled at 62 (±3) db with an oscilloscope and later verified with a MSA Soundscope (Model B) sound level meter. Stimulus material was presented through calibrated earphones to the subject's left ear.

After the infrared film had been processed by a commercial firm, film records were magnified by a factor of 4.5 cm via projection techniques, and pupil diameter from each frame was measured by hand with a millimeter ruler. Measurement calibration was accomplished by photographing a millimeter ruler placed in the viewing aperture between each subject. This enabled the magnified pupil measurements to be subsequently reduced to actual pupil size values.

The subjects were informed that the purpose of the experiment was to investigate changes in pupil size related to various types of mental activity, and the photographing technique was explained in general terms. Specific questions about experimental procedures and manipulations were deferred until after the session had been completed.

After initial equipment adjustments had been completed, the session was begun with a pre-test control period which consisted of three control trials containing 5, 9, and 13 digits presented orally at a constant rate of one digit per second. The subject was informed that the purpose of the control period was to collect "base line" measurements of individual differences in pupil size and was given assurance that no questions would be asked about the digits presented, thereby eliminating the need for attempting to remember them. Instructions were simply to fixate on the fixation slide and try to refrain from blinking.

Photographing began two seconds prior to the first digit in a trial and terminated two seconds after the last digit had been presented. Intertrial interval was 30 seconds at which time the subject was allowed to blink freely and otherwise relax her eyes while maintaining her position in the viewing aperture. At the conclusion of the three control trials a two minute rest period was granted during which time the subject could withdraw from the viewing aperture and relax.

The subject was next informed of the experimental task which consisted of listening to digit strings, similar to those presented in the control period, and attempting to recall the string at the completion of the trial. The digit strings/trials were described as "short ones which should be easy for everyone", "medium ones which might be fairly difficult for some people", and "long ones which are almost impossible to recall completely correct". The subject was not informed of the exact number of digits contained in the different types of trials but was encouraged to attempt to recall as many digits as possible on all trials.

The single difference between test trials and pre-test control trials was the word "Ready" which accompanied initial photographing for each trial (two seconds prior to the first digit) and the command "Repeat" which followed the final digit by two seconds. At this time photographing was terminated and the subject attempted to recall, unpaced, the digit string. A practice trial of five digits was given before beginning the test session.

The experimental test session consisted of 12 trials contained in three blocks of four trials each. There were four trials each of the three different trial lengths (5, 9, or 13 digits) and the presentation order was random. Intertrial intervals and two minute rest periods between trial blocks were identical to those in the pre-test control condition.

The subject was next presented with a post-test control period which was an exact duplication of the pre-test control period except for the order of presentation and actual digits heard. The subject was again assured that no questions would be asked concerning the control trial material.

Valid pupil data were obtained from 14 subjects. Measurements were not attempted for one subject because of poor quality film records (due to excessive movements by the subject), and records were not measured for another subject because of a partially closed eyelid.

Pupil measurements were averaged for all control trials of a given length, for both pre- and post-test control periods. The average decrement in pupil size (second 1 and 2) from pre-test control to post-test control trials was 0.4 mm (t = 3.44, 13 df, p<.01). This decrement has been previously observed (Kahneman and Beatty, 1967; Libby, Lacey and Lacey, 1973; Peavler and McLaughlin, 1967) and in fact constituted the rationale for having control trials both preceding and following test trials. Analysis of variance showed, however, no significant interactions between the two conditions; pre-test and post-test control trials were therefore averaged to provide a single control pattern with which to compare test trials.

Pupil measurements were averaged for all trials of a given length regardless of recall performance scores. Each subject contributed 4 trials of each length to the group average curves. Dilation from the time of presentation of the first digit (sec. 3, Figure 1) until one second after the final digit had been presented (sec. 8) was 0.5 mm for 5 digit trials. Analysis of the pattern beginning with the first digit (sec. 3) indicated significant differences between test and control trials (F = 6.37, 6/78 df, p<.0001). While some subjects achieved individual dilation peaks at slightly different times, the average peak time was after the fifth and final digit had been presented.

For the 9 digit trials, dilation from the first digit (sec. 3) until one second after the final digit (sec. 12) was 0.71 mm. Significant differences were obtained from a variance analysis beginning with the first digit (sec. 3; F = 17.89, 10/130 df, p<.0001). The average dilation peak was reached with the presentation of the final digit (sec. 11).

A similar pupillary pattern is present for 13 digit trials. The dilation score from the first digit (sec. 3) until one second after the final digit (sec. 16) is 0.56 mm. The smaller dilation is due primarily to earlier peaking in the 13 digit trials. The average peak dilation was reached when the 10th digit was being presented (sec. 12). An analysis of variance for the 13 digit trials yielded significance due to experimental conditions (F = 11.91, 14/162 df, p<.0001).

The similarities between pupillary response patterns was not unanticipated. Since subjects were not aware of the length of a

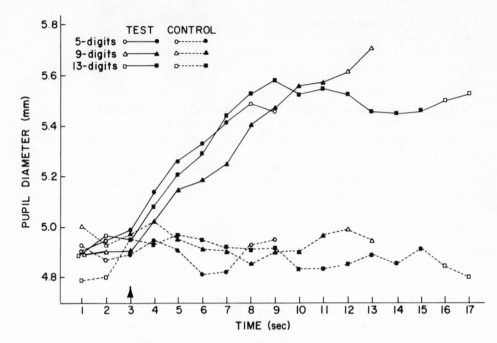

Figure 1. Pupillary patterns for 14 subjects during 5, 9, and
13 digit test and control trials. Digit strings began at the
arrow (sec. 3). Filled symbols represent pupil size during actual
digit presentations and unfilled symbols represent pupil size
for 2 seconds preceding and following digit strings.

given trial until it had been presented, there was no reason to
expect differences in dilation curves during the presentation of
the first 5 (or 9) digits in 9 (or 13) digit lists. Statistical
analysis confirmed that expectation. There were no differences
between the pupil patterns on 9- and 13-digit trials during seconds
9, 10, 11, and 12, which correspond to the presentation of the 7th,
8th, 9th, and 10th (for 13 digit trials) digits. Only at
second 13, when the 9-digit trial is ending and the 13-digit trial
is receiving the 11th digit, do the curves differ significantly
(t = 2.92, 13 df, p<.05).

Recall performance scores, based on one point awarded for
each correct digit recalled in proper sequence and one point subtracted from the total scored for intrusions and omissions (reversals of two adjacent digits was scored as one point), were
computed for each subject. Group average performance scores for
5-, 9-, and 13-digit trials were 4.86, 4.23, and 3.50 respectively.
Performance scores on 13-digit trials were significantly lower
than scores on 5-digit trials (t = 4.94, 15 df, p<.01).

An overall performance score was computed for each subject by weighting recall scores on trials by the trial length. Nine digit trial scores were multiplied by two and 13-digit trial scores were multiplied by 3 in order to assign a higher value to digits correctly recalled from a longer digit trial. The correlation between this score and cumulative dilation (using pupil diameter value at sec. 3 as the base line) was positive but nonsignificant (r = .42). Performance scores were positively correlated with initial pupil size (value at sec. 3; r = .61, 12 df, p<.01), average pupil size (r = .68, 12 df, p<.01), and the mean peak dilation value achieved on all trials (r = .71, 12 df, p<.01). The two latter measures are quite similar in that both reflect individual differences in initial size in addition to the dilation component. There were, incidentally, no observed relationships between initial pupil size and subsequent dilation achieved.

The consistent separation of pupillary response patterns between test and control trials clearly demonstrates that reliable dilations do not occur in the absence of a requirement to process the information even when sensory stimulation is identical. The response patterns on 5-digit trials, which was well within the capacity of the subjects, is typical of the loading function noted by previous research (Kahneman and Beatty, 1966). Nine digit trials proved to be a difficult but reasonable test of memory capacity since on several such trials recall was without error. The 13-digit trials, on the other hand, clearly exceeded memory capacity and resulted in the lowest performance scores.

Previous reports of relationships between dilation and task difficulty have had at least two common features in the experimental design (Kahneman and Beatty, 1966; Kahneman, Peavler, and Onuska, 1968; Kahneman, Tursky, Shapiro, and Crider, 1968). Trials which contained performance errors were excluded in an effort to avoid any possible emotional contamination of the pupil response and more importantly, the subject was informed of the nature (difficulty) of the task prior to its presentation. This fact, of course, allows for the possibility that the task requirements may have been anticipated in such a way as to influence the actual dilation observed. By contrast, the dilation patterns observed among the three trial categories in the present research were similar to each other during the early portions of the trials before the subject was able to identify the trial as either "short", "medium", or "long".

The pupillary pattern observed on 13 digit trials provides evidence against attributing the dilation responses to emotional factors during information processing. Inasmuch as the subjects were obviously overloaded with more than 8 or 9 digits, the perception of such an impending overload, if the dilation were due to anxiety associated with task performance, would have probably resulted in a significant dilation increase. There was no evidence of such a dilation increase in the present data.

The leveling pattern of the 13-digit trial curve occurred in close temporal proximity to the terminal digits in a 9-digit trial. In fact, close inspection reveals a temporary leveling in 9-digit trials between the presentation of the 8th and 9th digits. It is therefore tempting to suppose that when the subject perceived the number of digits presented as exceeding storage capacity, continued processing efforts were suspended while concentration was directed at "holding" digits already stored. This, of course, cannot be confirmed, although recall patterns from 9- and 13-digit trials indicated that successful efforts of sorting and recalling were centered around the early portion of a trial. Finally, the terminal dilation seen after the final digit had been presented in both 9- and 13-digit trials is typically observed when efforts are being made to regroup previously stored information for recall (Kahneman, Onuska, and Wolman, 1968). Evidence which suggests that the leveling does not reflect a pupillary ceiling effect is present in research which demonstrated larger dilation responses with a difficult transformation task (Kahneman, Tursky, Shapiro, and Crider, 1968).

A second alternative, although not mutually exclusive, interpretation of the leveling patterns is provided by the instructions given to the subjects. In order to prevent complete discouragement and ensure processing attempts on the entire 13 digit trials, these trials were described as "almost impossible to recall completely correct". This instruction may have had an effect of devaluing performance on 13 digit trials since correct recall was not really expected. Thus, the leveling pattern may be due to motivational decreases associated with the perception that it was in fact a "long" trial, although the subjects reported making genuine efforts on all trials.

However, the results suggest that presumed anxiety associated with information overload is not characterized by additional dilation resulting from momentary emotionality. In fact, the processing effort as reflected by the pupillary measure, seemed to be voluntarily suspended when an impending overload was perceived.

An interesting result of the study was the relationship observed between behavioral performance and various measures of pupil size. While Simpson and Molloy (1971) did not observe a relationship between pupil size and intelligence during a digit recall and digit transformation task, these results suggest that additional attention to individual differences in performance ability and pupillary characteristics is warranted.

The same subjects also served in other studies on two succes-
ive weeks. Rank correlations of initial pupil size at the beginning
of an experimental session were significant for the 13 subjects between the three weekly sessions (rho = .79 between the 1st and 2nd
weeks; rho = .64 between the 2nd and 3rd weeks). The interpretation of this individual consistency would not be difficult except
for the correlations observed between pupil size and performance.
One obvious explanation rests with the known fact that a large
pupil is typical of an individual who is in an especially alert
and attentive state which would also account for the relatively
superior performance on a mental task. However, when the same
individuals tend to exhibit larger pupils over a three week period,
it becomes tempting to talk of constitutional types which are
characterized by psychophysiological factors which influence pupil
size as well as performance abilities. This speculation must, of
course, be verified by additional data of a definitive nature.

Another aspect of the pupil measures which showed individual
consistency was the amount of decrement in base line measurements
obtained during the pre-test control trials and the post-test control trials, regardless of the experimental task. Individuals who
exhibited the largest decreases during the first weekly session
had similar patterns during the second and third weekly sessions.
Rank correlations between the first and second weeks, and the
first and third weeks of testing were .62 and .67, respectively.
This consistency prompted us to examine shifts in pupil size as
an indication of fatigue (Geacintov and Peavler, in press).

Objective measurement of fatigue has long evaded precise
specification (Bartley, 1947). One factor which has contributed
to the problem has been the notable absence of an acceptable definition of fatigue which has a specific scientific meaning
(McFarland, 1971). Fatigue has traditionally been inferred by
subjective reports of tiredness and/or by measurement of the presumed consequences of fatigue such as performance decrement
(Przystanowicz, 1970).

Attempts to identify objective measures of fatigue have included a variety of psychological and physiological variables
which range from reaction time, blink rate, CFF, and visual acuity
to biochemical, circulatory, and psychophysiological analyses of
bodily processes. The major difficulty with many of these techniques is that the human organism is able to temporarily overcome
effects of fatigue -- except in cases of extreme exhaustion --
during a test situation, thereby offsetting all or some of the
dependent variables (Cameron, 1971; Dearnaley, 1958).

An area of investigation which has been even more elusive
is the measurement of fatigue accruing as a result of normal work

activity at jobs which do not require an inordinate amount of
physical activity. This mental/psychological fatigue is presumably
a normal result of repetitive and/or monotonous tasks and may be
partially caused by boredom.

In a series of studies investigating pupillary dilation
patterns associated with psychological processes (Peavler, 1969;
Peavler and McLaughlin, 1967), a consistent observation was a
reliable decrease in baseline diameter between the onset and termination of an experimental session, regardless of the nature of the
task, which suggested that systematic diameter changes may be re-
flective of normal cognitive effort associated with typical job
activities.

Other investigators of the pupillary system (Lowenstein and
Loewenfeld, 1951) have indicated a close relationship between
pupillary patterns and fatigue levels. They state that pupillary
waves of dilation and contraction accompany arousal and drowsiness
in the tired individual and that the waves are ideal indicators of
fatigue because of their objective, quantitative nature and sensitivity (Lowenstein, Feinberg, and Loewenfeld, 1963). Under normal
light conditions, pupil diameter is maximum in a well-rested and
alert subject and diminishes as fatigue increases - finally reaching a minimum diameter just prior to the onset of sleep (Lowenstein
and Loewenfeld, 1964).

A review by Bell Laboratories of the Directory Assistance
Operation, in order to identify labor or time saving methods and
devices, resulted in a trial examination of new systems for storage and retrieval of customer numbers. One of the proposed systems
consisted of a microfilm viewer which enabled the operator to access
the telephone directory listings using an electronic keyboard. Customer listings were displayed on a screen prior to a final search.
Because the operator works many hours per day at this task, concern
was expressed that continuous usage of display devices could possibly induce fatigue on the part of the operator.

As a result of the reviewed evidence relating pupil size
to fatigue, we conducted a pilot study employing 10 subjects. Presumed fatigue was induced by exposing the subjects to three
Hollywood films, all shown on one day, with a total viewing time
of six hours interrupted by a lunch period and a short afternoon
break. Promising results of that study (reliable decreases in
base line diameter were observed) resulted in plans to obtain
relative measures from operators participating in the microfilm
trial while working at both the traditional book positions as well
as the microfilm positions.

The previous work by Lowenstein and his associates relating

pupil size to fatigue level was confined primarily to clinical evaluations of alert subjects and chronically tired individuals, whereas the purpose of our effort was to determine if the pupillary response sensitivity would permit discrimination between two similar job activities.

Seventeen operators participated in the study. Measurements on two of the subjects were not completed due to operator schedule changes. The data of four additional subjects were discarded because the pupils were unmeasureable for various reasons. As a result, the data are based on 11 subjects, five of whom normally used corrective lenses which were not used during data collection periods.

The pupillary data were obtained with the technique described in the earlier study. Measurements were taken with the room in darkness except for light from a desk lamp on the rearview screen of the viewing box. The subjects looked straight ahead at a set of three letters (ABC) after having been instructed to focus on the middle letter (B) located about 1/3 of the distance from the top of the rearview screen.

Each subject's pupil was allowed to adjust to the red light for one minute, after which it was photographed for three minutes at a rate of two frames per second during each of the four sessions, resulting in 360 measures at each session. Each subject was measured before and after a full day's work on the book and before and after a full day's work on the microfilm reader. The observations were taken on two consecutive days, resulting in four sets of measures for each subject. Half of the subjects were initially measured before and after working on the book position, while the other half were measured initially before and after working on the machine positions. Each frame of the processed film was projected on a screen 89 cm from the front of the lens of a Dunning Animatic single-frame projector and the pupil image, magnified 15X, was measured to the nearest millimeter.

As previously mentioned, the pupil is sensitive to many influences other than fatigue. In order to isolate the effect of fatigue, an attempt was made to minimize influences of extraneous variables by photographing the subject's pupil in a dark, quiet room, with only the experimenter present. Also, because cognitive relaxation is necessary in order to obtain data uncontaminated by the factors mentioned, data analysis was limited to the *final minute* of the recording period. We should add that continuation of the session in a partially sensory deprived environment would probably have resulted in some subjects going to sleep.

The mean pupil sizes for all subjects before and after work on the book position and the microfilm position are shown in Figure 2.

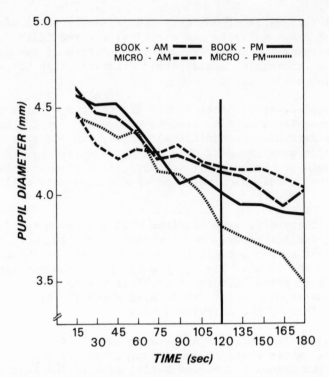

Figure 2.   Mean pupil diameter changes for 11 subjects across time
before and after working on book and microfilm positions.

The graph encompasses the entire three-minute recording period.
For easier graphic presentation, data points have been averaged
for every 15 seconds.   The initial mean pupil size for all subjects at the beginning of the workday was essentially the same at
the book and machine positions: book - 4.6 mm, microfilm - 4.5 mm.
Furthermore, individual pupil sizes obtained during the morning
session were not correlated with diameter differences between
morning and afternoon sessions.

        The mean difference in pupil size (0.32mm) between morning
and the evening measures for all 11 subjects across work conditions
was statistically significant (t = 2.78, p<.01).   Further analysis
of the data within each work condition indicated that the mean
decrease (0.43mm) was statistically significant (t = 2.64, p<.05)
when the subjects worked on the microfilm device, but not when
they worked on the traditional book positions.

        The purpose of the study within which the fatigue measures
were carried out was to compare the performance of operators who

worked on the microfilm machine with that of operators using the
paper telephone record. This principal study showed that using
the mechanized device resulted in improved performance by operators because of the inherently greater access speed of the mechanized microfilm device. Therefore, performance changes traditionally correlated with fatigue were confounded with the differences
in treatment conditions.

While subjective reports of fatigue from the specific operators participating in the study were not identifiable because of
guarantees of anonymity, the population from which they were
selected reported significantly more physical symptoms of fatigue
such as neckaches, backaches, eyestrain, and headaches, when working on the microfilm device than when working at the paper positions.
These complaints were somewhat contradicted, however, by an overwhelming preference for the microfilm device.

A difference in relative fatigue indices was not unanticipated because several plausible contributing factors associated
with the microfilm device had been identified both prior to and
during the study. The major factors, identified both by operator
comment and by environmental analysis, included poor overhead
lighting which created glare, excessive contrasts in the visual
field, specular reflections, inappropriate chair design which did
not provide proper support, and an inadequate physical design of
the microfilm device which precluded shifts into restful positions.
It should be indicated that operator acceptance of the device, as
evaluated, was generally very positive and enthusiastic in spite
of the noted problems.

The interpretation of fatigue rests primarily with the subjective reports, the environmental factors which were identified
as selectively affecting the microfilm operation, and the existing
literature. Reliable performance differences, even without the
previously mentioned confounding between tasks, are extremely
difficult to obtain in the live Directory Assistance environment
because of the nature of the task. Since the customer who is not
under experimental control, is the most potent determiner of speed
and accuracy in the transaction, data collection must necessarily
continue over weeks or even months before reliable individual
differences in operator performance may be identified.

The pupillary response shows promise as a reliable indicator
of fatigue, as shown in the literature and by this study. However,
in order to apply this technique to practical problems involving
groups of subjects, it will be necessary to correlate the degree
of fatigue as measured by performance decrement with changes in
pupil size and to develop quantitative norms which reflect individual differences. We are able only to speak of statistical sig-

nificance when comparing mean pupil size at the end of a day's work performed on two somewhat similar tasks, both of which are assumed to be normally fatiguing.

Finally, let me briefly describe some preliminary results from a study which is not yet fully analyzed. We have recently conducted a study to determine if the previously observed relationships between differences in pupil size and other indications of performance ability as well as inferred fatigue states could be replicated. Seventeen subjects were assigned a typing task for one day which was divided into four work periods. Three minutes of pupillary data were obtained from each subject before and after each work period and the Wonderlic Personnel Test was administered at the end of the day.

The pupillary data, averaged for 15 second intervals, revealed significantly more constriction for recordings obtained following a work period than those preceding a work period (F = 26.93, 1/16 df, p<.01). The constriction pattern during the three minute recording was also reliable (F = 8.44, 10/160 df, p<.01) as was the resulting interaction between rate of constriction and whether the data preceded or followed a work period (F = 5.81, 10/160 df, p<.01). These data again suggest utility of the measure as an indication of the fatiguing process, although much additional work needs to be done.

In addition, when the subjects are divided into two groups based on the Wonderlic Personnel Test scores and overall pupillary data are examined, two statistically distinct groups result (F = 8.14 1/15 df, p<.05). The average difference in pupil size for these groups exceeded 0.5 millimeters. While these results are not as readily interpretable as the fatigue indications, we feel the area of individual differences in pupil size certainly warrants additional examination and may very well possess considerable potential as a correlate of individual differences in both observed and potential behavior.

REFERENCES

Bartley, S. H. Fatigue and inadequacy. *Physiological Review*, 1957, *37*, 301-324.

Beatty, J., and Kahneman, D. Pupillary changes in two memory tasks. *Psychonomic Science*, 1966, *5*, 371-372.

Bernick, N., and Oberlander, M. Effect of verbalization and two different modes of experiencing on pupil size. *Perception and Psychophysics*, 1968, *3*, 327-330.

Bradshaw, J. Pupil size as a measure of arousal during information processing. *Nature*, 1967, *216*, 515-516.

Bradshaw, J. Pupil size and problem solving. *Quarterly Journal of Experimental Psychology*, 1968, *20*, 116-122.

Cameron, C. Fatigue problems in modern industry. *Ergonomics*, 1971, *14*, 713-720.

Carmichael, L., and Dearborn, W. F. *Reading and Visual Fatigue*, Greenwood, 1947.

Carver, R. P. Pupil dilation and its relationship to information processing during reading and listening. *Journal of Applied Psychology*, 1971, *55*, 126-134.

Dearnaley, E. J. Fatigue: A psychological review. Royal Air Force Institute of Aviation Medicine, I.A.M. Report 110, 1958.

Duke-Elder, E. S. *Textbook of Ophthalmology*, Vol. 1, St. Louis: C. V. Mosby Co., 1946.

Finan, J. L., Finan, S. C., and Hartson, L. D. A review of representative tests used for the quantitative measurement of behavior decrement under conditions related to aircraft flights. U. S. Air Force, Air Material Command, Dayton, Ohio. Technical Report, 5830, 1949.

Geacintov, T., and Peavler, W. S. Pupillography in industrial fatigue assessment. *Journal of Applied Psychology*, in press.

Goldwater, B. C. Psychological significance of pupillary movements. *Psychological Bulletin*, 1972, *77*, 340-355.

Hakerem, G., and Sutton, S. Pupillary response at visual threshold. *Nature*, 1966, *212*, 485-486.

Hess, E. H. Pupillometrics. In N. S. Greenfield and R. A. Sternbach (Eds.), *Handbook of Psychophysiology*. New York: Holt, Rinehart and Winston, Inc., 1972.

Hess, E. H., and Polt, J. M. Pupil size as related to interest value of visual stimuli. *Science*, 1960, *132*, 349-350.

Hess, E. H., and Polt, J. M. Pupil size in relation to mental activity during simple problem-solving. *Science*, 1964, *143*, 1190-1192.

Janisse, M. P. Pupil size and affect: a critical review of the literature since 1960. *Canadian Psychologist*, 1973, *14(4)*, 311-329.

Johnson, D. A. Pupillary responses during a short-term memory task: cognitive processing, arousal, or both. *Journal of Experimental Psychology*, 1971, *90*, 311-318.

Kahneman, D. Construct validity of the pupil response. Paper presented at American Psychological Association, Washington, D.C., 1967.

Kahneman, D., and Beatty, J. Pupil diameter and load on memory. *Science*, 1966, *154*, 1583-1585.

Kahneman, D., and Beatty, J. Pupillary response in a pitch-discrimination task. *Perception and Psychophysics*, 1967, *2*, 101-105.

Kahneman, D., Onuska, L., and Wolman, R. Effects of grouping on the pupillary response in a short-term memory task. *Quarterly Journal of Experimental Psychology*, 1968. *20*, 309-311.

Kahneman, D., and Peavler, W. S.   Incentive effects and pupillary changes in association learning. *Journal of Experimental Psychology*, 1969, *79*, 312-318.

Kahneman, D., Peavler, W. S., and Onuska, L.   Effects of verbalization and incentive on the pupil response to mental activity. *Canadian Journal of Psychology*, 1968, *22*, 186-196.

Kahneman, D., Tursky, B., Shapiro, D., and Crider, A.   Pupillary, heart rate, and skin resistance changes during a mental task. *Journal of Experimental Psychology*, 1969, *79*, 164-147.

Libby, W. L.,   Lacey, B. C., and Lacey, J. I.   Pupillary and cardiac activity during visual attention. *Psychophysiology*, 1973, *10*, 270-294.

Loewenfeld, I. E.   Mechanisms of reflex dilation of the pupil. Historical review and experimental analysis. *Documenta Ophthalmologica*, 1958, *12*, 185-448.

Lowenstein, O., and Loewenfeld, I. E.   Type of central autonomic innervation and fatigue. *Archives of Neurology and Psychiatry*, 1951, *66*, 581-599.

Lowenstein, O., and Loewenfeld, I. E.   The sleep-waking cycle and pupillary activity. *Annals of the New York Academy of Sciences*, 1964, *117*, 142-156.

Lowenstein, O., Feinberg, R., and Loewenfeld, I. E.   Pupillary movements during acute and chronic fatigue. *Investigative Ophthalmology*, 1963. *2*, 138-157.

McFarland, R. A.   Understanding fatigue in modern life. *Ergonomics*, 1971, *14(1)*, 1-10.

Nunnally, J. C., Knott, P. D., Duchnowski, A., and Parker, R.   Pupillary response as a general measure of activation. *Perception and Psychophysics*, 1967, *2*, 149-155.

Peavler, W. S.   Attention, processing load, and pupil size. Paper presented at Sixth Colloquium on the Pupil, Bethesda, Md., May, 1969.

Peavler, W. S.   Pupil size, information overload, and performance differences. *Psychophysiology*, in press.

Peavler, W. S., and McLaughlin, J. P.   The question of stimulus content and pupil size. *Psychonomic Science*, 1967, *8(12)*, 505-506.

Przystanowicz, A.   Effect of fatigue on the precision of positioning movements. *Przeglad Psychologiczny*, 1970, No. 19, 33-44.

Shakhnovich, A. R.   On the pupillary component of the orienting reflex during action of stimuli specific for vision and non-specific (extraneous) stimuli. In L. G. Varonin, A. N. Leontiev, A. R. Luria, E. N. Sokolov, and O. S. Vinogradova (Eds.), *Orienting reflex and exploratory behavior*, Vol. III. Washington, D.C.: American Institute of Biological Sciences, 1965.

Simpson, H. M.   Pupillary activity during imagery tasks. Paper presented at American Psychological Association, Washington, D.C., 1967.

Simpson, H. M., and Molloy, F. M. Effects of audience anxiety on pupil size. *Psychophysiology*, 1971, *8*, 491-496.

Simpson, H. M., and Paivio, A. Changes in pupil size during an imagery task without motor response involvement. *Psychonomic Science*, 1966, *5*, 405-406.

Simpson, H. M., and Paivio, A. Effects on pupil size of manual and verbal indicators of cognitive task fulfillment. *Perception and Psychophysics*, 1968, *3*, 185-190.

Snell, Peter A. An introduction to the experimental study of visual fatigue. *Journal of the Society of Motion Picture Engineers*, 1933, *20*, 367-390.

Weston, H. C. Visual fatigue. *Illumination Engineering*, 1954, *49*, 63-74.

CHAPTER VII:

TWO APPROACHES TO ATTITUDE ASSESSMENT USING THE PUPIL RESPONSE

Niles Bernick

Psychophysiology Laboratory
NIDA Clinical Research Center
Lexington, Kentucky

In 1965 Eckhard Hess published an article in the *Scientific American* entitled, "Attitude and Pupil Size", in which he described a number of studies relating the psychological content of various kinds of stimuli to changes in pupil size. While "attitude" was not rigidly defined, it was clear that it represented a number of dimensions such as: preference, interest, attractiveness, pleasantness, motivation, emotion, and arousal.

Attitude, in its normal usage, involves a predisposition to respond in a particular way to a particular set of stimulus conditions. The response is basically an emotional response, but when this response actually occurs, it is the product of both the pre-existing attitude and the immediate stimulus conditions. Attitudes, defined as predispositions to respond, might be innately based (what the ethologists call "innate releasing mechanisms") but they are usually considered to be learned, either through direct experience with the stimulus conditions or by indirect influences of culture or tradition.

With the possible exception of innately based attitudes, the cognitive activity involved in the activation of an attitude is a necessary condition for the production of a subsequent emotional response. While a physical insult to the organism may, for example, produce physiological activation and a subjective response of pain, it does not produce the emotional component, fear of pain, until cognitive processing occurs. On the other hand, an individual may be said to possess and express an attitude without necessarily experiencing an emotional response. Whether one accepts this theoretical position or not, it seems clear that in order to measure attitude, one must tap either the cognitive processing or the

177

emotional response associated with it (when it occurs). The pupil
response seems quite appropriate for this task. There is a wealth
of data supporting the use of the pupil response as a measure of
cognitive activity. Problem solving, memory tasks, and imaging
have all been well demonstrated as affecting pupil size. As an
indicator of emotional response it is well known that shifts in
autonomic balance, classically associated with emotional responses,
can easily be seen and practically defined by pupillary activity.

Like the other autonomic measures in use by psychophysiolo-
gists, the pupil response is an attractive measure for behavioral
research because it is involuntary. It is different from these
other measures in a number of ways: it can be measured remotely,
i.e., the subject is not threatened or incumbered by electrodes or
transducer leads; it requires very little cooperation by the subject, i.e., he need only place his head against a face cushion;
and most important, it appears to be more sensitive than the other
available measures to psychological kinds of variables.

The promise of this new technique to measure some of the more
elusive qualities of behavior has stimulated a great deal of research which has been recently reviewed by Goldwater (1972) and
Hess (1972). The real potential for students of behavior lies in
research with human subjects who are unable by virtue of verbal
ability or psychological state, or unwilling by virtue of social
pressure or lack of trust, to communicate with another human,
whether therapist, teacher, or researcher. This technique also
has the potential of being unbiased with regard to age, sex, race,
culture, or education within relatively broad limits.

The purpose of this paper is to describe some data which have
heretofore only been alluded to in the literature, mentioned in
passing as part of an unrelated study, or finally, recently completed and not yet prepared for independent publication.

The first of these studies was conducted when I was a graduate
student at the University of Chicago (Bernick, 1966). Upon reviewing the early findings relating the interest value of visual
stimuli to the pupil size which was observed in subjects viewing
them, it occurred to me that this technique had several unique
characteristics which would make it particularly useful for some
basic kinds of research on attitudes which has been technically
impractical previously. Having a basic interest in the development
of behavior and particularly human behavior, I took a naturalist's
view of the problem of how the developing human organism views his
environment, that is, his attitudes toward the objects around him.
From a technical point of view the measurement of behavior of this
type developmentally, was without precedent. How was one to apply
the same instrument to young children, adolescents, teenagers, and

adults? Even given a solution to this problem how could such a
measure be valid and equally valid across these different age
groups? Verbal measures which have been classically used in these
situations were clearly inadequate. For me, the answer was a
physiological measure which would reflect the emotional response
of an individual independent of that individual's age, sex, language or verbal ability, or even his honesty. While culture and
race could be included in this list, they present certain other
complications which would have to be dealt with first. The pupil
response showed promise of being the ideal technique for this
problem and had the additional advantage of being easily administered to potentially difficult subjects, i.e., young children.

My next interest in conducting such a study was to limit the
problem in some meaningful way in terms of the class of objects
to be investigated. The choice was fairly easy inasmuch as some
of the most common premises of theories of human behavior were
based on little, if any, evidence of a solid nature. Freud's
theory of psychosexual development, for instance, was based exclusively on clinical observations and has generated only the most
meager of subsequent research data in its support. With reference to Freud's theory, the bulk of anthropological data, again
subjective in nature, is not in agreement as to the development
of sexual interest or its dynamics during development. It is not
my intention to launch into an expanded discussion of these kinds
of data but only to point out the great potential for research
employing this psychophysiological approach in providing descriptive data relevant to the basic questions of psychology. Because
of considerations such as those mentioned above, the study which
grew out of these efforts was limited to an investigation into
social objects in the child's world. These were divided on an
a priori basis into the following categories - baby, boy, girl,
man, woman, father, and mother as in Table 1. The last two categories were each depicted by an adult with a baby, boy or girl.
In addition, since previous studies had employed pinup photographs
as stimuli, for the appropriate categories, that is boy, girl, man,
and woman, stimuli were prepared in both clothed and semi-clothed
conditions, in order that comparisons could be made along this
dimension.

The subjects for this study were white, middle class children
of both sexes from suburban schools in the midwest. As a part of
their selection children were visually screened and the sample
limited to those with normal uncorrected vision. The design called
for sampling equal numbers of boys and girls from the kindergarten,
first, second, fourth, sixth, eighth, tenth and twelfth grades.
Each cell was to have eight subjects; a total of 128 subjects.
Because of missing and/or unmeasurable data, this total was eventually reduced to 113 distributed as in Table 2.

TABLE 1

STIMULUS CATEGORIES FOR DEVELOPMENTAL STUDY

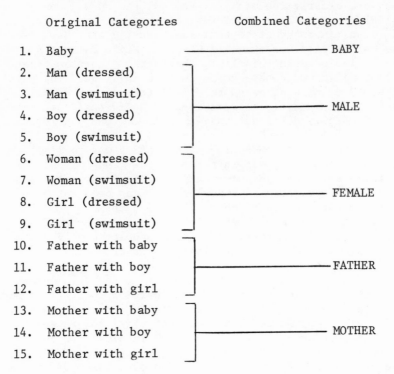

Original Categories   Combined Categories

1. Baby ———————————————————————— BABY

2. Man (dressed)

3. Man (swimsuit)

4. Boy (dressed)   MALE

5. Boy (swimsuit)

6. Woman (dressed)

7. Woman (swimsuit)

8. Girl (dressed)   FEMALE

9. Girl (swimsuit)

10. Father with baby

11. Father with boy   FATHER

12. Father with girl

13. Mother with baby

14. Mother with boy   MOTHER

15. Mother with girl

The stimuli consisted of photographs culled from popular
magazines which were prepared photographically to be of equal
overall brightness and of uniformly low contrast. The details of
this technique have been described by Hess (1972) and will not be
repeated here. Each of the stimulus categories described above
were represented by three photographs, one in each of three different sets of stimuli, that is there were 45 stimuli in all. The
stimuli in the first and second sets were ordered in such a manner
that stimuli from similar categories were not adjacent. The stimuli in the third set were arranged in an order opposite that of the
first stimulus set.

In order to assess subjects' verbal preferences for the stimulus pictures, following the presentation of each stimulus set in
the pupil response apparatus each subject was shown an array of
the same pictures he had just seen and asked to indicate which he
liked best, second best, third best, and fourth best. Similarly,
the same choices were made for pictures liked least. Each time

TABLE 2

DISTRIBUTION OF SUBJECTS BY SEX AND GRADE LEVEL

Grade Level	Boys	Girls
K	5	7
1	5	2
2	6	7
4	8	8
6	8	8
8	8	8
10	8	8
12	8	8
	56	56

TOTAL = 112

a choice was made the picture chosen was removed from the array so as to simplify subsequent choices. For presentation of stimuli in the pupil response apparatus 2 x 2 slides were prepared, and for the subsequent verbal response procedure 3" x 4" prints mounted on cardboard were prepared from the same materials. For pupil response testing, stimuli were presented for five seconds each via slide projector on a rear projection screen. This screen was mounted on the apparatus used to record pupil responses which has been described elsewhere (Bernick and Oberlander, 1968). A floodlight reflector with a 60 watt bulb was also directed on the screen and adjusted through its power supply so that it evenly illuminated the screen, thereby minimizing any differences in illumination which still remained between the stimulus materials. The screen's brightness measured with the floodlamp alone was 24 footcandles. With the brightest slide projected in addition to the floodlamp it measured 27 footcandles.

Subjects were tested individually in groups of three. While one subject viewed the first slide set, the other two waited nearby. The next subject then took his turn viewing the first stimulus set while the first subject indicated his verbal preferences for the pictures he had just seen. By alternating all three subjects in each group in this fashion, all of the subjects eventually saw all of the pictures in the pupil apparatus and indicated their

verbal preferences for them without exhibiting any fatigue or
boredom as a result of the experimental procedures. The writer
and his wife acted as experimenters and were both present at all
times during the testing sessions.

Upon initial perusal of these data it was obvious that there
were considerable differences in absolute pupil size at baseline
between subjects. These differences were found to be unrelated
to sex or age. In order to rule out the possibility that these
baseline differences might interact with the magnitude of changes
due to our stimuli as might be predicted by the Law of Initial
Values (see Johnson and Lubin, 1972), a correlation was calculated
between range of response and overall mean pupil size for each
subject. No significant relationship was found and it was concluded that under these conditions the Law of Initial Values did
not apply.

The results of this study are presented in terms of percentage change in pupil size due to the stimuli, that is, each stimulus picture was preceded by a control slide, which consisted of a
gray field with an X in the center, that was exactly matched in
brightness to that stimulus slide. Percentage change was calculated on the basis of the difference between each slide and its
preceding control slide.

In order to compensate for the differences in overall response level between the groups of subjects, it was assumed that
each subject had his or her own baseline and that the absolute
value of this baseline was not as meaningful as the distribution
of responses around it. Accordingly, all scores were converted
to deviation scores, that is, the mean score for each subject was
calculated, then, for each subject, individual scores were subtracted from each subject's own mean. This conversion equated the
mean of each subject's range of response. The biasing effects of
missing data on group means are also reduced considerably by this
conversion. Thus, the measurements obtained of pupil diameters
were processed for deviation scores, means, and finally in analyses
of variance.

A two way analysis of variance was performed for each of the
stimulus categories using percentage change deviation scores. The
basic design was a 2 x 8 matrix, that is, sex by grade. The odd
number of subjects in some of the cells of the matrix made it
necessary to use harmonic means for the analysis. For the purposes of this presentation, the more detailed analyses will be
omitted and the fifteen stimulus categories previously described
are reduced to five combined categories shown in Table 2, namely,
baby, male, female, father and mother. The F values and associated
probabilities generated by these stimulus categories in the analyses

of variance may be seen in Table 3.

TABLE 3

ANALYSES OF VARIANCE OF PUPIL RESPONSES BY

STIMULUS CATEGORIES (Deviation scores)

Category	Sex		Age		Sex x Age		Error
	F	p	F	p	F	p	
Baby	3.937	.05	2.026	.10	0.202	---	.075
Male	5.054	.05	0.865	---	1.489	---	.017
Female	1.615	---	0.487	---	0.494	---	.020
Father	3.387	.10	0.556	---	1.212	---	.036
Mother	6.938	.01	0.419	---	0.838	---	.048

The results are represented graphically in the next five figures. In Figure 1 "Pupil responses to stimulus category baby," there is no overlap between responses by the male subjects and those of the female subjects. Male subjects responded with more dilation than the female subjects across all grade levels. In Figure 2 "Pupil responses to combined stimulus category male," in all but one case, female responses are higher than the male responses. The single reversal occurs at the kindergarten level. A similar difference is seen in Figure 3 "Pupil responses to combined stimulus category female." In this case, however, there are two reversals and the overall sex difference does not reach statistical significance. Again, there is a reversal at the kindergarten level, but this time there is also one at the eighth grade. The direction of these responses is also opposite; male responses are, for the most part, higher than the female responses to this category. In Figure 4 "Pupil responses to combined stimulus category father," there is no consistent trend across age. Finally, in Figure 5, entitled "Pupil responses to combined stimulus category mother," a clear sex difference is observed. Male responses in all but two cases are much higher than the female responses. Reversals occur at kindergarten and eighth grade similar to those seen earlier in response to combined stimulus category female.

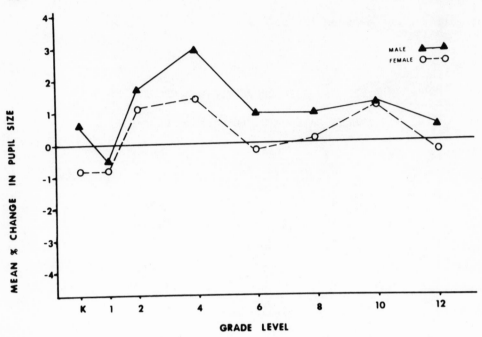

Figure 1. Pupil responses to stimulus category: Baby

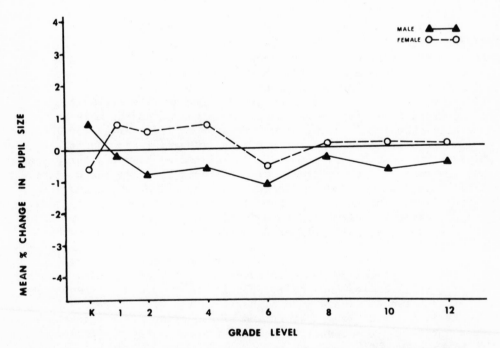

Figure 2. Pupil responses to combined stimulus category: Male.

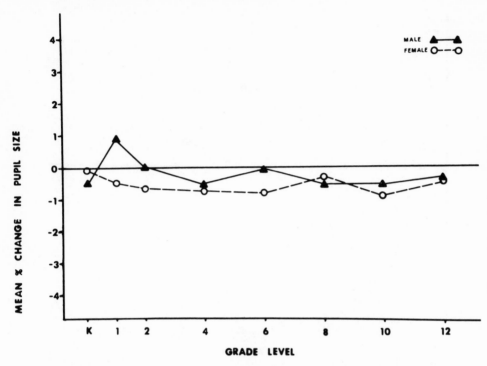

Figure 3. Pupil responses to combined stimulus category: Female.

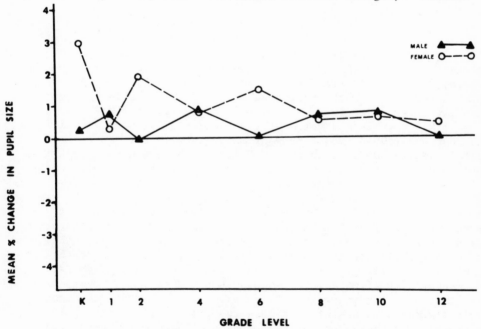

Figure 4. Pupil responses to combined stimulus category: Father.

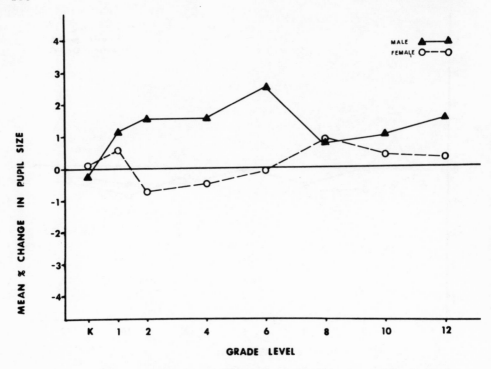

Figure 5. Pupil responses to combined stimulus category: Mother.

        The verbally expressed preferences for these same stimulus
categories provide an interesting contrast. As previously described, subjects verbally ranked the four best liked and the four
least liked of each set of fifteen stimuli. These stimuli were
then given values as follows: best liked was given a value of 1;
least liked was given a value of 15. Accordingly, each verbal
response was ranked from 1 to 4 or 12 to 15 with the non-ranked
stimuli each given a value of 8. Using these values, mean rankings
were calculated for each subject group and for each stimulus category
as well as combined categories. Mann-Whitney U tests (Siegal, 1956)
were made for each of the stimulus categories presented. The results of these two-tailed tests for the five combined stimulus
categories are presented in Table 4. Significant differences between the sexes are demonstrated for the categories baby, mother,
and male with female being marginally non-significant and father
being non-significant. These results can be observed graphically
in the next five figures. It should be noted that the verbal data
was limited to kindergarten through eighth grade. The tenth and
twelfth grade students did not have the time nor inclination to
participate in this stage of the study. In Figure 6 "Verbal responses to stimulus category baby," the females' responses are in

TABLE 4

MANN-WHITNEY "U" TESTS OF SEX DIFFERENCES IN

VERBAL RESPONSE DATA BY CATEGORY

Category	Probability
Baby	.052
Male	.002
Female	.078
Father	---
Mother	.002

marked contrast to the pupil responses observed earlier to the
same stimulus material. In Figure 7 "Verbal responses to combined
stimulus category male," there is no overlap between the responses
of the male and the female subjects. In all cases male responses
are higher than female responses to this stimulus category. In
Figure 8 "Verbal responses to combined stimulus category female,"
the opposite order of responses is seen with a single reversal in
the case of the kindergarten children. In grades 1 through 8 the
female subjects; rankings are higher than those of the male subjects. A single reversal is again seen in Figure 9 "Verbal responses to combined stimulus category father." With the exception
of the kindergarten children, male subjects show consistently
higher responses to these stimuli. In the corresponding data for
the combined stimulus category mother, Figure 10, there is no
overlap whatever. Female responses are consistently higher than
the male responses across all grade levels.

In order to facilitate the comparison between pupil responses
and verbal responses to the same stimulus categories, pupil responses were ranked on a dimension similar to that used with verbal
responses. In addition, since there was very little in the way of
developmental changes observed across the grade levels, all ages
were combined for this particular analysis. These data are presented in Figure 11. Male subjects consistently assigned higher
ranks to babies, mothers, and females; while female subjects
assigned higher ranks to father and male stimuli. Verbal responses
for the comparable data are presented in Figure 12 and show essentially the opposite trends. Male responses are highest to father
and male whereas female responses are highest to baby, mother and
female.

In summary then, the following observations were made. Both

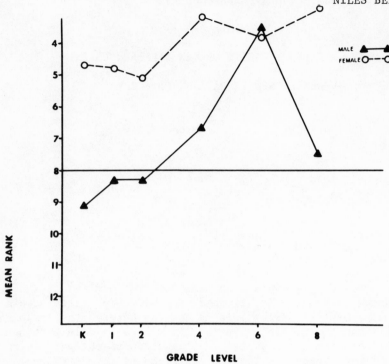

Figure 6.   Verbal responses to stimulus category: Baby.

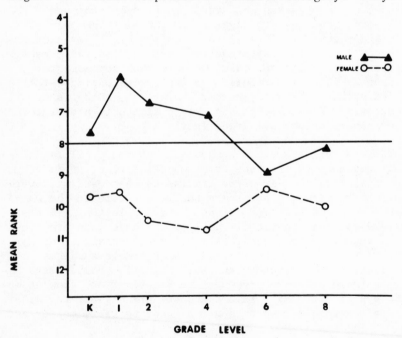

Figure 7.   Verbal responses to combined stimulus category: Male.

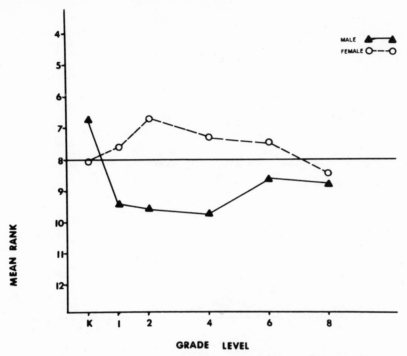

Figure 8.   Verbal responses to combined stimulus category: Female.

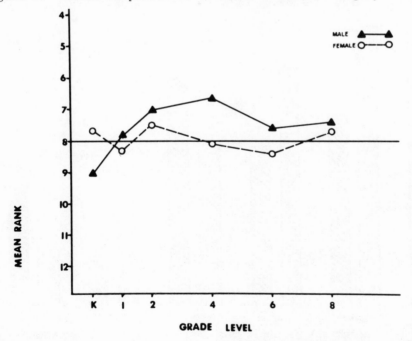

Figure 9.   Verbal responses to combined stimulus category: Father.

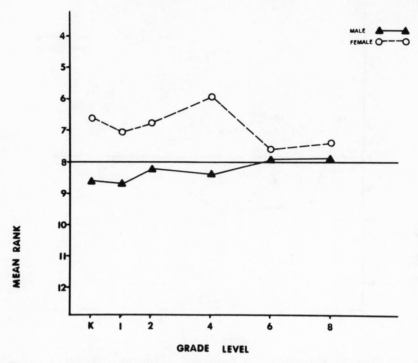

Figure 10.   Verbal responses to combined stimulus category: Mother.

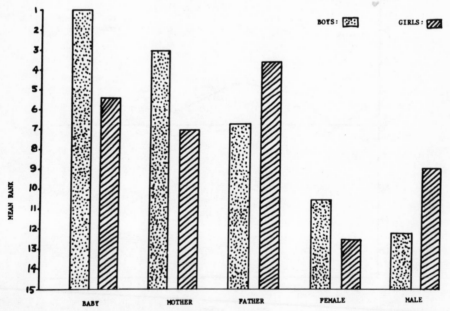

Figure 11.   Mean rank of pupil responses of combined age groups to
the five major stimulus categories.

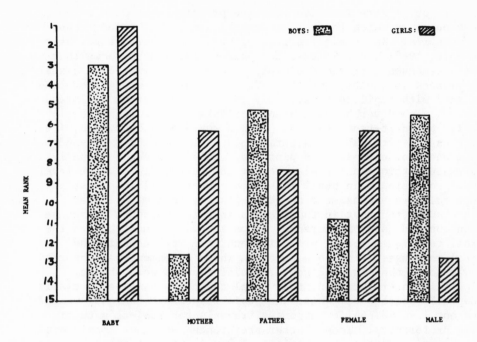

Figure 12. Mean rank of verbal responses of combined age groups
to the five major stimulus categories.

girls and boys of all ages respond positively to pictures of babies,
using both the pupil response and the verbal preference response
techniques. While the pupil responses indicate the boy's responses
to pictures of babies are higher than those of the girls, the
verbal data show the opposite order of preference. In general,
the pupil response data indicate opposite sex preference to peers,
adults and parents, while the verbal data show the same sex objects
to be preferred. Although the order of preference indicated by
the pupil responses to parents and adults is the same, the data
indicate that in general, parents elicit greater positive responses
than do single adults. No such ordering was seen in the verbal
data. In nearly 40 percent of the stimulus categories a marked
shift in preference is seen in the verbal responses between the
kindergarten and first grade. This shift is from opposite sex
preference in kindergarten to same sex preference in the first
grade. In a few cases a similar shift is seen in the pupil response data, however, the shift is observed to be from the same
sex preference to opposite sex preference.

These data have been interpreted in the following way. For
most of the stimulus objects presented, the pupil response data

and the verbal data indicate opposite preferences. Only a few
cases occur in which there is essential agreement between these
two measures. While the findings of Hess and others (e.g., Hess
and Polt, 1960; Hess, Seltzer and Shlien, 1965) have shown that
pupil responses correspond closely with verbally expressed sexual
preferences in adults, verbal preferences in this study show consistency with pupil responses only in the kindergarten children.
Presumably, had verbal data been available for our high school
sample, an adult-type response pattern would have been seen, i.e.,
the 10th and 12th grade subjects would have verbally expressed
preference for opposite sex pictures. This absence of verbally
expressed heterosexual preference at the intermediate grade levels
has no counterpart in pupil responses -- the pupil responses in
these children approximate an adult-like pattern at all ages.
It was suggested that in those cases in which the pupil response
technique indicated preferences opposite those found through the
verbal technique, social proscriptions were reflected in the
verbal responses. In those cases in which agreement was observed
it was noted that these kinds of social factors were absent.
Using this interpretation, the verbal technique assesses socially
acceptable preferences while the pupil response technique, which
does not involve public responses, reveals the subject's underlying preferences. These latter preferences are most consistent
with existing data on the biological development of the sexes
(Diamond, 1965). The observation of consistently larger opposite
sex pupil responses across the ages tested in this study, suggests
that the so-called boy-girl antipathy and latency period phenomena
may be products of social proscription and have no biologic,
genetic or psychological genesis within the child.

    In the next study to be described, the pupil response was
again used as a measure of attitude; however, this time, in the
context of a study specifically designed to physiologically discriminate the two emotional states sexual arousal and anxiety
(Bernick, Kling and Borowitz, 1971). In this study, in order to
produce situations wherein sexual arousal and anxiety were both
likely to occur, a heterosexual erotic movie, a suspense movie,
and a homosexual erotic movie were used in three separate test
sessions. The intent of this design was to maximize the likelihood of occurrence of sexual arousal, anxiety, or a mixed state
of both among our subjects, "normal" males between the ages of 22
and 30. Since we were also interested in changes in attitude as
a result of changed emotional states, a series of slides was presented to each subject before and after each of the stimulus
movies. The slides were selected from the slides employed in the
previous study and represented adult men and women. There were
twelve slides in all, six of men and six of women; half were semi-
clothed and half were clothed. Each slide and its corresponding
control slide was presented for ten seconds with a total time of

four minutes for the set. Again, brightness and contrast variations within this stimulus set were effectively eliminated by
the illumination of the rear projection screen to a constant minimum brightness level. Figure 13 shows a summary of the overall
results of this study irrespective of the content of the slides.
Although the pupil response to the pre-slides is smaller with each
successive session, it is not unreasonable to assume that responsiveness to stimuli with psychological meaning may, in general,
become attenuated upon repetition. No significant differences
were found between the mean responses to the male and female
slides within sessions. This was interpreted as being due to
the innocuous character of these materials, especially in contrast
to the movies presented. Due to the negative trend of responses
to slides already described, absolute comparisons of responses
to male or female slides between sessions are not possible.

In order to determine whether a subject's exposure to the
movies affected the balance of his responses to the male and
female slides, the following calculations were performed. As an
index of the male-female balance within each slide set, mean
responses to the male stimuli were subtracted from mean responses
to the female stimuli yielding scores described as "net female
response." To assess the change in this measure from before to
after each of the movies, the pre-score was subtracted from the
post-score. This final score was labeled "change in net response
to female slides." The data suggested that in subjects aroused
by the heterosexual movie, pupil size tended to increase when
viewing innocuous photographs of females. In subjects aroused
by the homosexual film, pupil size tended to increase when viewing
innocuous photographs of males. Though not statistically significant, this observation deserves further study.

From this more basic research orientation, our interest
shifted to an applied problem of measuring the attitudes of drug
addicts toward drugs and the drug culture. In 1965 B. E. Jones of
the Addiction Research Center attempted to measure the emotional
responses of addicts to drug argot, the special language of the
addict's subculture. He exposed words, some argot, some not,
tachistoscopically to a group of addicts and recorded their recognition thresholds. While his results suggested that addicts had
lower recognition thresholds for argot, the data was somewhat confounded by word familiarity and was accordingly equivocal. Lyle,
Miller, and Monroe in 1970, using a word association technique,
found they were able to reliably identify the extent of their
addict subjects' identification to the addict subculture. Unfortunately, their technique, while appropriate for their sample
and test situation, requires cooperative respondents and is particularly vulnerable to voluntary distortion. After searching the
literature and finding that no techniques other than these had

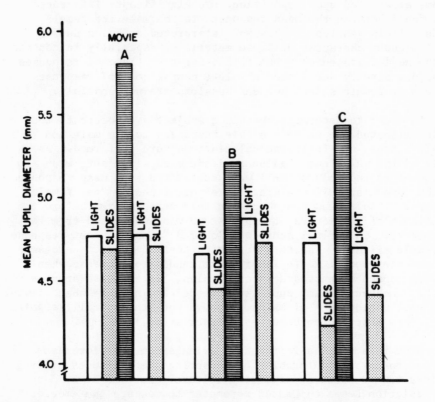

Figure 13. Mean pupil diameter during various stages of three experimental sessions. Reprinted with permission from Bernick, N., Kling, A., and Borowitz, G. *Psychosomatic Medicine*, 1971, *33*, 341-352.

been used for this purpose, it became clear that a psychophysiological approach to this problem might be profitable. In two
studies, we exposed the same type of materials Jones had used to
our subjects while recording changes in pupil size. (Altman,
Bernick, and Mintz, 1972; Bernick, Altman, and Mintz, 1972).

The design for the first study called for a comparison between
the responses of addicts and non-addicts to the argot and non-
argot words. The non-addicts or controls were chosen from a group
of staff members at the Clinical Research Center. They were all
familiar with drug argot but, we assumed, not likely to identify
with it, be committed to it, or show an emotional response to it.
We felt that using a naive control group for this study would not
allow us to answer the question: Were our addict subjects responding emotionally to the argot or were they responding to their
recognition of these words as being argot in the manner of a problem solving response? By using staff as control subjects, the
essential difference between our experimentals and our controls
was their involvement in addiction.

At another level we were still interested in the comparison
of our subjects with naive subjects and with this in mind, we
chose double entendre words for the drug argot. Unfortunately,
our results did not lead us in this direction and a naive subject
group was never tested.

The stimulus words were composed of ten control and ten experimental words; the latter being double entendre words, one of whose
meanings was from the drug argot. They were all highly familiar
and were matched on the basis of length and "straight" meaning.
The order of presentation was randomized. The words were presented via a tape recording under constant light conditions. Eleven
addict subjects and eight control subjects were tested individually.
Pupil size was continuously recorded every one-half second by means
of infrared cinematography as in the previous studies. .Following
a three and one-half minute adaptation period and a forty-five
second period when the screen before the subjects was alternately
at 15, 0 and then 15 footcandles (for the purpose of testing the
pupillary light reflex), a list of words was presented, one every
five seconds. Subjects were instructed during the adaptation period:
"Look at the center of the screen, think about what each word means,
and do not talk." The results of this study are shown in Table 5.
While both groups of subjects showed significant differences in
response to the stimulus categories (p<.01) the groups were not
statistically discriminable in this differential response. The
absolute difference in pupil size between groups is accountable
in terms of differences in subjects' ages. Without belaboring the
logic of our interpretation at this time, we tentatively concluded
that all of our subjects were exhibiting a cognitive response

TABLE 5

ARGOT STUDY I: MEAN PUPIL RESPONSES

STIMULI

		ARGOT	NON-ARGOT
	Addicts in Treatment	3.895	3.949
SUBJECTS			
	Controls (Staff)	3.775	3.814

that they found it easier to think about argot than non-argot, possibly because of the clear and frequent use of these words in our setting.

We felt that if we were to observe the emotional responses which were hypothesized, we would have to load the test conditions so that more stress and involvement might be obtained.   To accomplish this our second study employed stronger, less ambiguous argot.   These words were presented visually rather than orally, and subjects were required to read aloud each word as it was projected on the screen.   The design was changed so that each of our ten subjects served as his own control, and a third category of stimuli having *a priori* emotional impact was added to the test battery; namely sex-related words.   Words were typewritten and photographed in the form of slides for visual presentation. Stimulus slides were alternated with blank slides and each presented for five seconds.   The stimulus slides were presented in random order, corrected for split-half frequency.   Our initial analysis of these data was again disappointing.   Mean pupil size did not differ significantly between the stimulus categories.

At this point we were forced to question our naive assumption that the group labeled, "addicts" was a homogeneous group.   If these subjects represented a range of commitment to addiction, they should show a similar range of response to our stimuli.   We had available a series of psychometric tests routinely administered to addicts upon admission to the Clinical Research Center.   Included in these tests were several scales which relate to orientation to addiction and to sex.   By ordering our subjects on these dimensions and relating this order to that observed with our stimuli, we were able to test this heterogeneity hypothesis.

Two scales were used to estimate drug culture involvement,

Language of Addiction and Acceptability for Psychotherapy. The
Language of Addiction scale has been shown to reflect the commitment and specificity of an individual's abuse of opiates (Haertzen,
Monroe, Hooks, and Hill, 1970; Monroe, English, and Haertzen, 1971).
The Acceptability for Psychotherapy scale is used to select addicts
who are least committed to the life of the addict; that is, those
hypothesized to be most treatable (Berzins, Ross, and Monroe, 1970).
To measure sexual orientation, the MF scale of the MMPI was included in the analysis. Finally, on the chance that we might
only be tapping verbal intelligence, another scale specifically
designed for that purpose, called Vocabulary Estimate, was also
included. Our first perusal of the Language of Addiction and
Acceptability for Psychotherapy scales verified our suspicions
about the homogeneity of our addict sample. The scores were well
distributed. We accordingly ran correlations between pupil responses to drug and sex words with the four psychometric scales.
As expected, relative pupil responses to drug and sex words were
not significantly related to the Vocabulary Estimate scale. Pupil
responses to drug words were significantly correlated to both of
the drug related scales and in the expected directions: Language
of Addiction (r = .71 p<.025) and Acceptable for Psychotherapy
(r = -.62 p<.05). While pupil responses to drug words were un-
correlated to the MF scale, responses to the sex words did correlate significantly (r = -.61 p<.05) and in the predicted direction
with this scale which reflects sexual orientation. These results
support the hypothesis that pupil size reflects the emotional
impact of stimulation, however, it also suggests that unless the
differences one is examining are of a large magnitude, the data
may have to be analyzed on the basis of individual differences.

About this time we were also working on this problem from
another point of departure. One of the most reliable demonstrations of the pupil response in psychology has been in conjunction
with problem-solving activities. At the suggestion of one of our
staff members, Dan Mintz, we thought it might be possible to take
advantage of the phenomenon by imposing on a problem-solving situation the emotionally loaded material we were interested in. We
hoped that this material would differentially affect problem-solving
as a function of its content.

A pilot study was undertaken with eight subjects, four addicts
and four staff controls (Mintz, Bernick, and Altman, 1972). The
subjects were presented with a series of fifteen paired geometric
patterns and asked to manually indicate by means of a lever,
whether each pair of patterns was the same or different. Problem
slides were pre-tested and behaviorally determined to be of equal
difficulty. Three categories of pictoral stimuli were prepared;
neutral, sex, and drug. Each problem slide was preceded by a ten
second exposure of one of the stimulus slides. When the subject

responded to the problem by moving the lever, the problem slide
was replaced by the next stimulus slide. All slides were care-
fully matched for brightness and were of minimal, though acceptable
contrast.

The results indicate that addict subjects have the greatest
dilation to those problems preceded by drug related material,
while the non-addicts show their greatest dilation to problems
preceded by the sex-related material. It is also interesting to
note that the addict subjects, who are usually observed clinically
to be less active sexually, were least affected by the sexual
material.

By inference then, the addicts were most distracted by the
drug-related material since they showed more dilation to problems
which followed drug stimuli. The same inference may be drawn
from our control subjects' responses to sex-related material.
These observations are, of course, based on small samples. Although
an analysis of variance was performed and a significant categories
effect was obtained, there were too few subjects to test for differences between subject groups.

While the results of this pilot study are hardly conclusive,
we were encouraged enough to begin a program of development for
this new technique of attitude assessment. Now, rather than directly assessing emotional responses during stimulation, responses
to such stimuli may be assessed indirectly by observing their influence on well-defined problem solving situations. In order to
avoid the complications attendant with the use of visual stimulation in the problem solving task, we decided to employ simple
digit-span memory problems, similar to those used earlier by a
number of other researchers. For our purposes, however, we required maximum control of the experimental situation, particularly
with reference to the demand characteristics of that situation,
since we were most interested in manipulating emotional responses.

The following study was undertaken as a first step toward
developing a test situation whose parameters are well enough defined as to permit a definitive test of the proposed indirect
assessment technique (Bernick and Altman, 1973). Two basic conditions were employed. In the first condition, subjects were told
in advance that they would be required to repeat the digits which
they had heard previously upon cue. In the second condition,
subjects were told they would either have to repeat the digits
they had heard previously on cue or merely think the digits they
had heard previously. For this second condition two cues were
provided: "Repeat" and "Think". By these manipulations we hoped
to separate and thereby clarify the emotional and cognitive components of this relatively simple problem solving situation.

The subjects for this study were sixteen male post-addicts in treatment at the Clinical Research Center in Lexington. These subjects were randomly divided into two age-matched groups of eight subjects each. Each group was composed of five whites and three blacks. The instrumentation was essentially the same as that used in the previously described studies. Throughout the experiment a gray slide with a white "X" in the center was projected on the screen providing an illumination level of fifteen footcandles measured at the screen. A tape player and loud speaker were used to present the instructions and the auditory stimuli.

The stimuli consisted of 24 randomly selected series of numbers, eight containing four digits, eight containing five digits, and eight containing six digits. Four of the number series for each digit length were presented to the variable group followed by the instruction "Repeat" and hereafter referred to as "repeat" stimuli. The other four stimuli for each digit length were those followed by the instruction: "Think" and are designated as "think" stimuli. The order in which the number of digits and the instructions "Repeat" and "Think" were presented was randomized. The constant group received the same stimuli in the same order as the variable group but were instructed to "Repeat" for all of the stimuli.

The experimental group with the variable instructions heard the following: "This experiment will last about ten minutes. During the experiment you are to look at the "X" on the screen in front of you while we photograph your eyes. You will hear some numbers such as 1 0 0 9 or 3 2 5 3 3, or 2 6 8 9 8 0. Before you hear the numbers, you will hear the word "Ready." A few seconds later you will be asked either to say the numbers back or just to think the numbers. If the instruction is "Repeat" you are to say the numbers that you have just heard at about the same rate you heard them. If the instruction is "Think" you are to think the numbers you just heard at about the rate you heard them, but not repeat them out loud. When you have had enough time to respond you will hear the word OK". At that time you are to stop and wait until you hear the next ready signal. Remember, keep looking at the "X". Let's try a couple of examples. (Ready, 3 2 1 3 5, repeat. OK, ready, 3 2 5 3 3, think, OK.)"

The constant instruction group received essentially the same instructions except that they were told only to repeat each number series on cue. Upon completion of the instructions to the subjects the tape was stopped and the subject asked if he understood. Any questions were answered, whereupon the tape was restarted and pupil size recorded continuously for the remainder of the experiment. The time required to present the instructions served as an adaptation period.

The "OK" signal indicated the end of one trial and the start of the next. Five seconds later the next "Ready" cue was presented. The period between the OK signal and the Ready cue was used as a baseline period. The stimulus period, the time required to present the stimulus, lasted between three and four seconds. A delay period, lasting three seconds then followed, after which the appropriate response instruction was given. The time allowed for the response period was five seconds and was terminated by the "OK" signal initiating the next trial. Each trial accordingly lasted between sixteen and seventeen seconds. On the film record, the last frame of the baseline period and the first frame of the stimulus period were purposely fogged to provide a means of locating the stimulus at the time of analysis and were lost as data. Thus, each trial provided between thirty and thirty-two pupil size measurements. While the analysis of this data is soon to be published in considerable detail, I would like to present an overview of the results by means of the following set of graphs.

While not relevant to the present discussion, Figure 14 presents the differences between responses to different numbers of digits for the "think" stimuli by the constant instruction group. It is clear that the more digits presented, the more dilation observed. This data is in agreement with that of other studies and is presented here merely to indicate that we are dealing with the same phenomenon.

Figure 15 presents data from the same group of subjects but is limited to the stimuli with six digits (as are all of the subsequent graphs.) This data is typical of that seen in other studies using the digit span paradigm. Mean pupil size is on the ordinate expressed in mm, time is on the abscissa, with each point representing one-half second. The first period is recovery and baseline. During the second period, or stimulus period, the digits are presented to the subject. The third period is the three second delay, and the fourth period is when the subject responds. For all subjects, under all conditions, changes in pupil size are essentially identical up to the response period. This graph and the three graphs that follow are considered representative of the results of this study -- the findings they demonstrate have been extensively verified statistically.

During the first part of the baseline period there is generally constriction -- interpreted as recovery from the previous trial. During both the stimulus and delay periods pupil size increases, although most of the increase occurs during the stimulus period. For the constant instruction group a slight dilation is

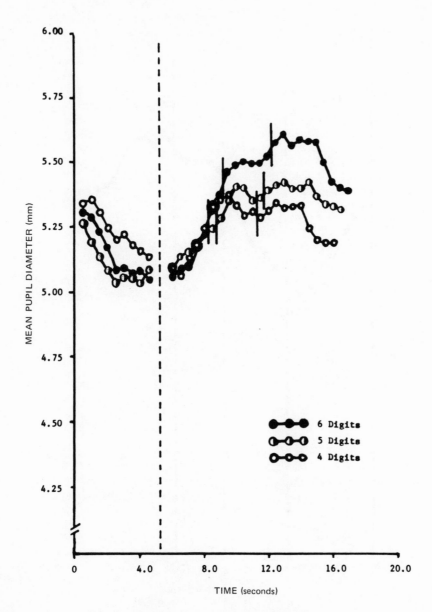

Figure 14. Effect of number of digits on pupil responses during the digit span task. Subjects: Constant Instruction Group (n = 8) Stimulus Set: Think (12 stimuli).

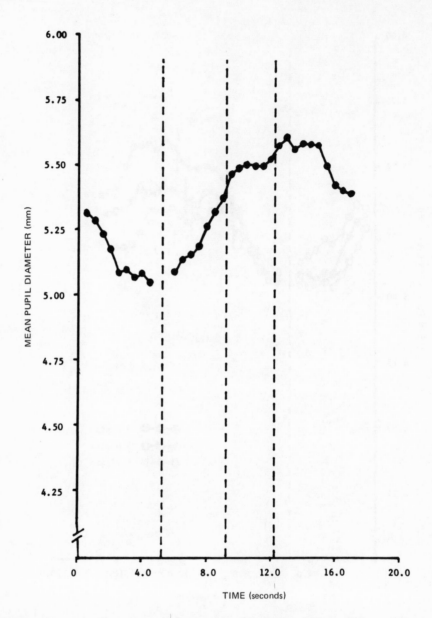

Figure 15. Pupil responses during the digit span task. Subjects: Constant Instruction Group (n = 8) Stimulus Set: Think (4 stimuli) Digits: 6.

observed during the first part of the response period, while constriction occurs during the latter part of that period. The same
response is seen in the next Figure (16) which presents the responses of the same group to the other set of stimuli. The first
part of the response period corresponds to the interval when the
subjects were actually speaking, while the second part represents
the time after completion of the utterance.

The variable instruction group shows two different response
patterns corresponding to the two instructions given. As seen in
Figure 17, the Repeat instruction appears to produce a marked and
immediate dilation followed by constriction. The Think instruction is followed by an immediate pupillary constriction as seen
in Figure 18. While the same cognitive responses were required
of the two groups which verbalized the digits, their pupillary
responses are clearly different. The uncertainty of the instructions given the variable group might be construed as producing a
problem solving situation, hence the dilation following the instruction might be due to the resolution of the uncertainty, however, since no such dilation is seen in the matched group in
which no verbalization was required, it appears that these results
may be most parsimoniously explained in terms of the emotional
response produced by the requirement for subjects to make a public
response without advanced preparation.

The next step in this research program will involve the in-
sertion of emotionally loaded material in the delay period of the
digit span paradigm. We would expect that the effect of such
material will be similar to that produced by the "Repeat" instruction in the variable instruction group although the possibility
exists that some kinds of materials might have the opposite effect.

What has been described in the foregoing has been a series
of experiments using primarily the direct approach and finally
the indirect approach for the assessment of psychological attitudes employing the pupil response as the primary measure. While
the results have not always been clear-cut and occasionally even
disappointing, on the whole, the evidence supports the original
contention that the pupil does indeed reflect changes in attitude.

In these studies we have used a relatively restricted range
of stimulation, and in almost all cases we have used stimuli of
low "intensity". The pupillary responses evidenced have been of
correspondingly low amplitude. When more intense stimuli have
been employed such as those used by Bernick, Kling and Borowitz
(1971), very large changes in pupil diameter were observed.
Whether or not these different magnitudes of response are qualitatively the same remains to be seen. The physiological mobilization associated with experimentally produced sexual arousal
and anxiety may be mediated in a different way than the small

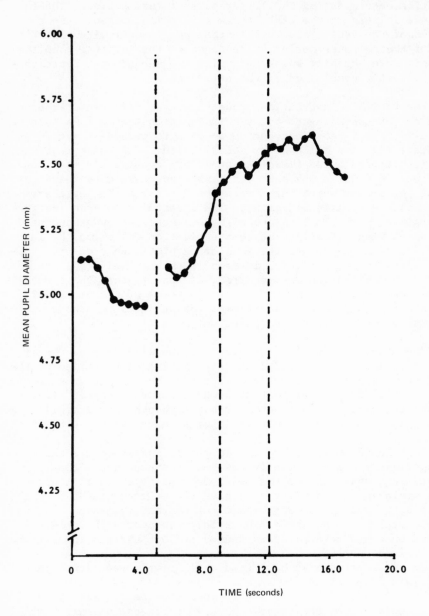

Figure 16. Pupil responses during the digit span task. Subjects
Constant Instruction Group (n = 8) Stimulus Set: Repeat (4
stimuli) Digits: 6.

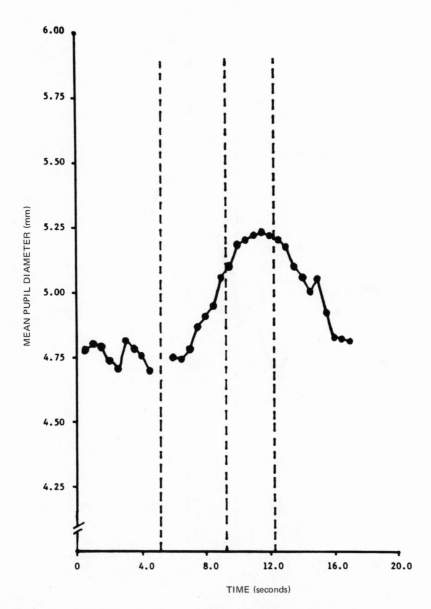

Figure 17. Pupil responses during the digit span task. Subjects: Variable Instruction Group (n = 8) Stimulus Set: Think (4 stimuli) Digits: 6.

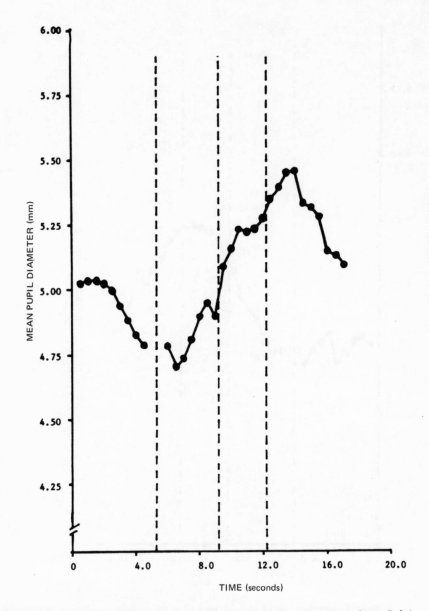

Figure 18. Pupil responses during the digit span task. Subjects:
Variable Instruction Group (n = 8) Stimulus Set: Repeat (4
stimuli) Digits: 6.

pupillary changes produced by our mild stimuli.

Since we are now able to identify the components of a response to the digit span task, a relatively simple memory problem, it is possible to predict responses in this situation with fairly high precision. By using the paradigm demonstrated in the pilot study described earlier in which emotionally loaded stimuli were inserted into a problem solving situation, it may be possible to discriminate subtle differences in emotional responses to these stimuli indirectly, thus avoiding the whole complex of variables associated with the presentation of stimuli whether visual, auditory or whatever. While it is the writer's view that the direct approach is superior in terms of gaining the greatest amount of information and can, with proper caution, be used practically, the indirect approach appears worthy of consideration, particularly for those who are most concerned with the complete control of the experimental conditions.

ACKNOWLEDGMENTS

The author would like to express his appreciation to all of those who have contributed to the research presented in this paper. In addition to those whose contributions are evidenced by co-authorship, special thanks are due to Dr. Eckhard H. Hess, Dr. Theodore Schaefer Jr., and Dr. Jerome S. Miller for their critical comments and encouragement.

REFERENCES

Altman, F., Bernick, N., and Mintz, D. L. Pupil responses of addicts in treatment to drug culture argot: I. Auditory presentation of double entendre words. *Psychonomic Science*, 1972, *28*, 79-80.

Bernick, N. Development of children's preferences for social objects as evidenced by their pupil responses. Unpublished doctoral dissertation, The University of Chicago, 1966.

Bernick, N., and Altman, F. Pupil size as an indicator of the cognitive and emotional components of a simple memory task. In preparation. (1973).

Bernick, N., Altman, F., and Mintz, D. L. Pupil responses of addicts in treatment to drug culture argot: II. Responses during verbalization of visually presented words. *Psychonomic Science*, 1972, *28*, 81-82.

Bernick, N., Kling, A., and Borowitz, G. Physiological differentiation of sexual arousal and anxiety. *Psychosomatic Medicine*, 1971, *33*, 341-352.

Bernick, N., and Oberlander, M.   Effect of verbalization and two
  different modes of experiencing on pupil size. *Perception and
  Psychophysics*, 1968, *3*, 327-330.
Berzins, J. I., Ross, W. F., and Monroe, J. J.   Crossvalidation
  of the Hill-Monroe acceptability for psychotherapy scale for
  addict males. *Journal of Clinical Psychology*, 1970, *26*, 199-201.
Diamond, M.   Critical evaluation of the ontogeny of human sexual
  behavior. *Quarterly Review of Biology*, 1965, *40*, 2.
Goldwater, B. C.   Psychological significance of pupillary movements.
  Psychological Bulletin, 1972, *77*, 340-355.
Haertzen, C. A., Monroe, J. J., Hooks, N. T. Jr., and Hill, H. E.
  The language of addiction. *The International Journal of the
  Addictions*, 1970, *5*, 115-129.
Hess, E. H.   Attitude and Pupil size. *Scientific American*, 1965,
  212, 46-54.
Hess, E. H.   Pupillometrics: A method of studying mental, emotional,
  and sensory processes. In, N. S. Greenfield, and R. A. Sternbach
  (Eds.), *Handbook of Psychophysiology*. New York: Holt, Rinehart
  and Winston, Inc., 1972.
Hess, E. H., and Polt, J. M.   Pupil size as related to interest
  value of visual stimuli. *Science*, 1960, *132*, 349-350.
Hess, E. H., Seltzer, A. L., and Shlien, J. M.   Pupil response of
  hetero- and homosexual males to pictures of men and women.   A
  pilot study. *Journal of Abnormal Psychology*, 1965, *70*, 165-168.
Johnson, L. C., and Lubin, A.   On planning psychophysiological
  experiments.   In, N. S. Greenfield, and R. A. Sternbach (Eds.),
  Handbook of Psychophysiology. New York: Holt, Rinehart and
  Winston, Inc., 1972.
Jones, B. E.   Visual recognition thresholds for narcotic argot
  in postaddicts. *Perceptual and Motor Skills*, 1965, *20*, 1065-1069.
Lyle, W. H., Jr., Miller, J. S., and Monroe, J. H.   A word association measure of knowledge of addict jargon as an indicator of
  identification with an addict subculture. *The International
  Journal of the Addictions*, 1970, *5*, 233-243.
Mintz, D. L., Bernick, N., and Altman, F.   Pupil responses to
  emotionally laden visual stimuli followed by a problem solving
  task. Unpublished manuscript. (1972).
Monroe, J. J., English, G. E., and Haertzen, C. A.   the language
  of addiction scales. Validity generalization of effects of
  labeling as drug addict or alcoholic. *Quarterly Journal of
  Studies on Alcohol*, 1971, *32*, 1048-1054.
Siegal, S.   *Nonparametric Statistics for the Behavioral Sciences*.
  New York: McGraw-Hill Book Co., Inc., 1956.

CHAPTER VIII:

THE PRESENT STATE OF PUPILLOMETRICS

Eckhard H. Hess and Elizabeth Goodwin

Department of Psychology, University of Chicago

PUPILLOMETRICS DURING THE PAST 13 YEARS

As is well known, Hess and Polt (1960) published the first modern report on pupillometrics, which demonstrated, even though the methodology, in terms of controlling completely for brightness contrast, had not yet been perfected, that sequential pupil size changes in response to an experimental situation provide a quantified method of measuring or scoring how appealing or interesting something is. In the subsequent five years Hess gave many lectures and colloquia on his research over the country so that many scientific people learned about pupil phenomena even though the published literature was not yet extensive.

In the mid-sixties wide public attention was brought to pupillometrics. Hess published an account of his work in *Scientific American* in 1965 and the *Saturday Evening Post* published an article on the subject in 1966. In 1966 the British Broadcasting Corporation produced a T.V. show on Hess' work in pupillometrics. Gerald Walker's *Best Magazine Articles* for 1965 reprinted the *Scientific American* article in 1966. As a result, not only laymen, but also some academicians became aware of psychopupil responses. There are now quite a few scientists doing serious research in pupillometrics, and the present Symposium is but one manifestation of this fact. There are now at least five different companies manufacturing and selling devices for pupillometric studies, according to the criterion that equipment that measures only one eye is intended to be used in pupillometrics rather than for the older and well established field of pupillography, which investigates pupil responses to light, drugs, and various neurophysiological conditions.

Many other investigators have used pupillometric assessment of differential psychological responses to stimuli. Among these investigators are Atwood and Howell (1971), Barlow (1969, 1970), Bergum and Lehr (1966), van Bortel (1968), Coss (1965, 1972), Coverdale and Leavitt (1968), Fitzgerald (1968), Fredericks and Groves (1971), Kennedy (1971), Krugman (1964a, b), Nunnally, Knott, Duchnowski and Parker (1967), Schwartz (1973), Sheflin (1969), Simms (1967), Tanck and Robbins (1970). Of particular interest is the use of pupillometrics in marketing research by Krugman, by van Bortel, and by Coverdale and Leavitt. There is now at least one market research agency in existence which is using pupillometrics as its primary research tool. This is the Perception Research Services company in Englewood Cliffs, New Jersey.

Of particular importance in the use of pupillometrics in advertising and marketing research is the measurement of attitude changes, as reported by Hess in 1965. Not only is this technique important in such research, but is also of considerable potential value in psychotherapeutic research. A recent example is Kennedy's (1971) study of alcoholics in treatment. Kennedy found that those patients under treatment who still dilated their pupils to their favorite alcoholic beverage when they had nearly completed treatment had a much higher rate of recidivism than did the treated patients whose pupils evidenced decreased pupil dilation in response to their alcoholic beverages.

Pupillometric assessment techniques were expanded to utilize filmed motion picture material when Niles Bernick, working in Hess' laboratory, developed a method of automatically controlling brightness at a constant level. This was done by setting up a photocell unit that scanned film just before it entered the filmgate of the projector. The photocell determined the overall brightness of each film section and opened and shut down a lens diaphragm fitted on the projector lens. This technique thus permitted the use of filmed motion material for pupillometric assessment rather than solely still photographs.

Figure 1 shows pupil responses to a T.V. commercial which was shown with its brightness controlled, with its brightness uncontrolled, and completely out of focus, thus producing a "brightness field". Inspection of the figure shows that the pupil responses to the commercial with its brightness uncontrolled reflect both the influences of the brightness level and the psychological responses depicted by the pupil responses to the commercial with its brightness controlled as described. One of the first things that we found in working with brightness controlled filmed material was that subjects' pupil responses to such material often were much stronger than to still material. It thus appears that filmed material is generally more appealing to viewers than still pictures.

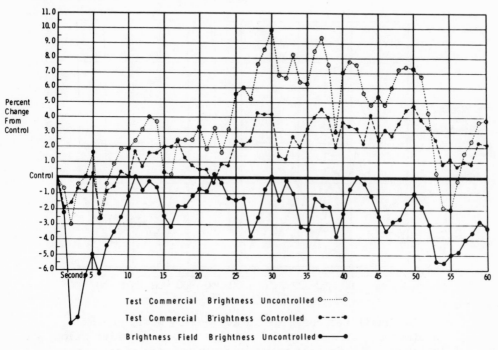

Figure 1. Pupil responses to a test commercial for television, under three viewing conditions: (a) with the brightness controlled by the automatic photocell-lens diaphragm method devised by Bernick and Hess, as explained in the text; (b) with the brightness uncontrolled, and (c) completely out of focus and brightness uncontrolled, thus producing a series of brightness changes.

Figures 2, 3, and 4 depict successive ten minute segments of a half hour television show that was presented in the Hess pupil Apparatus, with the brightness control method, to 50 men and 50 women. In general it can be seen that the men and the women had fairly similar pupillary responses to successive portions of the show. For all the subjects the interest reflected by the pupillary responses tended to reach increasingly higher levels. During the last ten minutes the average pupil dilation of 1 mm from the control size was greater than the average pupil response that has ever been obtained for 100 experimental subjects for any still picture stimulus. A mean pupil size change of 1 mm for 100 subjects is extremely significant, particularly when it is considered that most investigators work in terms of .1 or .01 mm size changes in such population sizes.

Another methodological advance made in Hess' laboratory (Hess 1965) was that of determining where in a visual stimulus a subject is looking during each frame of the filmed pupil record.

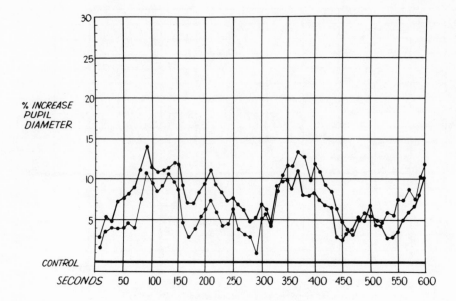

Figure 2. The pupil responses of 50 men and 50 women to the
first ten minutes (600 seconds) of a brightness controlled pilot
television show. The men and women had essentially similar pupil
responses

This permitted the assessment of the relative interest value of
each portion of the visual stimulus. For example, men often show
pupil dilation to pictures of mothers with babies or children.
Such analysis revealed that the positive pupil responsiveness was
elicited by the mother rather than by the child. Some of the new
commercial pupillometric devices now permit the automatic determination of where subjects are looking during experimentation so
that such information may be correlated with the pupil response.

Hess and Polt (1964) published the first quantified study
of arithmetic calculation effects upon the pupil. Heinrich (1896)
and Roubinovitch (1900, 1901) had done some work in this area.
However, Hess' work represented a distinct advance in that pupil
responses were found to correlate with the difficulty of the mental
calculation task and in that discrete stages in the process of
the task were discernable. Hess' (1964, 1965) reports, for example,
showed that pupil responses increased as a subject performed the
mental work and reached a peak when the answer was found. When
the answer was given the subjects' pupil sizes returned abruptly
to the control level. A subject who had reached a solution and
then recalculated to check the answer before reporting it was

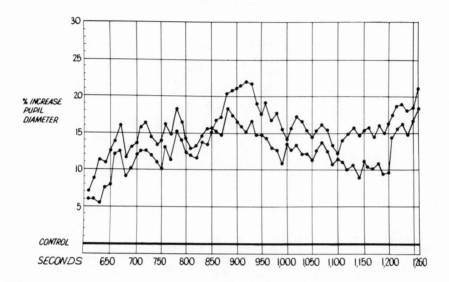

Figure 3. The pupil responses of 50 men and 50 women to the
second ten minutes (601-1260 seconds) of a brightness controlled
pilot television show.   The men and women had essentially similar
pupil responses.

found to have two distinct pupil response peaks in his pupil record.
After Hess reported these findings, Kahneman and his associates in
their several studies focussed upon these increases and decreases
in pupil size as a function of mental processing. Kahneman and
Beatty (1966, 1967) called the increasing pupil size during processing "loading" and the decreasing pupil size after the giving
of the answer "unloading". More recently Kahneman (e.g., 1973)
has replaced the term "unloading" with the term "dumping".

     Kahneman and his associates have indeed shown the fruitfulness
of using pupil size changes as a method of studying mental processes.
Among their studies are Beatty and Kahneman (1966), Kahneman (1967),
Kahneman and Beatty (1966, 1967), Kahneman, Beatty and Pollack
(1967), Kahneman, Onuska and Wolman (1968), Kahneman and Peavler
(1969), Kahneman, Peavler and Onuska (1968), Kahneman, Tursky,
Shapiro and Crider (1969), Peavler (1969), Peavler and McLaughlin
(1967).   Many other investigators have also studied mental pro-
cessing pupillometrically: Boersma, Wilton, Barham and Muir (1970),
Bradshaw (1968), Clark and Johnson (1970), Colman and Paivio (1970),
Elshtain and Schaefer (1968), Johnson (1970), McElvain (1970),
Paivio and Simpson (1966), Payne, Parry and Harasymiw (1968),

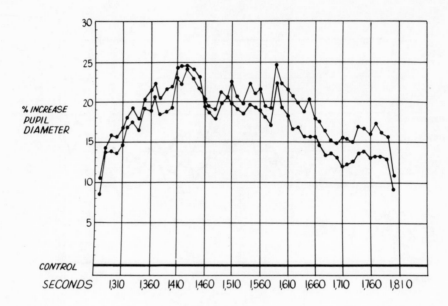

Figure 4. The pupil responses of 50 men and 50 women to the last
ten minutes (1261-1800 seconds) of a brightness controlled pilot
television show. The men and women had essentially similar pupil
responses. The observed dilations at the climactic portions at
1410-1430 seconds and at 1590 seconds are greater than any that
have ever been observed in Hess' laboratories for 100 subjects
viewing a still picture stimulus.

Polt (1970), Schaefer, Ferguson, Klein and Rawson (1968), Simpson
(1967), Simpson and Climan (1971), Simpson, Molloy, Hale and
Climan (1968), Simpson and Paivio (1966, 1968).

Not only has pupillometrics been used to quantify psychological responses to visual stimuli and to mental processing, but
also to quantify responses to gustatory (Hess and Polt, 1966),
olfactory (Hess and Polt, unpublished), and auditory stimuli
(Hess, 1965, and unpublished observations) such as music and baby
cries. Beck (1967) has investigated pupil responses to various
rates of soft click sounds.

PUPIL RESPONSES AND NONVERBAL COMMUNICATION PROCESSES

In recent years research in the area of nonverbal and nonconscious human communication has made important contributions to
our knowledge of human behavior. Body postures, arm, leg and hand
movements, and facial expressions have all been intensively studied.
Eye behavior has also attracted much attention as a means of non-

verbal communication with gaze direction and eye contact being the
subject of much investigation.

As may be recalled, the earliest findings in modern pupillometrics (Hess and Polt, 1960) were that men and women, even though
they looked at identical series of photographs, had different
patterns of different pupil responses to these pictures. Men's
pupils tended to dilate when looking at pictures of attractive
women but not when looking at pictures of babies or of men. Women's
pupils, on the other hand, tended to dilate when looking at pictures
of attractive men or of babies but not when looking at pictures of
women.

As an outgrowth of these findings, men were presented with
two pictures of an attractive young woman's face (Hess, 1965).
These two pictures were identical except that in one her pupils
had been retouched to make them extraordinarily large and in the
other they had been retouched to make them extraordinarily small.
Her expression was a noncommittal one. The men were shown these
two pictures as part of a larger series of slides in the pupil
apparatus (described in Hess, 1972). The subjects were interviewed
after they had seen the slides. They were asked if they remembered
seeing two pictures of a young girl. They all remembered having
seen her. Then they were asked if she had seemed any different
the two times she had been shown. Most of the men gave responses
that were much more positive toward the slide that had the large
eye pupils than toward the one that had the small eye pupils. Subsequently when the film records of the pupil responses toward the
slide presentations were examined, it was found that the men's
pupils during the viewing of the large-pupilled picture were significantly larger than they were during the viewing of the small-
pupilled picture. But when the men were questioned none of them
were able to identify the difference in the eye pupil size as the
source of the differences in their feelings toward the two slide
presentations. When they were shown large prints from these slides
they were again much more positive toward the picture of her with
the large pupils than toward the other one, they still did not see
that the eye pupils differed. In fact, in some cases this had to
be pointed out to them.

We hypothesized that the reason that the large-pupilled picture elicited more positive pupil and verbal responses from the
subjects is that the large pupils were, at least on the nonconscious
level, associated with positively toned sexual interest. Since then
several studies by other investigators as well as in our laboratories
have supported and elaborated upon these findings regarding the pupil
response as a nonverbal indicator of psychosexual interest.

For example, we hypothesized that the cross-sexual pupil response, if it truly were a psychosexual response, ought not to be

shown in the same way by homosexuals as by heterosexuals. That
is, homosexuals should show more positive pupil responses to
pictures of persons of their own sex than to ones of the opposite
sex. This appeared a reasonable hypothesis to investigate since
a few men in our early studies gave atypical pupil responses,
that is, showed pupil dilations to pictures of men and not to
pictures of women. In reviewing these atypical cases it appeared
possible that these particular men might be homosexual in orientation. We did a study of five men known to be heterosexual and
five men known to be homosexual (Hess, Seltzer and Shlien, 1965).
Several female and male pictures were shown to these subjects
among a set that also included abstract artistic representations.
None of the *specific* pictures consistently differentiated between
the heterosexual and the homosexual subjects, but we did find
that the mean total difference in response to the male and female
pictures did differentiate between the homosexuals and the heterosexuals. The mean total response difference was obtained by calcu-
lating, for each subject, his mean response to all the male pictures, and his mean response to all the female pictures, and then
the difference between these two mean responses. If the mean
pupil size in response to the female pictures was larger than the
mean pupil size in response to the male picture, the difference
was considered positive. If the reverse obtained, the difference
was considered negative. All heterosexual subjects had positive
response difference scores, whereas only one homosexual subject
did, and his positive response difference score was smaller than
the smallest positive response difference score for the heterosexual group. Hence, there was actually no overlap in the response difference scores of the two subject groups.

Simms (1967) did a study which replicated and extended our
findings. He made up facial photos of men and of women having
large and small pupil sizes and showed them to heterosexual men
and women. Both men and women had larger pupils in response to
the photo of the opposite-sex person with the large pupils than
with the small pupils, as would be expected. The pupils of the
male subjects increased very little in size toward the pictures
of men. The women subjects had the same pupil size in response
to the picture of the woman with small pupils as in response to
the picture of the man with small pupils, whereas their pupil
size in response to the picture of the woman with large pupils was
even smaller. These findings support the notion that pupil sizes
in a stimulus person are responded to in terms of implied sexual
interest.

Simms has conducted further pupillometric research, as yet
unpublished, which showed that Don Juans and homosexuals have the
same pupil response pattern toward pictures of women with large
versus small pupils. That is, their pupils show a preference for
women with small pupils over women with large pupils. Simms has

hypothesized that both Don Juans and homosexuals have an aversion
to women whose pupil responses indicate sexual interest, even
though their overt responses appear so different. Simms has
suggested that while homosexuals apparently avoid women, Don Juans'
seductions are essentially attacks upon them, particularly since
these seductions are followed by abandonment.

Atwood and Howell (1971) have extended pupillometric methods
to the study of pedophilia. They studied a group of men who had
been put in jail for nonviolently molesting young girls and another
group of men who were in jail for nonsexual offenses. The pedophiliacs' pupils dilated in response to pictures of immature females but constricted slightly to pictures of adult females. The
nonpedophiliac jail inmates, however, showed the normal pattern
of pupil dilation to pictures of the adult women, and very little
pupil response or a mild constriction to pictures of young females.
Sheflin (1969) has shown that paranoid schizophrenics have a normal
heterosexual pupil response to pictures of women, and therefore
cannot be latent homosexuals, as has for a long time been suggested
in the psychiatric literature.

Most of the studies employing verbal, or other responses
toward actual men and women, or to pictures of them, have supported
the pupil findings. Hicks, Reaney, and Hill (1967) reported that
women verbally expressed a preference for a photograph of a woman
with small pupils over one of her with large pupils. Stass and
Willis (1967) pharmacologically dilated the eye pupils of female
and male stimulus persons and paired them with another stimulus
person of the same sex with the normal eye pupils. An opposite
sex experimental person was asked to pick one of the two stimulus
persons as an experimental partner. Both male and female experimental persons were more likely to pick an opposite-sex partner
with enlarged pupils. Eye contact during introduction of the
experimental person to the prospective experimental partner also
influenced the selection of the partner. The subjects, just as
in Hess' (1965) report, were not necessarily able to report that
enlarged pupils or eye contact influenced them in their choice of
an experimental partner.

Jones and Moyel (1971, 1973), however, have obtained mixed
findings. In the earlier study they reported that male college
students reacted more favorably toward pictures of adult males
with light irides than toward ones with dark irides, but in the
later study they obtained different findings. The pictures of
men elicited more verbal affective responses from *both* men and
women subjects than did the pictures of women. However, the men
did show slightly more favorable responses to the pictures of
men with small pupils than to those with large pupils. The men
showed slightly more favorable responses to female pictures with

small pupils if the irides were dark and to show no difference
between the small and large pupilled women with light irides.
These findings are contrary to those of Hess (1965).   Jones and
Moyel (1973) also reported that the women showed the same degree
of verbally expressed affective responsiveness toward the four
male pictures, regardless of iride color or pupil size.   They
showed more affective responses to small-pupilled women than to
large-pupilled women, just as the female subjects in Hicks, Reaney
and Hill's (1967) report had.   The findings obtained with male
subjects therefore vary markedly with data in the pupil literature and those reported in other verbal response investigations.
Jones and Moyel cite a study by Fox and Steinmann (1966) which
reported that men and women putting themselves into the role of
a college admissions officer favored male candidates over female
candidates of equal qualifications.   It is possible that Jones
and Moyel's men felt expected to respond more favorably to pictures of men than to pictures of women, since facial portraits
rather than pinups were involved.   We already have found in our
own research that women often do not respond positively toward
male pinup pictures when asked to verbally indicate their preferences, even when their pupil responses show strong positive responsiveness toward these pictures.

Relevant to this interpretation are the findings obtained
by Bernick (1966) in his doctoral dissertation research conducted
at Hess' laboratory.   He studied the psychosexual pupil response
of children toward pictures of boys, girls, babies, mothers,
fathers, men, and women.   He also obtained verbal preference
ratings from these children for the pictures.   He investigated
children of both sexes in kindergarten, grades 1, 2, 4, 6, 8, 10,
and 12.   Boys and girls of all grades showed greater pupil responses to opposite-sex stimulus persons in stimulus category
pairs.   Their pupils dilated more to pictures of opposite-sex
peers than to same-sex peers, more to opposite-sex parents than
to same-sex parents, and more to opposite-sex adults than to same-
sex adults.   Hence it appears that the psychosexual pupil response
to opposite-sex stimulus persons is present at an extremely early
age, and it appears to remain constant between the age of 5 to 18
years.

However, the verbally expressed preferences of these children
were very different from the pupil responses and were much more in
conformity with classical notions regarding the psychosexual development of the child.   Contrary to the pupil data, the verbally
expressed preferences of the children were usually for persons
of the same sex within stimulus category pairs.   The verbal preferences of the girls, however, were for fathers rather than
mothers, perhaps because this appears to be a socially acceptable
cross-sex preference for them to have.

As was mentioned at the beginning of this chapter, women usually show positive pupil responsiveness to pictures of babies while men do not. The pupil responses of women to babies have provided us with a further indication of the nonverbal communication role of eye pupil size. A picture of a mother with her infant was so treated that in one print her pupils were quite small and in another print her pupils were quite large. Hess showed these prints to sixteen college and graduate students and asked them "which mother loves her baby more?" The students unanimously chose the one with the large pupils although they were not able to say that the large pupil was the deciding factor in their choice.

Several research studies, beginning as long ago as Silberkuhl (1896) and continued by workers such as Birren, Casperson and Botwinick (1950), Kumnick (1954, 1956a, b), Rubin (1961, 1962), and Wikler, Rosenberg, Hawthorne and Cassidy (1965), have shown that children have larger absolute pupil sizes than do adults and that age is inversely related to absolute pupil size. Larger pupil size thus would serve to make children visually appealing to adult caretakers and this would promote the formation of a caretaker-child affectional bond. It is possible, furthermore, that larger pupil size in a woman would not only serve to increase her sexual attractiveness but would also make her look younger, as Hess (1973b) has recently suggested.

Even schematic eyes can be used to demonstrate the nonverbal communication value of eye pupil size cues. Hess (1969) made up slides showing single, paired, or triple eyespots. These eyespots were constructed by drawing two concentric circles and filling in the inner circle to represent the "pupil". The paired eyespots were placed together to maximally resemble eyes in a human face, and the tripled ones were positioned in a horizontal row the same distance apart as were the paired eyespots.

The subjects who looked at the eyespots had larger pupil responses to the paired eyespots than to either the singleton or triple eyespots. Their response data are shown in Tables 1, 2, 3, and 4. In fact, in considering the mean pupil responses to the singletons and to the triples, in comparison with those to the pairs, it appears that the singletons and the triples as a whole tended to elicit pupil constrictions. There was no tendency for the pupil responses to be smaller to single or triple eyespots that had small "pupils" or for them to be bigger to the ones that had big "pupils". That is, a hypothesis that pupil responses should be larger toward schematic eyespots with large "pupils" because of the greater amount of dark area, particularly in the case of the triple eyespots, did not receive support, as the data in Table 3 show.

TABLE 1

PUPIL RESPONSES TO SINGLE, DOUBLE, AND TRIPLE EYESPOTS

REGARDLESS OF THEIR "PUPIL SIZE"

	◯	◯◯	◯◯◯
Male subjects	-.039	+.008	-.056
Female subjects	-.014	+.022	-.003
All subjects	-.027	+.015	-.030

TABLE 2

PUPIL RESPONSES TO SINGLE EYESPOTS OF DIFFERENT "PUPIL SIZE"

	◉	◉	◉
Male subjects	-.070	-.028	-.020
Female subjects	-.021	+.004	-.026
All subjects	-.046	-.012	-.023

TABLE 3

PUPIL RESPONSES TO TRIPLE EYESPOTS OF DIFFERENT "PUPIL SIZE"

	⦿ ⦿ ⦿	⦿ ⦿ ⦿	⦿ ⦿ ⦿
Male subjects	−.052	−.036	−.080
Female subjects	−.021	−.008	+.019
All subjects	−.037	−.022	−.031

TABLE 4

PUPIL RESPONSES TO DOUBLE EYESPOTS OF DIFFERENT "PUPIL SIZE"

	⦿ ⦿	⦿ ⦿	⦿ ⦿
Male subjects	−.008	+.002	+.029
Female subjects	+.005	+.020	+.042
All subjects	−.002	+.011	+.036

But the series of paired eyespots, resembling eyes in a human face, elicited a consistent pattern of pupil responses, as shown by Table 4. The subjects' average pupil responses to the pair with the smallest "pupils" were the smallest, and the average responses to the pair with the largest "pupils" were the largest.

A 1965 study by Coss (reported in Coss, 1972) also used schematic eyes to study pupil responses. Coss devised concentric circles having solid inner circles of different sizes. As in our study, the schematic eyes were presented in sets of one, two and three. On the average the group of pictures that consisted of paired eyespots caused greater pupil dilation responses than did the groups consisting of single or triple eyespots. The triple sets, as a matter of fact, caused the least pupil dilation. These findings are concordant with those from Hess' laboratory. Among the paired eyespots, Coss found that those that resembled dilated pupils the most elicited much more pupil dilation than did those that resembled constricted pupils the most. These findings, too, are in accord with Hess'. In Coss' study the women subjects had a greater difference in response to the "dilated" and "constricted" eyespots than did the men subjects. These eyespots produced pupil dilation scores of 1.90 and 1.55, respectively, from the women, whereas the corresponding scores from the men were 1.63 and 1.55.

Coss' data do not give as strong a difference between "pupils" of different size in the paired eyespots as there is in Hess' study. A probable cause of this is that Coss placed the schematic eyespots very close to each other whereas Hess placed them in the same relation as actual eyes have in a normal human face.

Since schematic eyes elicit differential pupil responses it appears that these responses are either innately released by specific releaser configurations or learned very rapidly in early life. A current study by one of Hess' students, which will be discussed subsequently, may be able to give some information on this question.

Not only do people's pupils respond to different eye pupil sizes in a stimulus person, but it also appears that many people actually have at least some nonconscious knowledge of the affective meaning of differential pupil size in a stimulus person. This hypothesis was already suggested by the experiment Hess conducted with the picture of a mother holding her baby, as was above described. To investigate this hypothesis further, Hess (1973b) made up two different facial drawings, one of a smiling "happy" face and the other of a frowning "angry" face. They were about three-quarters natural size and the eye pupils were left blank. They are shown, in reduced size, in Figures 5 and 6.

Figure 5. The smiling face stimulus used by Hess as one of the two blank-eyed faces shown to naive experimental subjects with instructions to draw in appropriate pupils.

Figure 6. The frowning face stimulus used by Hess as the other of two blank-eyed faces shown to naive experimental subjects with instructions to draw in appropriate pupils.

Hess showed these two faces individually to 20 experimental subjects
and gave them a #2 pencil with an eraser on it. Hess said to them,
"draw in the size pupil you think best fits the face."

The 20 experimental subjects consisted of 10 men and 10 women.
On the average, both the men and the women drew larger pupils for
the "happy" face than for the "angry" face. Table 5 shows the
average sizes of the actual pupils drawn by the men and by the
women for the two faces.

TABLE 5

MEAN ACTUAL PUPILS DRAWN BY 20 SUBJECTS (IN MM)

	(Face)	
	"Happy"	"Angry"
Men	4.0	2.9
Women	4.5	2.8

While there were no significant difference between the men
and the women for the pupil sizes that they drew for the same
kind of face, there were some subjects who made bigger differences in the pupil sizes of the two faces than the others did.
Hess then hypothesized that since pupil size changes function as
nonverbal communication signals, differences in the ability to
react to such signals could be related to the relative visibility
of a person's own eye pupils. Preliminary data from this group
of subjects suggests that there may indeed be such a relationship.

Since the initial experiment Hess has tested an additional
39 naive subjects. Twenty-seven out of the 39 drew larger pupils
for the "happy" face than for the "angry" face, a result which is
in the same direction as in the original experiment. Hence this
phenomenon can thus be demonstrated readily. A few children have
also been tested and they have been found to draw larger pupils
for the "happy" face than for the "angry" face. One ten year old
boy, after being tested, was asked why he drew a larger pupil
for the "happy" face than for the "angry" face. His reply was
that everyone knew that they were supposed to be that way.

Many pupil researchers believe that *all* emotions serve to dilate eye pupils. In other words, no emotion can result in pupil constriction. In view of this, it is extremely striking to find that the naive subjects in this research showed that they associated anger or displeasure with smaller pupils than they associate with happiness or pleasure. There is no question that further and careful research should be conducted on this question. Pupil constriction serves to sharpen visual detail and to increase depth of field and may thus be associated with threatening situations when seen in a stimulus person. Paul Leyhausen, a German ethologist, has reported (personal communication) that wild cat trainers have found that when a wild cat is being trained, as long as its pupils are large, the trainer has the situation well under control since the animal is afraid. But if the wild cat's pupils become very small, this presages the animal's intention to attack the trainer.

Thus it does very clearly seem that people do possess a covert knowledge of eye pupil size in relation to affective states. Current research by one of Hess' doctoral students, James Dickson McLean, is attempting to ascertain the developmental course of this ability to react appropriately to different eye pupil sizes in stimulus persons. Initial research by this student, in collaboration with Hess, reconfirmed that both male and female adult subjects tend to associate large pupils with happy faces, whether the faces are male or female. These adult subjects were also shown the two pairs of eyes depicted in Figure 7. Out of the total of 60 naive subjects that were shown these two pairs 47 reported that the pair with the small pupils appeared to be older than the pair with the large pupils and only 13 chose the pair with the large pupils as being the older. Hence, in congruence with the fact that children actually have larger pupils than

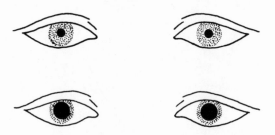

Figure 7. Two pairs of eyes shown by McLean to subjects who are asked which pair of eyes is older. The majority of subjects indicate that the pair with the smaller pupils is the older of the two.

do adults, adults definitely appear to associate small pupils
with greater age than they do with large pupils. McLean's
current research is focussing on the extent to which individuals
of different ages attend to the pupils, the age at which they
become aware of age-correlated differences in pupil size, the
age at which they react to maleness and femaleness in conjunction
with eye pupils of different size, and the age at which they
differentially interpret pupil size changes as indicators of
attitude states.

Another of Hess' doctoral dissertation students, Angelique
Sallas, is beginning an investigation of the effect of different
facial expressions and gaze directions of the stimulus person
upon experimental subjects' reactions to different eye pupil sizes.
This research should give further information regarding the ways
in which the eye pupils serve as nonverbal communication devices.
It should also shed some light on the affective response to the
perception of highly constricted eye pupils in a stimulus person.

Patrick Shrout, still another of Hess' students, is extending
Hess' face completion task to include other types of affective
states in a stimulus person. Shrout is conducting his research
by giving subjects several copies of the face shown in Figure 8.
The subjects are asked to create six expressions: very happy,
complacent, very angry and threatening, very tired, displeased,
and bored. While Shrout has so far tested only a few subjects,
his results with the happy and angry instructions are in line
with those obtained by Hess.

Figure 8. Face stimulus used by Shrout for subjects to complete,
filling in eyebrows, pupils, and mouth, and any other details
subjects may wish to depict specific expressions.

PUPIL CONSTRICTION PHENOMENA

The report by Hess and Polt in 1960 also indicated that the pupil can fail to dilate to certain classes of stimuli. Subsequent research, such as that reported in Hess (1965) and Polt and Hess (1968) has demonstrated that under certain conditions the pupil can actually constrict, even though there has been no increase in environmental illumination. Not only has it been found that some subjects' pupils decrease in size in response to specific visual stimuli, but doctoral dissertation research by Beck (1967) in Hess' laboratory showed that certain auditory stimuli cause pupil constriction in some subjects. Figure 9 taken from his thesis, shows the effect of different auditory click rates (in terms of number of clicks per second) at different sound intensity levels upon pupil size in four female subjects.

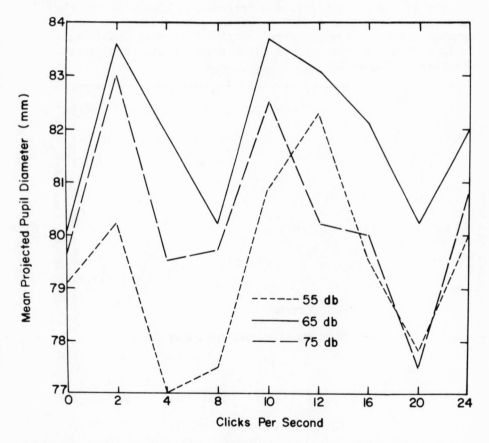

Figure 9. Effects of eight different auditory click rates at three different sound intensities upon the pupil responses of four female subjects, from Beck's 1967 thesis.

There were 24 click stimuli and each was presented for 12.5 seconds. The series was presented to each subject for a total of four times, in different orders. Figure 9 thus shows that ten of these stimuli resulted in pupil dilation, four caused pupil constriction, and ten caused little or no change in pupil size. The lowest sound intensity, 55 db, was involved in 3 of the 4 cases of pupil constriction. At 20 clicks per second, two of the intensity levels resulted in a pupil constriction and the third resulted in no change in pupil size in comparison with the silent condition. When the subjects' pupil responses to the different click rates, irrespective of sound intensity, are considered, it becomes apparent that they are closely related to brain function in some fashion.

Morgan and Stellar (1950) have published data upon the intensities of different cortical brain waves occurring at various cycles per second. Their data are depicted in Figure 10, which has been taken from Beck's (1967) thesis. These data are compared with the mean relative pupil sizes of the four female subjects in response to the various click rates at all three sound intensities in Figure 10.

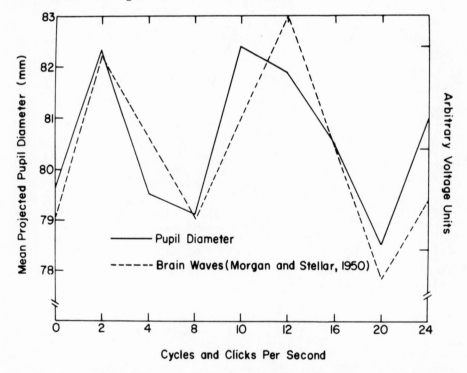

Figure 10. Average pupil response to various auditory click rates in comparison with intensity of brain waves occurring at various cycles per second, from Beck's 1967 thesis.

These two sets of data are astonishingly similar in topography.
There are dominant cortical rhythms at approximately 2, 12, and
24 cycles per second, and click rates of 2, 10-12, and 24 per
second serve to increase pupil size. In addition, 20 clicks per
second have a depressive effect upon pupil size and there are no
dominant cortical rhythms at 20 cycles per second. Beck (1967)
has suggested that the auditory clicks synchronize in some way
with dominant cortical rhythms (or their determinants) to produce the observed pupil response patterns.

Most important, however, is that Beck's research demonstrates
that there are indeed situations in which psychosensory pupil
constrictions can occur. For this reason we cannot accept
Loewenfeld's (1966) categorical statement that "all psychologic
and sensory stimuli, with the exception of light, dilate the
pupil and none of them contract it." It is certainly true that
it is much more difficult to obtain psychosensory pupil constrictions than to obtain psychosensory pupil dilations. Our own data
have shown that pupil constrictions are highly individualistic
in nature and that they are usually likely to be overridden by
strong negative emotional reactions through autonomic arousal.
Pictures that will cause constriction in one experimental subject
can cause strong dilations in another experimental subject. One
cannot make *a priori* judgments as to what pictures will be unpleasant for a specific individual. Not even their verbal reports can be trusted because people may have unconscious or
deeply rooted attitudes that conflict with their professed views.
The specific nature of the situation to which an individual may
respond also plays a role: for example, a picture of a can of
worms can cause a woman's pupils to constrict. But a real can
of worms might well cause her pupils to dilate because of the
additional component of autonomic arousal from fear.

In general it is highly difficult to find stimuli or situations which will reliably cause pupil constrictions in subjects.
One exception to this may be hypnotic induction. Seltzer (1969)
in his doctoral dissertation research in Hess' laboratory documented that the hypnotic induction process is accompanied by a
large pupillary constriction. Medical hypnotists use pupil constriction as a criterion for determining that their patients have
actually been hypnotized successfully. As is well known, some
persons are readily hypnotizable while others are practically
impossible to hypnotize even when they express willingness.

While most auditory stimuli, such as music, serve to dilate
pupils, preliminary research in Hess' laboratory has shown that
many people show pupil constriction to the sound of a baby's
distress crying in comparison with "white noise" of the same
sound intensity level. Hess and Petrovich have conducted preliminary research that showed that there is one visual stimulus

that often produces pupillary constriction. This was a picture
of an autistic baby, and it elicited pupillary constriction
responses in almost all of the adult subjects tested, whereas
other baby pictures shown in the same series produced pupillary
dilation.

A T.V. pilot show which Hess (1973b) showed to 50 men and
50 women was found to have a portion which elicited strong pupil
constriction responses in the male viewers and not in the female
viewers. Figures 11 and 12 depict the sequential pupil responses
of the men and the women to the first 520 seconds of this film.
The show began with a violent sequence, to which both women and
men had a pupil dilation response that peaked at the 50th second.
Subsequently, however, the men and women showed decreasing pupil
size, a trend which was not reversed until around the 450th
second. The men, however, actually had definite pupil *constriction*
in comparison with the control level. The difference in the men
and women's responses to the film appears to arise from the fact
that after the initial violent episode the show continued to deal
with a situation that made a man appear to be a fool. The men
therefore seemed to have a much greater distaste for watching
this material than the women did, presumably because of their
emotional identification with the show's subject. There can be

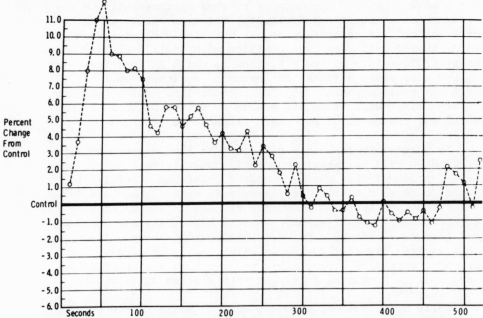

Figure 11. Pupil responses of 50 women to the first 520 seconds
of a brightness controlled pilot television show. The initial
pupil responses were high but steadily leveled off to near control
level after 300 seconds.

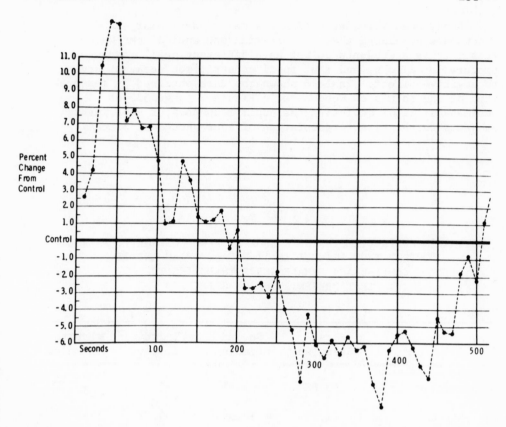

Figure 12.   Pupil responses of 50 men to the same brightness controlled pilot television show.   As in the case of the women subjects, the initial pupil responses were high.   However, the decline in pupil size was much more rapid, and the pupil sizes were
below control level from 210 to 500 seconds.   The men definitely
showed pupil constriction responses to portions of this show.

no question that their pupil responses to this portion of the show
were very different from those of the women.

     Other studies in addition to Hess' (Barlow, 1969; Atwood
and Howell, 1971; Fredericks, 1970; Fredericks and Groves, 1971)
have reported obtaining psychosensory pupil constriction from
individual subjects, while still others have obtained data which
they have interpreted as being against the hypothesis that the
pupil response is differentially affected by positive and negative
affect states (e.g., Peavler and McLaughlin, 1967; Stewart and
Jensen, 1966; Collins, Ellsworth and Helmreich, 1967; Vacchiano,
Strauss, Ryan and Hochman, 1968; Woodmansee, 1970).

   Woodmansee's research findings merit particular examination.
Woodmansee concluded that equalitarian and anti-Black* White
female college students do not have different pupil responses to
pictures of Blacks, and that pupil constriction does not occur
to negative affect. Table 6 shows the data obtained by measurement of the points on Woodmansee's Figure 2 (page 525 of
Woodmansee, 1970) depicting the pupil responses of experimental
subjects to the first presentation of four photos of Blacks.

TABLE 6

ESTIMATED PUPIL DIAMETER SIZE CHANGES FROM CONTROL TO RACIAL
CONTENT TEST STIMULI IN 11 EQUALITARIAN AND 11
ANTI-BLACK FEMALE SUBJECTS DURING THE
FIRST PRESENTATION OF STIMULI**

Subjects	First Stimulus	Second Stimulus	Third Stimulus	Fourth Stimulus
Equalitarian	+3.5%	+2.6%	+1.7%	+2.5%
Anti-Negro	+1.9%	+0.5%	-0.3%	-2.0%

---

*Although Woodmansee used the term "Negro" in his report, we
  prefer to use the term "Black" and therefore shall use it in
  discussing research on the subject.

**Data based upon measurement of points on Figure 2, page 525 of:
  Woodmansee, J. J. The pupil response as a measure of social
  attitudes. In: G. F. Summers, editor, *Attitude Measurement*.
  Chicago, Illinois: Rand McNally, 1970. The percentage changes
  for each stimulus were computed by taking the difference in
  pupil size during the viewing of the test stimulus and during
  the viewing of the control which preceded it, and then calcu-
  lating the percentage by which the pupil changed its size from
  that of the control period when the test stimulus was viewed

Inspection of these shows that there is no overlap between the
responses of the two subject groups toward the four stimulus
pictures. During the viewing of the fourth picture the anti-
Black subjects' pupils were 2.0% smaller than they had been during
the preceding control period. Since there were a total of 11 subjects in this group, some of the individuals must have had rather
extensive pupil constriction for a group constriction average of
2.0% to be obtained. Normally the pooling of data from more than
5 subjects, as has been observed in Hess' laboratory, results in
losing the evidence of negative pupil responsiveness.

The interpretation which Woodmansee (1970) has advanced regarding these data is very different from the one we would give.
In our opinion, the anti-Black subjects' pupils dilated in response
to the first Black picture principally because of the "first picture effect" that normally occurs in a series of stimulus slides
shown in a pupillometric apparatus. The anti-Black subjects show
a slight dilation to the second picture and a rather slight constriction to the third picture. They very definitely have a constriction to the fourth picture.

Woodmansee (1970) has proposed that the adequate assessment
of pupil constriction and pupil dilation necessitates averaging
together pupil diameters during the control periods both before
and after each specific stimulus picture. While the control
period pupil diameters decline slightly and gradually for the
equalitarian subjects, either because of slight boredom or relaxation, the anti-Blacks showed a rapidly decreasing control
pupil size. Woodmansee has hypothesized that arousal decrement
is responsible for this latter phenomenon, but we would hypothesize that it is caused by emotional carry-over from the stimuli
to the control periods, since the equalitarian subjects did not
show such a decrement. In our opinion, the anti-Black subjects
evinced an increasing avoidance of the negatively toned experimental situation. It is very obvious that after the second
Black picture the pupil behaviors of the two subject groups are
very different with respect to the control and stimulus presentation periods.

Such an interpretation of these data is similar to that given
by Nunnally, Knott, Duchnowski and Parker (1967) and Parker and
Mogyorosy (1967) in regard to their data upon the effect of lifting different weights upon pupil size. In this study the pupil
sizes during the period between weight lifting did not return to
the same control level. The magnitude of the pupil size during
the control periods between weight lifting corresponded to the
subjects' anticipation of the weight to be lifted next. The
subjects obviously were not at a "zero" state between the weight
liftings. It must therefore be concluded that "control" pupil
sizes are not always at the neutral level corresponding strictly

to the amount of illumination. A "control" interval not only
functions to account for total brightness effects but also aids
to partially control for emotional carry-over from previous
stimulus situations. Since emotional carry-overs dissipate, there
is always less emotional carry-over during the stimulus than during
the previous control period. Nevertheless the use of the immediately preceding control period pupil size permits more accurate
assessment of the effect of a particular stimulus than does the
use of illumination level effects only. Other sequential factors
also are controlled for through the use of the control period.
These include the subjects' getting bored, thinking of things
that are extraneous to the experiment, and so on, and these can
be at least partially controlled for by the use of the previous
control period. This methodology is the same as that used by
ethologists in studying the relative effectiveness of different
stimuli in releasing specific behaviors in animals.

The differing interpretations of research data by Woodmansee
and by us illustrate very clearly that data interpretation is
very much subject to biases that researchers have.

Barlow (1969), however, has obtained findings which differ
considerably from Woodmansee's and clearly demonstrates pupillary
constriction in groups of subjects. He used actual political
participation as a criterion for selecting subjects, and the subjects showed pupil constriction responses to pictures of major
opposition political figures. Three groups of subjects were
used: White conservative supporters of George Wallace, Black
and White liberal supporters of Lyndon Johnson. The Wallace
supporters had pupil dilations when they looked at Wallace's picture and pupil constrictions to pictures of Lyndon Johnson and
of the late Martin Luther King, Jr. Both Black and White liberals
had pupil constriction responses to Wallace's picture and pupil
dilation responses to King's and Johnson's pictures. The Blacks,
furthermore, had more extreme pupil constriction and dilation
responses to the pictures than did the White liberals, quite
probably because of their greater emotional and personal involvement.

The Atwood and Howell (1971) study described earlier has also
shown that it is possible to obtain both pupillary dilation and
constriction responses from experimental subjects. The constriction responses of their pedophiliac subjects toward pictures of
attractive adult females show that the psychopupil constriction
response does exist and can be obtained in some experimental
situations.

In addition, Fredericks (1970) and Fredericks and Groves
(1971) have obtained data showing that pupillary dilation is
associated with pleasant stimuli and that pupillary constriction

is associated with unpleasant stimuli. Coverdale (1970) has reported that while pupillary constriction responses are relatively low in frequency among normal subjects those normal subjects who have high neuroticism scores have a significantly higher frequency of pupillary constriction responses than do any of the other personality groups studied, which included introverts, extraverts, and stables.

Most of these demonstrations of psychopupil constriction response to psychologic stimuli have involved the use of the visual modality. Hence if the controversial question of whether the apparent psychopupil constriction response is actually an experimental artifact in the studies that have reported it is to be resolved, it is not only necessary to utilize rigid stimulus preparation controls such as those employed in Hess' laboratory (Hess, 1972), but also additional experimental methods which bypass the difficulties of the visual modality.

For example, it is possible to use hypnosis to suggest various objects or states to experimental subjects without there being any actual changes in visual illumination or patterning. In our laboratory we have used hypnosis and suggestion to produce pupil constrictions and dilation. A hypnotized subject was first told that he was extremely hungry. He had, in fact, eaten recently. Then we showed him pictures of food, and his pupils *dilated* to the pictures. Then he was told that he had eaten a large meal and was completely satiated. Then we showed him the same pictures of food, and his pupils *constricted* to these pictures. Since the food pictures were identical in the two hypnotic suggestion conditions, the different pupil responses could have been caused only by the correspondingly different psychological states induced by the hypnotic suggestions. Similar findings have been obtained at the Pupil Research Center of the University of Michigan (personal communication, 1966). They told hypnotized subjects that they were looking at an extremely pleasant picture, without mention of any specific subject matter. The subjects' pupils dilated. Then for another blank slide the subjects were told that they were seeing something very unpleasant and distasteful, again without mention of any specific subject matter. Their pupils constricted.

Hess (1973a) has developed still another method of studying pupillary constrictions and dilations. This has been based upon the tachistoscopic presentation method. The controversial "perceptual defense" phenomenon has been based on the fact that tachistoscopically presented words which are socially disapproved, anxiety-arousing, or taboo are not recognized as readily as are neutral words. Hutt and Anderson (1967) and Hutt (1968) have investigated whether the psychopupil constriction response may be a mechanism responsible for the recognition differential. Hutt

determined the subjects' tachistoscopic recognition thresholds
for words of three different categories of emotional response --
pleasant, unpleasant, and taboo. He also showed these words
projected on a screen to the subjects and recorded their pupil
sizes in response to these words. There was a significant negative correlation between pupil size and recognition threshold
values for the words. The correlation coefficients were significant in the taboo and pleasant categories whereas they did
not reach significance within the unpleasant category. Of course,
this is in no way a demonstration that differential tachistoscopic recognition thresholds are *caused* by the different pupil
size responses. It may be that both the differential tachistoscopic recognition thresholds and the different pupil sizes are
functions of the anxiety-provoking characteristics of the material
viewed. Our experimental investigation, conducted in collaboration
with Benjamin Beck, is relevant to this question.

In this investigation Hess and Beck tachistoscopically
presented plain light, neutral, positively toned, and negatively
toned pictures. These pictures were presented in the Hess Pupil
Apparatus (Hess, 1972). A Wollensak Alphax shutter was used on
the lens of a Bell and Howell Slide Master 35 mm projector to
control the tachistoscopic presentations. The projector was so
placed that there was a total luminance of 32 footlamberts (color
temperature = 3600°K), as measured just behind the 2.5 mm diameter
black circle serving as the fixation point on the screen of the
Hess Pupil Apparatus, whenever the .2 second flashes occurred.

Both male and female adult subjects were utilized in these
experiments. They were between the ages of 20 and 37 years.
After an interview to obtain demographic information such as age,
sex, and occupation, individual subjects were seated in front of
the Hess Pupil Apparatus in a dimly lit room, and told that they
would see a series of flashes.

In the first experiment .2 second light flashes were presented
to the subjects. Figure 13 depicts the pupil response of one subject to the light flash. Photographic records of the pupil size
were taken at the rate of 16 per second. However, it became
apparent that four frames per second also provide good reliability
for recording the course of the photopupil reflex. This is shown
by the circled points on the figure. Hence Hess and Beck subsequently used a rate of 4 frames per second for the tachistoscopic studies. The ordinate on the graph gives the pupil size
as magnified 16.5 times. This is because the pupil sizes were
measured from an enlarged projection of the successive frames of
the film record. The enlargement was 16.5 times and thus we used
the raw data measurements for construction of the graphs. Therefore, at the beginning of the experiment the pupil size of the
subject averaged slightly less than 5 mm in diameter and then con-

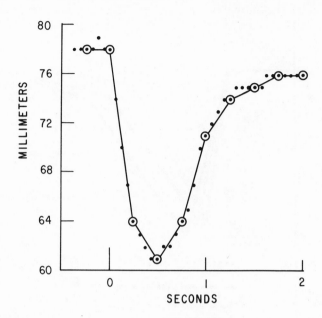

Figure 13. Pupil responses of a single subject to a .2 second flashed light that had its onset at 0 seconds. Constriction was at the lowest level in .5 second, after which recovery proceeded. The circled circles represent every fourth frame in the series.

stricted to slightly less than 4 mm in diameter in response to the flashed light. The constriction response reached its maximum in .5 second and recovery was almost complete 2 seconds after the flash.

Since it was noticed that the film transport mechanism in the pupil recording apparatus made a clicking noise which varied with the speed at which the frames were exposed, Hess and Beck decided to examine whether these various click rates had an influence upon the photopupil reflex. They then recorded the photopupil constriction reflex to the .2 second flashed light at two different filming speeds, 8 frames per second and 4 frames per second, and also with the camera so muffled that the subjects did not report hearing the film transport clicks when asked later. Five subjects were utilized in each of the auditory conditions.

The photopupil reflex response data were used to construct the stylized response curves shown in Figure 14. These response curves were stylized by drawing straight lines for the average

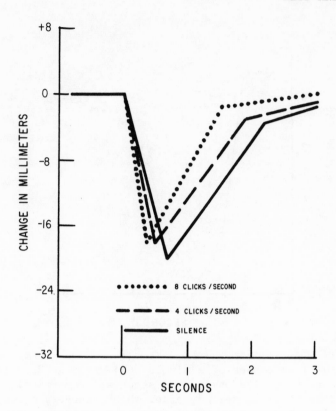

Figure 14. Pupil responses of human subjects to a .2 second
flashed light under three filming conditions: (a) 8 clicks per
second; (b) 4 clicks per second and (c) silence. See text for
explanation of stylized response curve construction.

resting pupil sizes, from the resting pupil size to the maximal
constriction size, from maximal constriction to the beginning of
the "E" wave (which is the second redilatation phase described by
Lowenstein and Loewenfeld, 1950), thus describing the "D" wave
(which is the first redilatation phase described by Lowenstein
and Loewenfeld, 1950), and from the beginning of the "E" wave to
the point where the pupil size begins to stabilize. As Figure 14
shows, the effect of the auditory stimulation is to keep the pupil
from constricting as fully as it does to the .2 second flashed
light under conditions of apparent silence, and tends to cause an
earlier return to the resting size.

Subsequently Hess and Beck tachistoscopically flashed plain light and picture slides, to 5 men and 5 women. Like the light, the slides were flashed for .2 second. One was a picture of a female nude and the other was of concentration camp victims. There was a ten-second interval between the flashed presentations. Figures 15 and 16 depict the stylized (by the same method as in Figure 14) photopupil responses of the male and female subjects to the light and to the two pictures. Both the men and the women had a photopupil reflex response to the flashed light very similar to that shown for the 4 clicks per second auditory condition in Figure 14. They also had essentially similar photopupil reflex responses to the concentration camp picture: the pupils constricted to a much smaller size than for the simple light flash and at the end of the third second the pupils were still well below the original control size and were beginning to stabilize at the lower level.

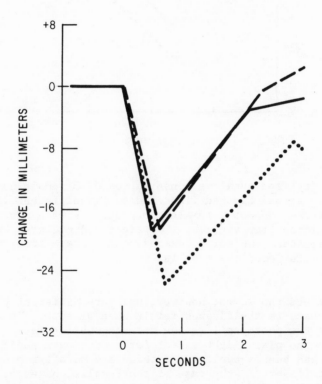

Figure 15. Stylized pupil response curves of 5 male human subjects to a .2 second flashed light (solid line) and to two different .2 second flashed pictures, one of a female pinup (dashed line) and one of a scene depicting concentration camp victims (dotted line). The light and pictures had their onset at 0 seconds.

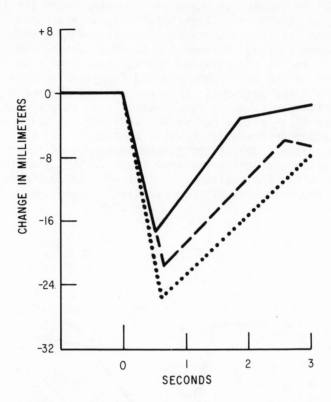

Figure 16. Stylized pupil response curves of 5 female human subjects to a .2 second flashed light and to two different .2 second
flashed pictures, one of a female pinup and one of a scene depicting concentration camp victims. The light and pictures had their
onset at 0 seconds. The solid, dashed, and dotted lines represent
the same stimulus conditions as in Figure 15.

       The men and the women, however, had very different photopupil
reflex responses to the flashed female nude picture. In the case
of the males the photopupil reflex was not substantially different
from that to the plain light except for producing a pupil size
larger than had been shown for the third second after presentation
of the light flash. In the case of the females, however, pupillary
constriction proceeded as long as it had for the concentration
camp picture, but not to quite as small a size. Redilatation thus
occurred at an earlier time than for the concentration camp picture, as shown by the data for the end of the third second after
presentation.

Just as in the case of the viewing of ten-second slides, the positive-negative aspect of the emotional responses elicited by tachistoscopically presented pictures is an extremely individualistic matter in general. It cannot be over-emphasized that the psychopupil constriction response normally cannot be demonstrated by pooling subject data regarding pupil responses to negatively toned pictorial stimuli. In addition, it should be pointed out that the classical photopupil reflex curve, as published in the literature, normally cannot be obtained on a single trial with a single human subject. The classical photopupil reflex curve, as is well known, is based upon pooled subject data and therefore is an abstraction. Real pupils in individual subjects have only tendencies to follow the course shown by the classical curve, and other factors intervene to cause the pupils of individual subjects to deviate from the classical curve during the course of individual trials. It appears to us that an important reason why these deviations occur during individual trials is that subjects are prone to having various notions and ideas occurring to them whenever they are in an experimental situation. When these various notions and ideas occur, they can exert dilating or constricting effects upon the pupil and thus result in the observed deviations. Hence it seems to us that what the tachistoscopic picture presentations do is to control somewhat just what it is that crosses the subjects' minds during the photopupil reflex response.

The actual *perception* of the content of the flashed pictures is also demonstrated by these results, since the consequent photopupil reflex responses deviate consistently from those shown for simple light. Unrecognizable visual patterning cannot be responsible for the observed phenomena since flashed landscapes have produced the very same photopupil reflex responses as do the plain light flashes. Furthermore, the consistency of the direction of deviation for specific flashed pictures demonstrates that the observed deviations are not randomly caused. In addition, these findings are in accord with those reported by Hakerem and Sutton (1966) that pupil dilations occur during the recognition or detection of visual stimuli that are near to the visual threshold.

Since the content of the flashed pictures are actually received by the experimental subjects, this supports the hypothesis that the *verbalized* recognition thresholds for anxiety-provoking materials and the pupil size in response to these materials when tachistoscopically presented are both a function of *actual* recognition and hence also of the anxiety-arousing characteristics of the material.

The research in Hess' laboratory has served to provide quantification of pupillary dilation and constriction response. However, it is still necessary to set up an adequate means of comparing these quantified responses. For example, is a 10 percent dilation twice as much as a 5 percent dilation? Furthermore, it also appears that if the pupil response measure is to yield maximum information regarding a subject's response to a specific situation, it must also be complemented by other autonomic measures such as the GSR. This is particularly important in assessing the relative role of autonomic arousal in unpleasant situations, since autonomic arousal serves to produce pupillary dilation which overrides the pupillary constriction effects that may be produced by unpleasant situations.

In our laboratories we are now conducting preliminary research utilizing "horror" visual stimuli. In monitoring GSR simultaneously with the pupil, it appears that when such pictures elicit pupillary dilation responses, there is also a large GSR. But when pleasurable pictures are shown, there may be no autonomic arousal evident through the GSR. Simultaneous EKG, EMG (electromyograph), and EEG would also add maximal usefulness to pupillometric data. We feel that behavior cannot be adequately measured or understood by the use of only one yardstick. Some of the literature has already shown the use of multiple measures. Colman and Paivio (1969) have simultaneously recorded pupillary responses and GSR during an imagery task; McElvain (1969) used the same measures during the course of noncompetitive paired associate learning; and Kahneman, Tursky, Shapiro, and Crider (1969) have studied heart rate and GSR with the pupil responses. Currently Paul Beaver, one of Hess' doctoral students, is beginning an investigation of eyeblink rate during the viewing of positive and negative visual stimuli. It is possible that eyeblink rate, as well as GSR, can provide additional and differentiating information upon the psychological processes responding to specific situations.

Furthermore, in considering the question of positive and negative psychopupil responses, it should be fully realized that in an absolute sense we can only speak of more dilation versus less dilation of pupils in response to specific situations. In the realm of physics one cannot speak of hot or cold, but of more heat and less heat, nor of brightness or darkness, but of more light and less light. Nevertheless the terms "hot" and "cold" or "brightness" or "darkness" are ones that are readily understood and used in relation to what we experience. In the same way the terms "dilation" and "constriction" must be understood and used: they indicate opposing tendencies in pupillary responses to specific situations.

ACKNOWLEDGEMENTS

Because of an illness, the author has asked Dr. Goodwin, his research associate, to assume responsibility for completion of this manuscript.

REFERENCES

Atwood, R. W., and Howell, R. J. Pupillometric and personality test score differences of pedophiliacs and normals. *Psychonomic Science*, 1971, *22*, 115-116.

Barlow, J. D. Pupillary size as an index of preference in political candidates. *Perceptual and Motor Skills*, 1969, *28*, 587-590.

Barlow, J. D. Pupillary size as an index of preference. *Perceptual and Motor Skills*, 1970, *31*, 331-336.

Beatty, J., and Kahneman, D. Pupillary changes in two memory tasks. *Psychonomic Science*, 1966, *5*, 371-372.

Beck, B. B. The effect of auditory stimulation on the photopupil reflex. Unpublished doctoral dissertation at The University of Chicago, 1967.

Bergum, O., and Lehr, J. Prediction of stimulus approach: Core measures experiment I. Research Report R66-8. Rochester, New York: Xerox Corporation, 1966.

Bernick, N. The development of children's preference for social objects as evidenced by their pupil responses. Unpublished doctoral dissertation at The University of Chicago, 1966.

Birren, J. E., Casperson, R. C., and Botwinick, J. Age changes in pupil size. *Journal of Gerontology*, 1950, *5*, 216-221.

Boersma, F., Wilton, K., Barham, R., and Muir, W. Effects of arithmetic problem difficulty on pupillary dilation in normals and educable retardates. *Journal of Experimental Child Psychology*, 1970, *9*, 142-155.

Bradshaw, J. L. Load and pupillary changes in continuous processing tasks. *British Journal of Psychology*, 1968, *59*, 265-271.

Clark, W. R., and Johnson, D. A. Effects of instructional set on pupillary responses during a short-term memory task. *Journal of Experimental Psychology*, 1970, *85*, 315-317.

Collins, B. E., Ellsworth, P. C., and Helmreich, R. L. Correlations between pupil size and the semantic differential: An experimental paradigm and pilot study. *Psychonomic Science*, 1967, *9*, 627-628.

Colman, F. D., and Paivio, A. Pupillary response and galvanic skin response during an imagery task. *Psychonomic Science*, 1969, *16*, 296-297.

Colman, F. D., and Paivio, A. Pupillary dilation and mediation processes during paired-associate learning. *Canadian Journal of Psychology*, 1970, *24*, 261-270.

Coss, R. G. Mood provoking visual stimuli: Their origins and applications. Los Angeles: Industrial Design Graduate Program, University of California, 1965.

Coss, R. G. Eye-like schemata: Their effect on behaviour. Doctoral dissertation at University of Reading, November, 1972.

Coverdale, H. L. Pupillary response, connotative meaning and personality. *Dissertation Abstracts International*, 1970, *31*, 5045B.

Coverdale, H. L., and Leavitt, C. Pupil size as a predictor of coupon return performance: A directional trend approach. *Proceedings of the 76th Annual Convention of the American Psychological Association*, 1968, 673-674.

Davidson, B. Your eye can't lie. *Saturday Evening Post*, January 15, 1966, 239, No. 2, 76-79.

Elshtain, E. L., and Schaefer, T. Effects of storage load and word frequency on pupillary responses during short-term memory. *Psychonomic Science*, 1968, *12*, 143-144.

Fitzgerald, H. E. Autonomic pupillary reflex activity during early infancy and its relation to social and nonsocial visual stimuli. *Journal of Experimental Child Psychology*, 1968, *6*, 470-482.

Fox, D. J., and Steinmann, A. Decision-making and the contrast between thought and behavior in sex-role interaction. Presented as part of a symposium on Perception, Decision-making and Behavior in Sex-role Interaction in the United States and Abroad, at the American Psychological Association Convention, New York City, September 3, 1966.

Fredericks, R. S., and Groves, M. H. Pupil changes and stimulus pleasantness. *Proceedings of the Annual Convention of the American Psychological Association*, 1971, *6*, 371-372.

Hakerem, G., and Sutton, S. Pupillary response at visual threshold. *Nature*, 1966, *212*, 485-486.

Heinrich, W. Die Aufmerksamkeit und die Funktion der Sinnesorgane. *Zeitschrift für Psychologie und Physiologie der Sinnesorgane*, 1896, *9*, 343-388.

Hess, E. H. Some relationships between pupillary activity and mental activity. Presented at the American Psychological Association Meeting, September, 1964.

Hess, E. H. Attitude and pupil size. *Scientific American*, 1965, *212*, No. 4, 46-54.

Hess, E. H. Paper presented at the Eleventh International Ethological Conference at Rennes, France, 1969.

Hess, E. H. Pupillometrics. In N. S. Greenfield and R. A. Sternbach, (Eds.), *Handbook of Psychophysiology*, New York: Holt, Rinehart and Winston, 1972, pp. 491-531.

Hess, E. H. Some new developments in pupillometrics. In E. Dodt and K. E. Schrader (Eds.), *Die normale und die gestörte Pupillenbewegung*. Symposium der Deutsche Ophthalomologische Gesellschaft vom 10-12 März 1972 in Bad Nauheim. Munich: J. F. Bergmann Verlag, 1973, pp. 246-262 (a).

Hess, E. H. What people know about the size of eye pupils. Paper presented at the Eighth Colloquium on the Pupil, Detroit, May 24-26, 1973 (b).

Hess, E. H., and Polt, J. M. Pupil size as related to interest value of visual stimuli. *Science*, 1960, *132*, 349-350.

Hess, E. H., and Polt, J. M. Pupil size in relation to mental activity during simple problem-solving. *Science*, 1964, *143*, 1190-1192.

Hess, E. H., and Polt, J. M.   Changes in pupil size as a measure of taste difference. *Perceptual and Motor Skills*, 1966, *23*, 451-455.

Hess, E. H., Seltzer, A. L., and Shlien, J. M.   Pupil responses of hetero- and homosexual males to pictures of men and women: A pilot study. *Journal of Abnormal Psychology*, 1965, *70*. 165-168.

Hicks, R. A., Reaney, T., and Hill, L.   Effects of pupil size and facial angle on preference for photographs of a young woman. *Perceptual and Motor Skills*, 1967, *24*, 388-390.

Hutt, L. D.   Selective attention: The relationship between pupil size and recognition threshold. *Dissertation Abstracts*, 1968, *29*, 338B-389B.

Hutt, L. D., and Anderson, J. P.   The relationship between pupil size and recognition threshold. *Psychonomic Science*, 1967, *9*, 477-478.

Johnson, D. A.   Pupillary responses during a short-term memory task: Cognitive processing, arousal, or both? *Journal of Experimental Psychology*, 1971, *90*, 313-318.

Jones, Q. R., and Moyel, I. S.   The influence of iris color and pupil size on expressed affect. *Psychonomic Science*, 1971, *22*, 126-127.

Jones, Q. R., and Moyel, I. S.   Men's and women's affective response to photographed subjects who differ in iris-color, pupil-size and sex. *Perceptual and Motor Skills*, 1973, *37*, 483-487.

Kahneman, D.   Construct validity on the pupil response. American Psychological Association Meeting, September, 1967.

Kahneman, D.   Attention and Effort. Englewood Cliffs: Prentice-Hall, 1973.

Kahneman, D., and Beatty, J.   Pupil diameter and load on memory. *Science*, 1966, *154*, 1583-1585.

Kahneman, D., and Beatty, J.   Pupillary changes in a paired-associate learning task. American Psychological Association Meeting, September, 1967.

Kahneman, D., Onuska, L., and Wolman, R.   Effects of grouping on the pupillary response in a short-term memory task. *Quarterly Journal of Experimental Psychology*, 1968, *20*, 309-311.

Kahneman, D., and Peavler, W. S.   Incentive effects and pupillary changes in association learning. *Journal of Experimental Psychology*, 1969, *79*, 312-318.

Kahneman, D., Peavler, W. S., and Onuska, L.   Effects of verbalization and incentive on the pupil response to mental activity. *Canadian Journal of Psychology*, 1968, *22*, 186-196.

Kahneman, D., Beatty, J., and Pollack, I.   Perceptual deficit during a mental task. *Science*, 1967, *157*, 218-219.

Kahneman, D., Tursky, B., Shapiro, D., and Crider, A.   Pupillary, heart rate, and skin resistance changes during a mental task. *Journal of Experimental Psychology*, 1969, *79*, 164-167.

Kennedy, O. A. Pupillometrics as an aid in the assessment of
  motivation, impact of treatment, and prognosis of chronic
  alocholics. *Dissertation Abstracts International*, 1971, *32*,
  1214B-1215B.

Krugman, H. E. Pupil measurement at Marplan. *The Brewer's Digest*,
  November, 1964, 26-28 (a).

Krugman, H. E. Some applications of pupil measurement. *Journal
  of Marketing Research*, 1964, *1*, 15-19 (b).

Kumnick, L. S. Pupillary psychosensory restitution and aging.
  Journal of the Optical Society of America, 1954, *44*, 735-741.

Kumnick, L. S. Aging and pupillary response to light and sound
  stimuli. *Journal of Gerontology*, 1956, *11*, 38-45 (a).

Kumnick, L. S. Aging and the efficiency of the pupillary mechanism.
  Journal of Gerontology, 1956, *11*, 160-164 (b).

Lowenstein, O., and Loewenfeld, I. E. Role of sympathetic and
  parasympathetic systems in reflex dilatation of the pupil.
  A.M.A. Archives of Neurology and Psychiatry, 1950, *64*, 313-340.

McElvain, J. L. Pupillary dilatations and galvanic skin response
  activity during competitive and noncompetitive paired association
  learning. *Dissertation Abstracts International*, 1970, *30*,
  3410B-3411B.

Morgan, C. T., and Stellar, E. *Physiological Psychology*. New York:
  McGraw-Hill, 1950.

Nunnally, J. D., Knott, P. D., Duchnowski, A., and Parker, R.
  Pupillary response as a general measure of activation. *Perception
  and Psychophysics*, 1967, *2*, 149-155.

Paivio, A., and Simpson, H. M. The effect of word abstractness
  and pleasantness on pupil size during an imagery task. *Psychonomic Science*, 1966, *5*, 55-57.

Parker, R. K., and Mogyorosy, R. S. Pupillary response to induced
  muscular tension. American Psychological Association Meeting,
  September, 1967.

Payne, D. T., Parry, M. E., and Harasymiw, S. J. Percentage of
  pupillary dilatation as a measure of item difficulty. *Perception
  and Psychophysics*, 1968, *4*, 139-143.

Peavler, W. S. Attention, processing load, and pupil size.
  Unpublished doctoral dissertation at the University of Delaware,
  1969.

Peavler, W. S., and McLaughlin, J. P. The question of stimulus
  content and pupil size. *Psychonomic Science*, 1967, *8*, 505-506.

Polt, J. M. Effect of threat of shock on pupillary response in a
  problem-solving situation. *Perceptual and Motor Skills*, 1970,
  31, 587-593.

Polt, J. M., and Hess, E. H. Changes in pupil size to visually
  presented words. *Psychonomic Science*, 1968, *12*, 389-399.

Roubinovitch, J. Du reflexe ideo-moteur de la pupille. *Revue
  neurologique*, 1900, *8*, 740-741.

Roubinovitch, J.   Des variations du diamètre pupillaire en rapport
avec l'effort intellectuel.   In P. Janet, (Ed.), *Quatrième Congrès
Internationale de Psychologie, 1900.*   Compte rendu des séances
et textes des mèmoires, publiés par les soins du docteur Pierre
Janet.   Paris: Alcan, 1901, 522–523.

Rubin, L. S.   Patterns of pupillary dilatation and constriction
in psychotic adults and autistic children.   *Journal of Nervous
and Mental Disease,* 1961, *133,* 130–142.

Rubin, L. S.   Autonomic dysfunction in psychoses: Adults and
autistic children.   *Archives of General Psychiatry,* 1962, *7,*
1–14.

Schaefer, T., Ferguson, J. B., Klein, J. A., and Rawson, E. B.
Pupillary responses during mental activities.   *Psychonomic
Science,* 1968, *14,* 137–138.

Schwartz, D.   Problems in identifying emotional stimuli by
pupillography.   Paper presented at the Eighth Colloquium on the
Pupil, Detroit, May 24–26, 1973.

Seltzer, A. L.   Hypnosis and pupil size.   Unpublished doctoral
dissertation at The University of Chicago, 1969.

Sheflin, J. A.   An application of Hess' pupillometric procedure
to a psychiatric population: An approach utilizing sexual
stimuli.   *Dissertation Abstracts International,* 1969, *29,* 1907B.

Silberkuhl, W.   Untersuchungen über die physiologische Pupillen-
weite.   *Albrecht von Graefe's Archiv für Opthalmologie,* 1896,
42, 179–187.

Simms, T. M.   Pupillary response of male and female subjects to
pupillary difference in male and female picture stimuli.
Perception and Psychophysics, 1967, *2,* 553–555.

Simpson, H. M.   Pupillary activity during imagery tasks.   American
Psychological Association Meeting, September, 1967.

Simpson, H. M., and Climan, M. H.   Pupillary and electromyographic
changes during an imagery task.   *Psychophysiology,* 1971, *8,*
483–490.

Simpson, H. M., Molloy, F. M., Hale, S. M., and Climan, M. H.
Latency and magnitude of the pupillary response during an imagery
task.   *Psychonomic Science,* 1968, *13,* 293–294.

Simpson, H. M., and Paivio, A.   Changes in pupil size during an
imagery task without motor response involvement.   *Psychonomic
Science,* 1966, *5,* 405–406.

Simpson, H. M., and Paivio, A.   Effects on pupil size of manual
and verbal indicators of cognitive task fulfillment.   *Perception
and Psychophysics,* 1968, *3,* 185–190.

Stass, W., and Willis, F. N.   Eye contact, pupil dilation, and
personal preference.   *Psychonomic Science,* 1967, *7,* 375–376.

Stewart, R. W., and Jensen, D. D.   GSR, pupillary dilation, and
response latency to words differing in entropy.   Midwest Psychological Association Meeting, Chicago, 1966.

Tanck, R. H., and Robbins, P. R. Pupillary reactions to sexual, aggressive, and other stimuli as a function of personality. *Journal of Projective Techniques and Personality Assessment,* 1970, *34,* 277-282.

Vacchiano, R. B., Strauss, P. S., Ryan, S., and Hochman, L. *Perceptual and Motor Skills,* 1968, *27,* 207-210.

van Bortel, F. J. Commercial applications of pupillometrics. In F. M. Bass, C. W. King, and E. A. Pessemier, (Eds.), *Applications of the Sciences in Marketing Management.* New York: Wiley, 1968.

Walker, G. (Ed.) *Best Magazine Articles, 1965.* New York: Crown, 1966.

Wikler, A., Rosenberg, D. E., Hawthorne, J. D., and Cassidy, T. M. Age and effect of LSD-25 on pupil size and kneejerk threshold. *Psychopharmacologia,* 1965, *7,* 44-56.

Woodmansee, J. J. The pupil response as a measure of social attitudes. In G. Summers (Ed.), *Attitude Measurement.* Chicago: Rand McNally, 1970, pp. 514-533.

AUTHOR INDEX

Numbers in *italics* indicate the page on which the reference is listed.

SUBJECT INDEX